"I've been on the bottor  gree
that being on top is muc
—Sherry Argov, Author

"Out of the box thinking that will take you on a spiritual journey of self-fulfillment, love and completeness. For women and men ready to revamp their thinking about themselves in relationships and in our modern society."
—Linda Anderson, President, ***Elite Fitness, Murrieta, CA***

"Barbara Wright Abernathy tells it like it is. So much truth given in such a no-nonsense, factual way that men are sure to love it as much as women. And anyone who quotes Doris Day and John Gray on the same page is tops."
—Mimi Donaldson, Internationally-renowned speaker, co-author of ***Negotiating For Dummies***

"Move over Betty Friedan...Barbara Wright Abernathy's book is the long awaited sequel to The Feminine Mystique! This is required reading for all women, young and old(er)."
—Ellen Reid, ***Book Shepherd, CA***

"*Venus On Top* edifies and encourages the driven, career oriented woman by revealing to her that marriage, love and romance are possible in her life if she can overcome traditional societal expectations by embracing her inner female power. Barbara Wright Abernathy intelligently and correctly reveals that the aggressive, dominant woman is at the head of the curve of a growing societal trend where women are in charge and men are their helpmates. I highly recommend this book."
—Elise Sutton, author of ***Female Domination: An Exploration into the Male Desire For Loving Female Authority***

"This book is a 'must read' for any guy who wants to understand today's women. And for those men who find themselves attracted to dynamic, successful women, this book may truly be the key to their happiness."
—Simon Menkes, ***C.P.A., Los Angeles, CA***

"Great book! *Venus On Top* fills the gap for women who need to hear of alternative ways to look at life. Things change, including interpersonal relationships and cultural mores, so thank you for letting women (and men) know it's OK to not play the same roles as our mothers!"
—Kajira Djoumahna, author of ***The Tribal Bible***

Women Who Are Born To Lead
And The Men Who Love Them

Women Who Are Born To Lead And The Men Who Love Them

Barbara Wright Abernathy

First Edition

Oakhill Press
Winchester, Virginia

10 9 8 7 6 5 4 3 2 1

Edited by Carolyn Allen

Jacket design by Kathi Dunn

Book design & production by Robbie Bos, Mountain Creative Services, Big Bear Lake, CA

Indexing by Michelle Graye

Library of Congress Cataloging-in-Publication Data

Abernathy, Barbara Wright, 1947-
Venus on top : women who are born to lead and the men who love them / Barbara Wright Abernathy. – 1st ed.
p. cm.
Includes bibliographical references and index.
ISBN 1-886939-66-7 (pbk : alk. paper)
1. Leadership in women. 2. Women–Psychology. 3. Man-woman relationships. 4. Marriage. 5. Self-realization in women. 6. Femininity. I. Title

HQ1233.A24 2005
306.7–dc22

2004056839

Oakhill Press
1647 Cedar Grove Road
Winchester, VA 22603
800-32-books
Printed in the United States of America

About the Book

There's A Relationship Revolution Brewing...

Which Side Will You Be On?

There are men who can accept nothing but the dominant role. They need to attract women who prefer being led. Barbara Wright Abernathy suggests that that arrangement is a hangover from the past.

There is a growing number of take charge Star Women who have broken through the glass ceilings at work, but when it comes to romantic relationships they are inclined to submerge their authentic selves, believing all men are uncomfortable with accomplished, powerful women. Not true! Just as there are more leadership women emerging, so are there more men willing to let their partners take the helm. It's not a question of masculinity/femininity; it's a matter of temperament.

While some of you are already there, most women are just beginning the climb or wondering where they should start. This book will help you make the most of who you are.

The author knows whereof she speaks. You'll read about how she graduated from The School of Hard Knocks into the arms of a man who celebrates her strengths. The revelations gained from this transcendental journey inspired this breakthrough book.

About the Author

Barbara Wright Abernathy

From Relationship Hell To Relationship Heaven

Ten years ago Barbara Wright Abernathy was the last person you'd want to listen to about emotional equilibrium. Hers has been an arduous journey from the depths of despair to the heights of happiness.

By any criteria, Ms. Abernathy deserves to be counted among that emerging class of leadership women. After graduating from Syracuse University and postgraduate studies at the Wetterhoff Institute in Finland, she parlayed six years in the fashion and retail industries into a successful career designing commercial interiors, specializing in optical interiors. Her business accomplishments have been acknowledged with an array of awards as well as financial success.

However, her entrepreneurial success didn't translate into anything resembling a satisfactory personal life. By the time forty-five came along, she had gone through three divorces and innumerable false starts with men. "I was destroyed on all fronts–physically, emotionally, financially, and spiritually. And the hangover from these

failures lasted for five long, dark years." During which time she went in and out of one self-help regime after another.

Now that she has emerged from that tunnel of discontent, and found her soul mate waiting at the far end, Barbara felt she could help other Star Women avoid the pitfalls that tripped her up. The author knows of what she speaks. While her accomplishments in the business world qualified her early on as a powerful woman, three divorces left her pretty much an emotional basket case.

And for those of you who may already be in the throes of confusion and discontent, she provides ways and means to lift you out of the depths of depression into a well-rounded and rewarding new life.

The proof is in the pudding, of course. But as Barbara discovered, you first have to come to the table. So pull up a chair and sample her recipe for renewal.

Table of Contents

Dedication

To Stephen Abernathy—
my husband, soul mate and best friend.
Without his constant love,
infinite patience, and complete support
this book could not have been written
or even conceived.

Acknowledgements

My book shepherd, Ellen Reid, gets a very special thank you from this first-time, but certainly not last-time author. She guided me gently but firmly through the unfamiliar wild forest of possibilities and pitfalls, which I had to navigate in order to produce this book. Without her help I surely would have stumbled and lost my way.

No one could ask for a finer editor than Carolyn Allen, whose razor-sharp insights and probing questions helped me shape my ideas into a well-organized work, of which I am very proud.

I am especially grateful to Chandra (Sky Bear Weaves Her Path, elder) Smith, M.S.W., who first introduced me to the Native American personality archetypes noted in this book at our annual Women of Wisdom conference in Big Bear Lake, California. These concepts were passed down to her from her elders in the Native American oral tradition.

Many thanks to all the wonderful spiritual teachers who assisted me along the way in my personal spiritual journey, especially Rev. Jean Sweet of the Bear Valley Church of Religious Science Center for Spiritual Enrichment.

And, of course, I am very grateful to my mother, Dorothy Siracusa, my brother, Tom Campanelli, and the rest of our extended family. They are always 100 percent behind me no matter what my next madcap endeavor might be. Growing up with all your love was truly a blessing for me. Thank you.

"Women who seek to be equal with men lack ambition."

— Timothy Leary

Introduction

Women have come a long way, baby, but we still have a long way to go. Too many women today are successful at work but curiously unsuccessful, unhappy, and dissatisfied in their relationships with men. There is a reason for the problem and there is a solution. It's all laid out for you here in these pages. Women are about to learn how to find happiness in a new way of life at the leading edge of the relationship frontier.

No longer must women choose between being loved and being the leader. No longer must women furtively manipulate their men in order to have power. Men and women are forging a new kind of partnership where both partners make a conscious choice for the woman to be the leader of the household. This is the wave of the future. Is it right for you? Is this the missing ingredient in your otherwise satisfying life?

Some women will read this book just to learn how to get their man to do the laundry. Others will recognize themselves and be enthralled at the prospect of being totally in charge and totally loved for it. More and more couples every day are discarding the old model of male-dominated marriage and embracing a new lifestyle.

"But I don't necessarily want to dominate my partner or be the leader in our relationship," you may say. "I just want to be equal." We've been trying to be equal for decades and we're still not there. Most men are not volunteering to "empower" us to be equal, are they? I dislike that word empower. Nobody can "empower" anyone else.

We women need to rediscover and reclaim the feminine power that we already have within us, and learn to express it and use it in meaningful ways. Whining, playing the victim, and pleading for fairness and equality haven't won us the results or respect we want. Feminine power exercised with grace and strength elicits respect from men. Men expect those with power to act powerful without asking permission. We are never going to be equal unless we first get on top! From that position we can then create the kind of equality we want.

> ***"She's the leader...I'm like the monkey on the piano. I do the jumping. She plays the tune."***
> ***—Ozzy Osbourne on wife, Sharon***

If your partner gave you this book, you owe it to yourself to temporarily suspend your judgment and read it all the way through. He's telling you that this "woman as leader" lifestyle is what he wants. That means you're way ahead of most women — you've already got the right partner for a woman-led marriage! His job now is to back off and let you gradually come into your power on your own terms and at your own pace.

If you pick up this book, prepare yourself for some startling insights into your cultural heritage as a woman, and a new perspective on what our feminine-led future can be. It's awesome!

All women are inherently powerful, but that power is expressed differently through different personalities. Using the simple system of personality archetypes I have refined for men and women will help you identify your archetype, and understand which type of man is the best match for you.

If you are single, you will learn which kind of man is right for you and how to evaluate the men you date for long-term compatibility. If you are married you will learn how to tell if your man is worth keeping, and how to improve your relationship if he is. If he's not a keeper you'll be able to develop the inner strength you need to shed your partner — if necessary — and find a better one who is in harmony with your needs, in support of your goals, and respectful of your feminine power.

Don't accept that poppycock about good men being scarce. There are tons of good men out there who want to be in partnership with a powerful woman, but there is a shortage of women who have accepted and embraced their true feminine power.

When I finally discovered my real power, I was 54 years old with three painful divorces behind me. I now have a tall, handsome, kind, and loving husband who treats me like a queen and does all the housework. I never need to be anything less than all that I am and my husband loves me for it. I'm free to let my light shine brightly instead of masking it for fear that I won't be loved. I'm happy at last and you can be happy too!

For too many of us women the old models of relationships don't work. When the old ways aren't working there are always a few brave souls willing to open their minds and hearts and try a new way of doing things. That's why a quiet revolution has been brewing on the home front in America over the past decade.

Women are taking their place as head of the household. And, yes, there are plenty of good men out there who want a powerful woman to respect and love — stay-at-home dads are just the tip of the iceberg.

If you had known me back in 1994 and I told you that some day I'd be writing a groundbreaking book on marriage and relationships, you would have laughed yourself silly, and then had me thrown into the loony bin. There I was at age 47, deep in the throes of menopause, emotionally bruised, and reeling from divorce number three. I was losing my home, my health, and my mind all at the same time.

Wouldn't you think an intelligent woman should have learned how to pick a good man and have a decent, stable relationship by this time in her life? Instead, my life was shattered into a million pieces for the third time, and I was faced with the daunting task of somehow putting myself back together again.

There's another way, my sisters. I found it and I'm going to show you how you can too. I'm writing this book because I remember how hard it was and how long it took to learn what I needed to learn on my own. I don't want you to spend decades in the dark like I did. I trudged through years of frustration wondering why my relationships with men always turned into a power struggle. I spent too much time and money in therapy complaining, "I'm successful at work, so why am I not successful at love?"

Well, at last I'm out of the woods and into the light. Here in these pages is the information about men, women, and relationships I wish I'd known 30 years ago. You won't have to suffer as long as I did. I'm giving you a relationship map to new territory that boldly goes way beyond "Venus & Mars." You may be jolted a bit by what I tell you, but the stories are all true examples from my life. These principles work and all you have to do is try them for yourself with an open mind.

> ***"Challenging existing social codes takes a kind of brilliance, a laser beam slicing through the old frames of reference to a new clarity about what is possible."***
> ***—Sherry Ruth Anderson, Ph.D. and Paul H Ray, Ph.D., authors of The Cultural Creatives***

Want to see for yourself the impact feminine power can have on a man's mind and soul? Read the poem on the next page, written to me by my future husband on the night we first met. When he allowed me to read it several months later I was amazed and delighted and grateful that the feminine qualities I had worked so long and hard to bring out in myself were so readily seen by him. He read the poem to me as part of our wedding ceremony—a moment I will treasure forever!

You deserve to have a man whose greatest pleasure and main goal in life is pleasing you. Now you're going to find out just how to make that happen! Your new life is waiting for you. Just turn the page.

– Barbara Wright Abernathy

A Poem Just For You, Barbara

Azure Blue Eyes

By Stephen Abernathy

Not Emerald green, but the brightest blue:
They remind me of the Sea;
I could gaze, to see therein, get lost eternally;
Windows clear, into your Soul, I wonder as I see;
I can't imagine any place that I would rather be!

They capture light and magnify, the depth I do behold;
The Sun pales in comparison, they surely are TOO bold!
The Moon, she hides behind the clouds, She REALLY is in envy!
For I have told HER (in so many words), your eyes have snared,
they hold me!

The stars above, have known my love, they sing a sweet refrain;
But even THOSE, above so high, know they love me now in vain!
My love for all these Celestial Ones, they surely know and see;
They've been long forgotten now, there's no escape for me!

I enter in, and am amazed, the SIGHT that I now see;
Stretched before, in vast domain, another WORLD does greet me!
Deep blue waters, cool and clear, wavelets wash my members;
Encompassed now, I dive so deep, COOL liquid, HOT as embers!

Deeply now, I do descend, HOT blue is getting COOLER;
I really could not be in here, if DECEIT was 'ere to fool HER.
So, knowing that my heart is PURE, intentions forth and upright;
We've allowed our journey to BEGIN, I see we've gained some insight!

Deeper still, and diving smooth, I see that we can breathe here;
The SERENITY I sense so deep, the STILLNESS, total lack of fear!
Tells my ESSENCE, OH TO EXPERIENCE...noteworthy to surprise;
The totality of PEACE there in the bluest of blue eyes.

Significance of the Symbols

Feminine Power

Some of the oldest prehistoric art known to mankind inspired the graphic symbols designed by the author for Venus On Top. The inverted triangle symbolizes the feminine principle as embodied by the womb. The spiral is the symbol for power exemplified by the coiling of a snake. In those times snakes signified life energy and were thought to bring good fortune.

Star Woman ***Earth Mother***

These two basic archetypes of the female personality are characterized by how a woman relates to her world. Star Women are the leaders and visionaries, whose energy is active and self-oriented. Earth Mothers are the nurturers and caretakers, whose energy is receptive and other oriented. The sign for feminine power is at the center of both symbols because both types of women are equally powerful, each in her own way.

Venus
ON TOP

SECTION ONE:

Understanding Women

"It takes a kind of genius to name a problem that has no name, because if you do it honestly and if the timing is right, millions of people who have been stupified or hypnotized by that problem will wake up."

— Paul H. Ray and
Sherry Ruth Anderson, Ph.D.

Chapter 1

Totally Powerful and Totally Loved

Every woman has the potential within her to be totally powerful and totally loved. Just imagine for a moment what it would be like to be respected and loved for your talents and your intelligence by a man you respect and love.

Imagine being seen and known and accepted as your whole self, with no need to hide your greatest gifts or your quirkiest quirks. Imagine what might happen if you were given free rein to follow your dreams with a partner who is your head cheerleader.

We women all know what it is like to be the head cheerleader for a man. We've been playing that role for ages. What if your man did that for you as well? Imagine how wonderful your life would be and what great things you could accomplish. Imagine the kind of world we could create if all our dormant female power were unleashed to do good!

Imagine being seen and known and accepted as your whole self, with no need to hide your greatest gifts or your quirkiest quirks.

This kind of relationship is no pipe dream. It is possible and it is an everyday reality for many women, including me. This can be your everyday reality, too.

The Powerful Woman

If you already think of yourself as a strong and powerful woman, but that exceptional relationship has so far eluded you – take heart. It is indeed possible to create a rewarding relationship using the information in this book.

> ***"Many women have more power than they recognize, and they're very hesitant to use it, for they fear they won't be loved."***
>
> ***– Patricia Schroeder***

If you are a woman who doesn't yet think of herself as strong and powerful, who is afraid that becoming powerful might make you less attractive to men, let me assure you – that old stereotype is no longer the case.

You may not have the type of personality that needs to be the leader in your marriage. However, if you ever hope to be in an equal partnership where your opinions and desires hold just as much value as the man's, you still need to develop your feminine power in a positive way.

The great thing about being a woman who knows her power is that you then have the tools to create a relationship that's right for you. The power in your relationship can be properly balanced and both partners will be free to work out the responsibilities according to individual strengths and weaknesses. For example, if your husband is a great money manager, the two of you can decide he will handle the bill paying and checkbook balancing. However, you must make sure that you have sufficient influence over how that money is spent. Your feminine power, when exercised correctly, will not only insure that your influence is felt, but that it will also be enjoyed and welcomed by your man.

What is Feminine Power?

The dictionary definition of power is: 1. The ability, skill, or capacity to do something, 2. Control and influence over other people and their actions. A great many of us have been working too hard toward the first definition while paying too little attention to the second. I believe that the best way to wield power is to influence others and their actions – this is the way of feminine power.

> ***"True power comes from within, and it has a spiritual rather than a material foundation."***
>
> ***– Deepak Chopra***

Have you ever noticed that there are some women who seem to have a certain knack with men? I've seen women who are not exceptionally beautiful but are treated like queens by their partners. They have a quiet, not boastful, self-confidence, and a kind and cheerful manner. Genuine serenity seems to radiate from the center of their being. This kind of woman is never rushed, driven, or stressed out.

Seeing one of these women at a party, I would initially think: "What a weak little pushover she must be! I could never be like that." Then I'd see her attentive husband happily bringing her a drink and asking if he could do anything else for her. "Hmmm," I'd grump to myself, "What's she got that I haven't got?"

Then I'd try to rationalize my doubts away. "Well, she probably just sits at home with the kids all day. She doesn't have to run a business like I do. I've gotta be tough!"

I began to see that acting like a man was not winning me the kind of man I thought I wanted. However, I was still buying into the idea that to make it in the business world, I'd have to lead with the most masculine traits I could find in myself, and suppress those I thought too soft and feminine. Back then I didn't understand that feminine power is about being; masculine power is about doing. Feminine power is inner directed; masculine power is outer directed.

Feminine power is about being: masculine power is about doing.

Most of our problems with men stem from the fact that we act too much like the old traditional male. We are caught between two worlds. We don't want to go back to the old world where women depended on men to bring home the bacon. Being financially self-sufficient is a goal to which most modern women aspire. Certainly we don't want to go back to the days when women weren't supposed to work outside the home. Our mental picture of a powerful person is based on what we know of powerful men. We think that the only way to win is to beat men at their own game.

Good Men

Is it at all surprising that women have trouble creating a good relationship these days? A woman who is ambitious, smart, and competent at work does not want to be in a relationship that requires her to stifle her talents at home, so that the man in her life won't be upset or feel inferior.

The good news is that there are good men out there who want a powerful woman to love. And these men aren't weak or wimpy or losers. They are men who have a deep and abiding respect for women in general, and whose greatest pleasure in life is making their women happy.

The good news is that there are good men out there who want a powerful woman to love.

Any woman who sincerely wants to have a fulfilling and supportive relationship with a good man can have it, providing she is willing to make the changes needed within herself to attract and hold the right man for her.

There are many reasons why your relationships aren't bringing you the satisfaction you seek. In the coming chapters I will shed light on these problems and, more importantly, show you how to overcome them. As I see it, these are the top three mistakes we make in relationships:

1. Expecting that having a perfect partner will fix everything.
2. Getting entangled with a partner who is incapable of meeting our needs.
3. Allowing resentments to build up and erode the respect we once had for each other.

The number one mistake people (both men and women) make is clinging to the idea that if you just had a perfect partner everything would be great, all your problems would be solved, and you'd finally feel okay about yourself. I can assure you that it actually works just the opposite way.

When you are happy with whom you are and your life is good and in balance *that's* when you'll attract (or maintain and enjoy) a great partner. This is the Law of Attraction – one of the most fundamental Universal Spiritual Principles in this physical world. The people and things that you attract into your life are like a mirror of your consciousness. You can only attract someone who is on your same level. If you are desperate and fearful, the man who is attracted to you is going to be desperate and fearful, too.

The people and things that you attract into your life are like a mirror of your consciousness.

However, if you are emotionally healthy, kind, and loving (that *is* the kind of man you want, isn't it?), then men who are emotionally healthy, kind, and loving will be attracted to you.

It's smart to put off even thinking about looking for a man until you can honestly say that you truly embody within yourself the whole laundry list of qualities that you want in your man. First you need to *be* the right person – to know what your values are and to live by them. Next you need to understand your personality archetype and the personality archetype of your most compatible mate, which we'll cover in Chapter 3. If you know what to look for in a man you will be able to attract the right man for you.

Role Models

There are very few role models of women who are strong, capable, feminine, and successful both personally and professionally. High profile women who make it to the top in politics or business, like Margaret Thatcher, often appear to be even tougher than the men they beat out to get there. Oprah Winfrey is one of the most accomplished and admired women in America, but she doesn't have a husband or kids making daily demands on her.

For most of my life I labored under the belief that being feminine meant being weak. Show any sign of caring or compassion in a business deal and you'd be run over by a man (or tough woman), whose only focus was getting to the bottom line and making sure their side came out on top. In those days, tension and stress were my constant companions. I even tried to use sex as a stress-reliever the way men do. No matter how hard I worked or how many wins I chalked up, I still wasn't happy.

Like many women in my generation, I've been involved in numerous short-term relationships. I'd meet someone new (or give an old beau another go), be happy for some period of time and then watch the relationship crumble. Yet I sometimes ran across women who were happily married or in a satisfying long-term relationship. What did they know that I didn't know? Was there some secret to having a good relationship that no one was willing to share?

As much as I loved and respected my mother, I didn't want to be like her. I dreamed of having my own business and knew I would never be happy "just" being a mother and homemaker. My mother had plenty of feminine power and strength, but as a child I did not understand or appreciate those qualities. I saw a world where men were in charge and thought women had to be aggressive to make it different. None of the men (or women) in my family ran their own businesses or even had a position of real leadership or authority at work. We were blue-collar working class, salt of the earth sorts.

Where was the role model of a woman who was powerful, successful, AND feminine? I couldn't look to my mother for my model. A product of the Depression and World War II, she was a stay-at-home Mom (for which I am very grateful — but, to be honest — I lacked respect for her quiet achievements of grace and family survival. But that's another story!). She genuinely enjoyed the domestic arts of cooking, decorating, sewing, and gardening. Her skills as a homemaker were outstanding. Her whole life centered on the family.

Not until my Dad became unable to work because of a heart condition, did Mom go to work. He died when I was thirteen and my mother kept the family going as a single working mom with a job as a salesperson in a department store. I was the first in our family to go to college, graduating from Syracuse University in 1969 at the height of the Flower Child Era.

Back then we thought that we could slough off the old limiting ideas about women as easily as a snake sheds its skin. We fully expected to charge off into the adult world and make our dreams a reality. The world of "equal pay for equal work" was just around the corner. We were free, weren't we?

We didn't realize the stranglehold that centuries of cultural conditioning still had on us.

But we didn't realize the stranglehold that centuries of cultural conditioning still had on us. On the surface it looked like we were free, but we weren't.

The vision of equality for women advocated by feminists in the last half of the 20th Century is still far from the everyday reality of most American women. We are now at the beginning of the 21st Century. We have entered a new millennium, and yet the way that men and women relate to each other is not significantly better than it was before.

After several decades of attempting to do it all and have it all, some women are closer to being paid equitably. More women are in leadership roles in business and politics. But most of us still have the same problems and complaints about men. Only now the men expect us to work full time, bring in the money, take care of the kids, and run the household too!

In the name of equality, we traded in the last vestiges of respect for feminine sensibilities. We believed that the way to be equal was to act like a traditional man.

We believed that the way to be equal was to act like a traditional man.

The feminist movement also affected men, many of whom are deeply committed to the traditional mentality, but a growing number of men are "modern men," striving alongside feminist women for a more egalitarian world. And they have lost their way in the unknown chaos of our changing society, just like women. Trying to do battle in the workplace under men's rules does nothing but turn women into tough, hard-boiled, stressed-out pseudo-men. Among other gains, women are also having more heart attacks and suffering from increased stress-related diseases.

Everywhere you turn, the media presents images of abrasive women, ready to cut down any man with a punch, a kick, or a verbal slash. We've been acting this way for decades now in the mistaken belief that the only way to get what we want in a male-dominated society is to adopt male-style tactics of violence and aggression. This "win or lose" mentality is unnatural for women. When left to our own devices, we find ways to cooperate with each other and create "win-win" solutions.

Most women who work in the business world competing with men in traditionally structured hierarchical organizations believe they have to play by the rules invented by men. The problem is that when you've been acting that way all day, it's difficult, if not impossible, to shift gears in your personal life after work. We come home battle-weary and exhausted to face the "second-shift" of childcare and household duties. Have you ever wished you could have a wife?

"Some of us are becoming the men we wanted to marry."
— Gloria Steinem

Is it any surprise we're having trouble in our relationships with men? We're trying to behave like them! But both traditional and modern heterosexual men want to be with a woman, not another man. They all want to enjoy their woman's sensuous side. But who has time to relax enough to feel sexy? Doing it all has just about done us in. Are you fed up enough to consider doing it a different way?

Doing it all has just about done us in.

Our Collective Roots

Back in the 1930's, psychoanalyst, Carl Jung, first proposed the concept of the "collective unconscious," which means that there is a common field of human thought to which we are all connected on a deep subconscious level. This consciousness holds all the stereotyped beliefs and thoughts of the entire human species. It influences the ideas we accept to be true on a deep level. These unconscious beliefs are so powerful and pervading that we don't even realize they are operating within us. We simply act on them as being "the truth."

Throughout the ages, human beings thought slavery was an acceptable practice. The idea was so ingrained in the collective unconscious that it never occurred to our freedom-loving forefathers that slavery was wrong. We finally abolished slavery, but the descendants of those freed slaves still suffer from the remnants of those beliefs. It takes a long time to impress a belief into the collective unconscious, and a long time to change it once it is established there.

On the surface women have made progress. We're able to work in just about any field we desire. We've made some strides in getting paid on a more equal par with men that do the same work. But our Western culture is still dominated by the values of the traditional man.

Western culture is still dominated by the values of the traditional man.

The Killer Woman

Now we see new images of women being thrust on us by the media. These ideas are just as destructive as the old ones. They are simply at the other end of the spectrum. We've now gone from the "female = weak and powerless" model to the "female = tough and violent" model.

One of the earliest examples is Princess Leia in the very first *Star Wars* movie. She was always putting down the males with a wisecrack or a derisive look. With her tough-cookie demeanor, she'd grab a weapon and show the guys how it should be done. But her antics are kindergarten level compared to what we see in movies and television today.

Later came *Thelma and Louise*, the story of two women who are fed up with being used and betrayed by men, and decide to get their revenge. Their newly discovered power is expressed by robbing stores and killing. On the run with nothing left to lose, they choose to drive themselves over a cliff to their own destruction, rather than surrender to the pursuing lawmen.

Another kind of "Killer Woman" is the woman who uses her sexuality in a cold-blooded, calculating fashion as exemplified by Sharon Stone's character in *Basic Instinct*. Giving her interrogators a fleeting glimpse of her private parts completely unnerved the men and thus accomplished her goal.

In advertising, movies, and TV we see more references to the leather-clad, stiletto-heeled dominatrix, an image of female sexual dominance that many men find titillating. But all these concepts of female power are clichéd versions of women acting like men or women dressing sexy for men. There is no pure feminine power there.

The original goal of feminism was to achieve gender equality. In his book *Killer Woman Blues*, Benjamin DeMott says, "releasing the sexes from imprisonment in fixed gender roles would mean richer, more amply imagined lives for all." The way to accomplish this goal is to accept that both sexes are capable of a full range of emotional and intellectual expression. Individuals have differing combinations of traits and talents, and none are the exclusive property of either men or women.

But our culture finds it too difficult, too challenging, or simply not profitable enough to present us with images that support gender equality and flexibility. Instead DeMott says that in the media "smart, career-minded, theoretically liberated women are depicted as driven by rage to scorn and humiliate men."

This may sound discouraging but there is some hope on the horizon. The media has also begun to report on other trends that are happening now, which show promising signs of a shift in our culture. About one third of top women executives and CEO's surveyed recently reported that they had stay-at-home spouses who handled domestic duties, so they could manage the demands of their careers and still have an intact family. Women are outpacing men when it comes to college enrollments too. More and more colleges and universities are finding that over 50 percent of their students are now women.

Changing our male-dominated culture is a slow process, but an inevitable one that cannot be stopped. New definitions and models of women, men, and relationships are being formed right now and you can be part of this new world.

Which Relationship Fits You?

Single Women

Consider yourself lucky if you are single right now. Single women have an advantage because they will be able to magnetize the right kind of man once they have completed the plan outlined in this book. If you are already dating a man, you will be able to test him to see if he is the right kind of man for you. And if he isn't, you'll have the courage and the confidence to move on. Do the work to become the real feminine woman who resides in your heart, and you will attract a man who has the desire and the ability to make you deliriously happy.

Married Women

Married women may have a more difficult task ahead of them. First, you need to determine whether the man you are married to is a keeper. If you love and respect your husband, but have a few issues that bother you, you certainly don't need to break up your marriage. If you have small children and your husband is a good father, you certainly don't want to break up your family. You may have to proceed slowly in developing and exercising your power. One thing is for certain. If you are making changes within yourself, your relationship cannot stay the same. And you will not stay the same.

> ***"In olden times sacrifices were made at the altar, a custom which is still continued."***
> ***— Helen Rowland, Reflections of a Bachelor Girl, 1909***

Maybe your man is a keeper but your marriage has lost that spark and you feel disconnected from him. Do not try to change your partner; that never works. Just work on yourself. You may be pleasantly surprised at what happens with your man when you begin to believe and act differently. A woman who is unshakably centered in the power of her femininity is a woman who is irresistible to a man.

A woman who is unshakably centered in the power of her femininity is a woman who is irresistible to a man.

Abusive Relationships

If you or your children are being physically or verbally abused, then do whatever it takes to get help and GET OUT! No matter how bad you think being alone could be, you will survive. If you stay, it's not going to get better; it's only going to get worse.

An abusive man is not worth the dirt under your heel. You will never be able to build a healthy sense of self-esteem as long as you are under his influence. Ask God for help and your prayer will be answered. A better life is waiting for you, but it will not happen until you make your escape.

I hope that reading this book will help you find the courage to do what you must do. There is a better way to live. I pray that you find the strength to take that first step toward the light. I was physically threatened and abused in one of my marriages and I know how difficult and frightening it can be to make that break. I found the courage with the help of professional counselors and friends, and I know you can too.

The Path to Power and Love

Now is the time for women to come to the forefront. It's time for us to discover our true potential and the enormous power we have to influence the people and the world around us. It's time to change the balance of power between men and women, and the purpose of this book is to show you the way.

We have outlined the basic individual problems and cultural influences that make it difficult for men and women to develop good relationships. Let's start learning how to overcome these difficulties and develop satisfying relationships. Before we look at a new way of understanding men (which you'll find in Section Two), we first need a new way of understanding ourselves as women. That's what Section One is all about.

The next chapter explores how to find and embrace our feminine power. Are you ready to deepen your appreciation of your inborn feminine qualities and widen their expression in your life? That's just what we're going to do next!

Chapter 2

Embracing Your Feminine Power

"The seat of a woman's power is her relationship to her own erotic nature."

— Regena Thomashauer

We live in a culture that uses sexual images to sell everything from music to automobiles. At first glance we appear to be a sexually liberated society but we Americans are very conflicted about sex. We get mixed messages from everywhere. There's more sex and nudity now on cable TV shows and in the movies than ever before, and more teens are having sex at increasingly younger ages. However, when it comes to feeling good about our sexual nature and really enjoying its pleasures, we have a long way to go.

A Woman's Power

Every woman has a power within her that no man can match—the power to create and nourish a new human being within her womb. Our menstrual cycle connects us to the rhythms of Nature, regularly reminding us that a potential miracle lies within us every month – the miracle of egg uniting with sperm to create a new life.

This undeniable fact that it is woman who births new life was most likely the reason that at the dawn of human history, God was thought to be female. Our earliest human ancestors saw this miracle happening before them and did not know how to explain it. It was natural that they would want to worship the mysterious and unseen source of power that was inherent in every female. And it was logical for them to assume that the great and powerful unseen deity was female.

Worshiping the Great Goddess

During the thousands of years that the Great Goddess was worshipped and revered, human beings, both male and female, had very different attitudes toward sex and reproduction than we do. Some of the oldest works of art found on the walls of caves are symbolic of the female vagina. In fact the very opening of the cave was itself a symbol of the vagina, and going into the depths of the cave to perform sacred rituals was, for those people, a way of entering into the mystery of life itself.

Women had lots of power in those days, but the archaeological evidence shows that they shared power with men. Most tribes and settlements lived peaceably. The women's power was usually concentrated in the temples of the Great Goddess. The temple priestesses often controlled much of the land and conducted the business of the community. In some communities the head priestess or Queen chose a male to be her main consort for a year or more. When she wanted a change she simply chose a new consort. The temple women were free to do as they wished sexually. No one was concerned about who the father of their children was. Every child was legitimate because he or she was born of a woman, and property was inherited through the mother only.

Sex as Religious Experience

Rituals in the temples often included sex between the priestesses and young, virile men as an expression of union with the Great Goddess. It is hard for us to imagine that sex and pleasure could be such an integral part of a religious experience. And yet, if we have any hope of rescuing ourselves and our male-dominated culture from the damage that centuries of sexual repression and violence have done, we must go beyond our cultural programming.

In the last 5,000 years nearly all cultures on earth became male-dominated. Men used both politics and religion to gain control over women. Women had to be virgins before marriage and were closely controlled by their husbands and religious laws for their entire lives for one basic reason. There was no other way a man could be sure of the paternity of his sons. As all property and power were now handed down through the father, women were treated like chattel. Women's power was so feared that the church had to control people's sex lives with threats of banishment to everlasting hell should they have sex for any reason other than to procreate. In Chapter 4 we will explore more fully how male-dominated politics influenced religion to help bring women under control.

It has taken them thousands of years and untold numbers of laws and edicts to continue the effort to keep women down. That should be proof enough for you that we are indeed powerful. Why would they be so afraid of us if we weren't! Are you starting to get some idea now of how much our attitudes and beliefs have been formed by these thousands of years of oppression? I'm not telling you these things to make you angry or upset. You must understand that you have a lot of unconscious thought to overcome if you are to step into your true power.

Feminine power is something we all have within us simply by virtue of having been born female.

Feminine power is something we all have within us simply by virtue of having been born female. What we need to do to reclaim it is to peel away the cultural conditioning and find the truth at the core for ourselves.

Body Image

The first obstacle we have to address is body image. Only a tiny percentage of women come close to meeting the ridiculous standards of beauty that are foisted on us by the media. The average woman in the United States is a size 14, not a size 4. To show you how utterly ridiculous and how insanely deep our disapproval of our own bodies can go, let me use myself as an example.

In my younger days I was a size six, but always thought my breasts were too small and my hips and tummy too big. After menopause my body changed. My waist got thicker, my belly got larger. I gained weight and my whole body became softer and rounder. What was happening to me was a perfectly natural and normal process but I hated it. I am now a size eight and I think I'm fat. Is that crazy or what? The only good thing I saw in it was that I finally had some womanly breasts.

Most women who are over 50 like me would kill to be a size eight. After doing all the research into human history and prehistory while writing this book, I know better than most how brainwashed we are about our bodies. And yet that brainwashing is still at work in me, even though I see it for what it is.

Learning to Love Your Belly

I knew that if I really wanted to own my feminine power I had to find a way to stop criticizing my body. I wanted to accept myself as I am and not try to fit myself into someone else's idea of beauty. The part of my body that I criticized the most was my belly. I had long been fascinated by belly dancing but never tried it. Dancing has always been my favorite form of exercise; I took ballet, jazz, and tap classes at various times. For years I studied ballroom dancing to the extent that I even became a professional teacher of ballroom dance. But now belly dancing beckoned me. I decided I would face squarely the part of my body that I had made my enemy and learn to love it.

I started taking belly dance classes and fell madly in love with the dance. It is truly a womanly art, and it really looks best when the dancer has some curves and some meat on her bones. This is no dance for skinny bitches! There were all sizes and shapes of women in our class, and I was really impressed with how beautifully many of them could dance. I went to a Middle Eastern dance convention where lots of student troupes performed and got my first taste of a totally new form of belly dance that transformed my life: American Tribal Belly Dance.

American Tribal Belly Dance

This uniquely American dance form began in San Francisco in the late 1980's with Carolena Nericcio and her "Fat Chance Belly Dance" troupe. They developed a style of costuming and a movement vocabulary that is a fusion of many styles from around the world. I bought one of their videos and sat transfixed as I watched them for the first time. Decked out in turbans and layers of antique jewelry and textiles from exotic places like Afghanistan and Pakistan, their elegant and sensuous movements riveted my attention. They danced in synchronized movement as a group and were utterly mesmerizing to watch. That did it for me. I went totally Tribal and never looked back.

The Dance for Every Woman

The more I learned about Tribal, the more I loved it. One of the best things about the style was that women of every age, shape, and size could learn the movements and look great doing them. And the same went for the costumes. Every dancer assembled her own unique costume from the old and the new, and could adapt any of the folkloric clothing styles that looked best on her. It is not even necessary to show your belly in this style of dance unless you want to. Your costume can show as much or as little skin as you are comfortable with. Most of us Tribal babes start out with our torsos covered and let our costumes evolve to show more as we become more confident in our dance skills and learn to love and accept our womanly bodies as they are.

American Tribal Belly Dance is not about being overtly sexy or seductive in the way that we usually think of belly dancing. It is more about dancing together as a group and making each other look good. It is certainly sexy too, but in a way that is dignified, sensuous, and respectful of all that is female. It is improvisational, not choreographed, so dancers can express themselves spontaneously with the music. There is a leader whom everyone follows, but the leader role is constantly changing so each dancer gets a chance to be the leader.

What a perfect metaphor this dance is for the way that women naturally relate to each other and the world.

When I learned how it worked, I marveled at what a perfect metaphor this dance is for the way that women naturally relate to each other and the world. In American Tribal style there are no individual "stars," no hierarchies, and no competitions. Subtle gestures by the leader cue the dancers to which step comes next. The leader voluntarily gives up the lead to the next dancer by traveling smoothly out of the lead position, signaling the whole group to shift positions as the new leader moves into the lead position. To the casual observer it all seems like magic as if the dancers are reading each other's minds. What a beautiful expression of teamwork in the feminine style! Most men would find it difficult to cope in a group where the leader role is always in flux, but women revel in it.

Non-competitive

Every other dance style appears to have numerous competitive events and titles that dancers can aspire to such as "Belly Dancer of the Universe." So far American Tribal Style has resisted the all-American (and typically masculine) desire to start a contest to see who is number one, the champion. There are a number of large Tribal conventions around the country you can attend, but the program consists of dance workshops, performances by Tribal troupes, and shopping in a colorful exotic bazaar of Tribal clothing, jewelry, and music. Tribal style belly dance teachers are known for their willingness to freely share steps, patterns, and techniques, rather than jealously guarding their trade secrets as other dance teachers often do. Competing for trophies has no meaning for Tribal dancers, and I personally hope it never will.

Belly Power

I love watching women with round, womanly bodies dancing with such strength and power. Learning this dance has really transformed my opinion of my body and especially my belly. For women the belly is the center of our feminine power and when you can really love and respect that part of yourself you can then command that love and respect from the rest of the world. In belly dancing you learn to isolate different muscles and different parts of the body so they move independently of each other but always in rhythm with the music. It is so much fun to learn. As you gain more control over your

For women the belly is the center of our feminine power and when you can really love and respect that part of yourself you can then command that love and respect from the rest of the world.

body it gives you an awesome sense of power to be able to move whatever part you choose in time to the music and to look good doing it.

When a whole group of women is doing the same movement perfectly in sync with each other and the music, the dancers and the audience are transported to another realm. Like a flock of colorful exotic birds we undulate, spin, and change directions together in perfect rhythm. You really feel that you and your sister dancers are a tribe. The music is primal and exotic with lots of drums, percussion, and strange sounding instruments that make you believe you've been magically teleported back in time to some ancient nomad encampment.

Few things make you feel more like a Goddess than belly dancing. If you have a secret wish to try it (and a great many women do), don't wait any longer. Find yourself a class, a Tribal class if possible (but any belly dance class will do), and get started. Your body will love you for it and you will learn to love your body.

To stay fit and healthy we all need to move and use our bodies on a regular basis. If dancing is not your thing, maybe there is a sport you enjoy. Even the simple habit of walking every day brings you great benefits. Physical activity is absolutely necessary for every Goddess, and it is up to you to find something you enjoy and then make it one of your top priorities right up there with eating and sleeping.

Asking and Receiving

If there's anything that disturbs me about how women act these days, it's when I see a woman refuse to let a man open a door for her. How did we go so wrong in our thinking that we believe we shouldn't allow men to help us? We have to teach our daughters and ourselves that it is essential to be respected by men, and to give them every opportunity to show their respect in daily life. The good men of the world love to show their respect by helping and serving us. We do them and ourselves a great disservice when we refuse to allow them to make these gestures of respect. Allowing a man to open a door, pay for your drink or dinner, move a heavy box for you, and help you in every way possible is enjoyable for him. You are not obligated to do anything in return but be polite and appreciative. That's enough for a good man. He loves feeling useful and your gracious smile of appreciation is all the payment he needs.

How did we go so wrong in our thinking that we believe we shouldn't allow men to help us?

When you allow a perfect stranger to do a little thing like hold the door open for you, it makes you feel respected as a representative of the female gender. If men are not voluntarily offering these little respectful gestures to you, then you need to adjust your attitude. When you become connected to your feminine power and have a deep knowing that you are worthy of respect just because you are a woman, men pick up on your attitude on an unconscious level and treat you with respect.

Woman's Divine Purpose

Asking for help is another thing many women are reluctant to do. When you ask for help from a man it doesn't mean you are helpless. It means you understand the male need to be helpful. We women have an advantage over men in that we are born with a divine purpose woven right into our identity as a female. If we do nothing else in life but bear a child and be a good mother to that child, we have fulfilled the divine promise of being born female.

When you ask for help from a man it doesn't mean you are helpless. It means you understand the male need to be helpful.

A Man Needs a Purpose

The male is not so lucky. He does not have the luxury of having such an obvious destiny. He has to find a purpose for himself and ful-

Males need females to give them a sense of purpose and direction.

fill it through his own efforts. Haven't you noticed how single males often seem to be lost puppies without a direction in life and no idea of how to get one? Males need females to give them a sense of purpose and direction. They are so much happier when they have a woman to please and are shown just how to please her. It sets up a cycle where the man is able to feel successful. A man has all kinds of wonderful talents and abilities, but without a woman to help focus his energies toward worthwhile goals, he flounders.

A man loves having a clearly definable mission to fulfill.

So when you ask a man for help, you are doing him a favor. You are giving him a specific task that he knows he can do. A man loves having a clearly definable mission to fulfill. When it's done, he's a hero and all he craves in return is your appreciation for his efforts.

Feminine power is all about being able to communicate and receive what you want and need from a man, and bestowing your sincere appreciation on him in return.

If you haven't discovered this little secret yet, you have been working way too hard by trying to do everything yourself. Let a man help you! Feminine power is all about being able to communicate and receive what you want and need from a man, and bestowing your sincere appreciation on him in return.

Earth Mothers and Star Women

There are two basic female personality types. One is the Earth Mother, the nurturer, who is predominantly focused on caring and growing. The other is the Star Woman, the leader, who is predominantly focused on envisioning the future and inspiring others. They have different strengths and weaknesses, which will be covered thoroughly in the next chapter.

Feminine Power for Earth Mothers

Earth Mothers may have an easier time identifying with their feminine power. They know they have the power to bring forth children and to nurture and guide them into adulthood. They are often less than thrilled when they find out that their adult husband needs similar nurturing and guidance too. I'm sure you've heard your women friends complain that managing their husband is too much like having another child in the family.

If a woman perceives her husband this way, he seems like a burden. The truly wise and powerful woman sees her husband as a bundle of energy and potential who just needs direction.

A woman of integrity who has a sense of purpose larger than herself can influence her man to direct his energy in ways that are good for the family, the nation, and the planet. This is the challenge for Earth Mothers. You may not want to take the reins of leadership in your relationship as fully as a Star Woman might, but you should not abdicate establishing the standards and values in your family and insisting that everyone live up to them.

> ***"A man's wife has more power over him than the state has."***
>
> ***— Ralph Waldo Emerson***

> ***The truly wise and powerful woman sees her husband as a bundle of energy and potential who just needs direction.***

Your husband probably enjoys being the family strategist and planning how and when things are to be done. It's fine to let him do that, but you must be sure that you have exercised your influence in establishing the goal for him in the first place. Does he put too much energy and time into work while neglecting to spend enough energy and time on you and the children? This is the kind of issue where your influence is critical. This is when you use your feminine power to steer him in the direction you know is best for your family.

Be the Spiritual Compass

Every woman has the right and the obligation to be the spiritual compass for her family. Problems arise when you start out a marriage without a clear idea of what your values are or when your values change over time. A man who is used to you just going along with his program is likely to get upset when you develop a backbone and a mind of your own.

Every woman has the right and the obligation to be the spiritual compass for her family.

Values Count

It is so much easier if you wait long enough to really develop your own personal sense of values and integrity before you get married. When those values are firmly established in your mind and heart you will attract a partner who has similar values. If you see that a potential mate has values that are not a match for yours you will have the strength to walk away from that relationship knowing that it cannot work.

It's more difficult for a husband to adjust to the fact that you have suddenly discovered your power; you now know what is important to you and are no longer willing to blindly follow his lead. If he loves you enough, he will make the adjustment and start respecting your opinions and accepting your influence. If he won't, you are faced with a tough choice – stay and live with the tension and conflict, or leave and face the difficulties of breaking up your family and starting over. Neither one is a great choice, but finding our way through situations like this is what makes us grow. One thing is for certain. When a woman who has been too much of a doormat discovers and embraces her power, her relationship with her man must inevitably change.

Feminine Power for Star Women

For Star Women the issue of finding our feminine power is a little more complex. We are born to lead, but our role models for leadership are mostly men (or women who act like men). We have to learn to dig down and find the female wisdom and power at our core, then develop ways of expressing that power that allow us to be our true feminine selves. Leadership and femininity are not mutually exclusive qualities.

Leadership and femininity are not mutually exclusive qualities.

We can and should put the male strategies we learned in the workplace on the back burner, bringing them out only when absolutely necessary. It is much more effective to come from the quiet but enormous reservoir of strength and wisdom that is at our center. When you have your own set of values and priorities clearly established in your mind, the people around you tend to respect and abide by your standards. You have to be like a rock rooted deeply in the earth. Nothing can sway you from what you know is right, and you expect proper conduct from the people around you.

Let us stop fighting and struggling to crawl up the male hierarchies so prevalent in business and government. We can step away from that battlefield and set up our own businesses and networks to accomplish the things that are important to us. Instead of trying to capture the titles and the power all the men are vying for, we simply need to use our feminine power and influence on the men who hold the titles and the power. Changes in our society and in the world will not happen by the power of might, but by the power of right thinking by enough individuals.

Changes in our society and in the world will not happen by the power of might, but by the power of right thinking by enough individuals.

Star Women need to pay more attention to being rather than doing in their quest for feminine power. Let others, especially your man, take care of the doing part. Let the intuitive, deep, spiritual wisdom at your center radiate, and you will be truly unstoppable. Let us be like the priestesses and queens of prehistoric times. Our wisdom and influence is what is needed in the world right now. We have only to connect with it on a deep level.

Let the intuitive, deep, spiritual wisdom at your center radiate, and you will be truly unstoppable.

Star Women are usually self-confident people who are not afraid to hold opinions that differ from the mainstream. They are able to withstand disapproval from other people, and have developed the strength to follow their own dreams. The danger for Star Women is that if all this self-confidence is not tempered with compassion, it can turn into arrogance. That is why it is so important for Star Women to find and integrate their feminine power into their already powerful personalities. When the yang (masculine) qualities of leadership and vision are balanced with the yin (feminine) qualities of compassion and nurturing, the result is a compelling combination that can truly inspire others to action.

Nurture Your Sensuous Side

Both Star Women and Earth Mothers alike need to take time to nurture themselves and enjoy the sensuous side of the feminine. Giving ourselves the time and attention we need to look and feel beautiful is not mere self-indulgence. It is a necessity in order for us to stay grounded in our feminine power. Sensual pleasure and sexual satisfaction are meant to be as natural as breathing. We have to find our way back to the highest values of our ancient sisters, whose womanly bodies and feminine power were respected

We have to find our way back to the highest values of our ancient sisters, whose womanly bodies and feminine power were respected and revered by all.

and revered by all. I enjoy being the queen of my household and my husband enjoys being the queen's consort. That's a much sexier role than the conventional role of husband, don't you think?

A number of good books are available on the subject of getting in touch with our feminine power, and my favorites are listed in the bibliography. I encourage you to explore your own feminine nature in whatever way appeals to you. There are many avenues and approaches that can help you connect to your feminine power, but you need to experiment to find the right way for you.

The Modern Goddess

The Great Goddess may be an ancient echo in the collective unconscious of the human race, but her legacy still lives in every woman. Our goal is not to try to recapture the past, but to go forward and create a new model for women – the "Modern Goddess." The 20th century ushered in the modern era of more freedom and more rights for women. Another big push came in the 1960's and 1970's with the "Women's Liberation" movement, which helped to open up more opportunities for women to work in previously male-dominated fields.

We focused so intently on getting money and position and things that we lost sight of what it really means to be female. We forgot that men are meant to serve us. We forgot how to be gracious and serene. That is why, now that we have entered the 21st century and the next millennium, it's time for us to take another leap forward and become proud examples of the truly Modern Goddess. Cultivating the proper Goddess attitude naturally attracts good into your life. Struggle becomes a thing of the past. With the right attitude you can harness the flow of good that is your God-given right and ride it gracefully toward your desires.

> ***"Life is a banquet, and most poor suckers are starving to death"***
>
> ***— Auntie Mame***

The Four Pillars

The four pillars of the Modern Goddess are the foundation on which your new life is built. As you create and cultivate the four pillars in yourself, your life begins to move and change in magical and mysterious ways. To be a woman is to be an earthbound vessel for the unseen power that is the true nature of our reality. That power is meant to be honored and cherished, as is every woman on this planet. The Four Pillars give us some simple guidelines for remembering how beautiful and special each one of us is.

To be a woman is to be an earthbound vessel for the unseen power that is the true nature of our reality.

Pillar I: Never Rush.

A Goddess has time for everything that is important to her. She stays calm and relaxed. If you are stressed out and harried, stop and take a deep breath. You always have all the time you need if you believe you do. Learn how to say no. Don't over-commit yourself. Live life at your own pace.

Pillar II: Never Worry.

A Goddess knows that she always has everything she needs. Worry is needlessly borrowing trouble from the future. She knows that things always have a way of working themselves out if we allow them to. She has a deep and abiding faith that God is her source and she always has enough.

Pillar III: Receive Graciously.

A Goddess graciously receives all gifts and compliments with a simple, "thank you." She never belittles or criticizes herself or her accomplishments. When someone wants to give you something or help you, accept the gift with a smile. A Goddess always remembers that allowing men to assist and serve her is the gift she gives to them.

Pillar IV: Appreciate Continually.

Accept and appreciate all the good that comes to you, especially the little things. Whatever you appreciate increases. Make it a habit to say, "how usual!" whenever something good happens to you. The more you express your gratitude, the more good the universe sends your way.

Today these Four Pillars are the foundation of my everyday life. They are all ingrained in me as habits of thinking and action. Not only do they make daily living a joy, they also make it possible to attract a great man who thinks the same way. It should be no surprise to you that my husband has these very same habits and beliefs.

How Usual

Most people react to something good happening to them as an out-of-the-ordinary event. How often have you said, "I don't believe it!" or, "that's amazing!" when you receive a delightful surprise. Words and thoughts have great power, so if your words convey to the universe that this is an unusual occurrence, it will comply. Your subconscious will make sure that "it's amazing" that anything good ever happens to you.

In our house we have adopted a more positive way of responding. My husband and I love to exclaim (often in unison), "how usual!" whenever something good happens to either of us whether it is a parking spot, a good news phone call, or a nice fat check in the mail. Receiving good is "how usual" in our life because we are in the habit of mentally creating it. Why not get into the "how usual!" habit yourself. Let the universe know that receiving good is a regular, everyday thing for you, too. "How usual!"

The path to a happier life as a woman starts with discovering, accepting, and embracing your own feminine power. Remember the Four Pillars of the Modern Goddess and adopt those attitudes as your own. Do that and you will begin to see changes in how you feel about yourself and how others treat you.

The first step on this path is in the next chapter where you will discover your personal identifying archetype. We begin by exploring the two basic types of female personalities: Star Woman and Earth Mother. Which one are you and how does that affect your relationships?

Chapter 3

Star Women and Earth Mothers

The Native American tribes of the Southwest treasure and hand down many legends and stories about Corn Mother and Rainbow Woman. Corn Mother symbolizes the nurturing aspect of womanhood, the part that grows and cares for life. Corn was the staple of their diet—and it was a revered symbol of life. Rainbow Woman symbolizes the leader, visionary, and idealist who inspires others to action.

These beautiful and inspiring images of womanhood can help us understand our own natures. Images like these are called archetypes, which means they are an ideal example or model. In the psychological theories of Carl Jung, an archetype is an inherited memory represented in the mind by a universal symbol and observed in dreams and myths. To make these two concepts more easily understood in our contemporary Western culture, I shall call them Earth Mother and Star Woman. We already hold the image of Earth Mother in our race consciousness. The Native Americans who originated this concept estimate that 80 percent of American women would likely consider themselves predominantly Earth Mothers, and have this nurturing imperative as the driving force in their personalities. The other 20 percent are the Star Women who are natural born leaders, who are more driven to set and accomplish goals, and who persuade and inspire others.

> ***"Anyone who thinks women are the weaker sex has never met my wife."***
>
> ***— Ozzy Osbourne***

All women have both Earth Mother and Star Woman aspects in their personalities in differing, not equal, amounts. One aspect is always stronger than the other. The stronger part is the personality type with which we most identify. This is the face we present to the world and this is how we approach everyday living; however, when the situation requires it, we can call forth the other part to help us.

Shifting Identities

Some women retain their primary identity as an Earth Mother or Star Woman for their entire lives. Others shift their primary identity from one to the other (and sometimes back again) according to their circumstances and priorities during particular periods of their lives. These days we increasingly hear about women who spend their younger adult years avidly pursuing career goals until they have a child. Then they realize that no corporate version of the "mommy track" is going to be an acceptable alternative to raising their child themselves during his or her formative years. They change their priorities, throw off the Star Woman mantle, and wholeheartedly embrace the role of Earth Mother. Parenting their child becomes more important than any outside-the-home career.

On the other hand, you probably know at least one woman who was a devoted mother until her children grew up and left the nest. Then she started a business, took up some artistic pursuit, or assumed a community leadership position with great energy and focus, surprising her family and creating a whole new role for herself, in addition to her role as mother. The female sex is outstanding in our ability to adapt to changes in circumstances by being flexible in the roles we play.

The Earth Mother

For the Earth Mother woman, giving comes as easily and as naturally as breathing. It is in her nature to give. She loves doing for others, especially her husband and children. She's the one who brings the most delicious casserole to the potluck. She's quick with a hug for a crying child. She notices if you're feeling down and tries to cheer you up. She loves being a mother and strives to be the best mother she can be. She derives great satisfaction from selflessly serving and helping other people, and usually doesn't require that a great deal of fuss be made over her contributions. The power and leadership abilities of the Earth Mother are directed toward others, especially in service to her immediate family. Thank goodness that a great majority of women are strong Earth Mothers. We need the nurturing, sustaining energy these women bring to the world. They are the ones who grow, attend to, and care for the people and environment around them, for their families, and for their communities.

The Star Woman

In many Native American tribes, women leaders were called Rainbow Women and were highly respected. They were recognized as potential Rainbow Women early in their lives and groomed to be leaders and shamans for their people. Our culture is less enlightened. We seldom recognize or encourage the leadership gifts of our girls in the same way. We have no respectful title like *Rainbow Woman* in our culture for female leaders, so let us crown her with one: *Star Woman*.

The Star Woman is generally possessed of talents and skills that desire interaction and recognition in the outer world. She tends to be more oriented toward self and intent on finding ways to express her gifts and gain approval or status. It is her nature to lead and inspire others to follow her cause. She sees the big picture and wants to have an effect on it. To others she can appear self-centered at times because she is so focused on her goal.

Star Women often feel they are destined for greatness if they can just find the right way to use their talent and leadership abilities. They are ambitious dreamers who long to make their mark on the world someday. While they can be excellent mothers, they also need to find some success and applause in the world outside of the family, in order to feel truly satisfied with their lives.

> ***"In politics, if you want anything said, ask a man; if you want anything done, ask a woman."***
>
> ***– Margaret Thatcher***

The Little Star Child

I always knew I was meant to be a visionary leader. In fact one of my earliest memories is deciding, at age three, to lead a parade around the block. I was playing in the backyard alone at the time and wasn't allowed to go out of the yard, but I never let petty, little details and stupid rules stop me (and still don't!). So I found a stick and had my parade all by myself, proudly strutting my stuff just like Robert Preston in *The Music Man*. With cars honking and people smiling and waving at me, I had a grand time and made it completely around the entire block without a mishap. My mother never knew about this little adventure of mine (until she reads this!). Even as a tiny child, my leadership potential and Star Woman nature burst forth into expression.

Earth Mother Leadership

Until quite recently in modern history, women's opportunities were culturally limited. So, unless she was prepared to fight against prevailing customs, the best way that a woman could express her Star Woman aspect was to become the matriarch and leader of her family. My feisty grandmother was one of these. She was the General, Drill Sergeant, and CFO (Chief Financial Officer) all rolled into one. In her home her word was law. My ten aunts and uncles and my Grandpa had to toe the line – or else! When things were going well, she tended to be somewhat moody and unpredictable. Her hot temper was legendary in the family. I think she was trying to cover up and ignore an underlying sense of frustration at her lot in life.

During her childhood her immigrant family was so poor that she was forced to quit school after 8th grade and go to work. She married before she was 20 and started having babies. Being a good Catholic, she kept on having babies. As a child she had dreamed of being a nurse, but was never able to realize that dream.

She was essentially an Earth Mother who concerned herself exclusively with every aspect of family life. With ten children to raise during the Great Depression of the 1930's, she had plenty with which to be concerned. My grandfather was a truck driver who was away from home for long stretches at a time. Her heart was so big that not only did she raise her own ten children, she also took in three foster children! Running that household and feeding all those children on a shoestring budget required incredible leadership, fortitude, and strategic planning skills that any military officer would admire.

When there was a big problem or crisis, my grandmother, Nonnie, was at her best. She would organize her resources, rally the troops, and sally forth to save the day. I remember when my little brother's tonsils were removed. He came home from the hospital and seemed to be recovering just fine on his first day at home. On the second day he started hemorrhaging and we all panicked. My Mom called Nonnie, who lived a block away. Nonnie ran straight through our neighbor's yard and somehow hopped over their tall fence into our backyard – flowered dress, apron, and all! She arrived at our house in a flash and immediately took over. She always knew just what to do, no matter what the problem. We always knew we could count on her when the chips were down.

Nonnie was my hero. She pushed me to go to college and become whatever I wanted to be. And she encouraged me to bypass having children. My Nonnie could surely have been a great businesswoman or community leader, in addition to caring for her family, if she had had access to the education and opportunities (and birth control!) women have today.

Female Personality Wheel

The Female Personality Wheel on the next page organizes the characteristics of these two types of personalities. You will probably easily recognize the archetype you most identify with. All four of the archetypes within the wheel are present within every woman, but at any given moment our actions and attitudes tend to reflect strongly just one of the four.

Earth Mothers emphasize the traits that are thought of as feminine in our society.

Star Women exhibit many traits that we think of as masculine.

These opposite poles are called yin (feminine) and yang (masculine) in Eastern thought. The Star Woman has more yang in her than the Earth Mother, and those yang qualities are not often appreciated or encouraged in our modern women.

The Light Side

Earth Mother	*Star Woman*
Nurturer	Leader
Protector	Visionary
Receptive	Active
Comforting	Inspiring
Soft Energy	Hard Energy
Yin	Yang

The Shadow Side

Volcano Woman	*Crazy Woman*
Over-Controlling	Out-Of-Control
Destructive Energy	Scattered Energy

Female Personality Wheel

Each of the two basic female types has an opposing shadow side. Native Americans characterize the shadow aspect of Earth Mother as a destroyer. Volcano Woman is our name for this archetype. Volcano energy is hidden beneath the Earth's surface until it is released to cause destruction. Volcano Woman undermines growth; she can destroy everything that Earth Mother has created and nurtured.

If an Earth Mother is unaware or refuses to entertain the thought that she could be anything but sweet and motherly, the Volcano Woman shadow side is free to work in secret behind the scene. For example, a woman can become an overprotective, smothering mother who ruins her children under the guise of being loving. Volcano

Woman is the controlling mother who will not let her children grow up; the gossip who spreads rumors that hurt others; or the critical wife who undermines her husband's masculinity. Volcano Woman is protective energy taken to the extreme.

Crazy Woman

The shadow side of Star Woman is Crazy Woman. She's out of control, her energy scattered, her emotions overblown. We all have seen Crazy Woman in action. She's the one who creates all that insane drama in your life. She can explode in anger from pent-up frustrations of which she is not even aware. If the Crazy Woman is repressed and never allowed to be spontaneous, she is free to work in the background. She will express herself using your everyday life as her canvas with disastrous results. Crazy Woman is creative energy gone awry.

Separation and Integration

We live in a world of duality. We need the contrast of opposites in order to distinguish differences. We can't understand what light is unless we compare it to dark. Our world is built on opposite poles: up and down, right and left, male and female. The reason we experience separateness is that we cannot appreciate togetherness unless we know its opposite. So we are born into an experience of being separated – separate from God and separate from others.

Our assignment here in earth school is to integrate the separate parts of us and regain awareness of our oneness with all life. As you seek to become a whole person who knows all of him or herself – the shadow side and the light side – your task is to become a person who is not afraid to bring those aspects out of the shadow and dance with them.

Our assignment here in earth school is to integrate the separate parts of us and regain awareness of our oneness with all life.

When you choose to become conscious of your shadow aspects, they can no longer hide and express themselves without your knowledge. You no longer deny their existence. Make friends with your shadow side, and you can harness that energy selectively. You can consciously choose to express the shadow aspect when it is appropriate. For example, if someone threatens your children, you call out Volcano Woman to defend them fiercely and, if necessary, destroy the threat. If you want to be creative, you bring Crazy Woman out to play, sing, dance, or paint, and to express your feelings in a creative, constructive way.

When you choose to become conscious of your shadow aspects, they can no longer hide and express themselves without your knowledge.

You are a unique and wonderful combination of all four of these feminine aspects. Get to know and work with all parts of you. When you become conscious of the shadow aspects of your personality, they are exposed to the light of your awareness, and you no longer expend emotional energy to keep them hidden and repressed. You become more openly diverse and have more innate talents at your command.

We have few well-known models of women who are truly respected and admired for exhibiting all the positive qualities of the Star Woman. Some men have an unconscious fear of Star Women, especially men who lack confidence in their own masculinity. To witness a woman who is a better leader than he, can make that kind of man even more insecure (we'll discuss types of men in a later chapter). Our modern culture has never before had a positive name for this kind of woman, although we have a number of negative terms that she is often called: bitch, ball-buster, battle-axe, etc.

> ***"We still think of a powerful man as a leader and a powerful woman as an anomaly."***
>
> ***—Margaret Atwood***

When I first learned about Rainbow Women, the whole concept of natural feminine leadership resonated as truth deep within my soul. I recognized myself in her image and was delighted to have a positive way to refer to myself. When I talk to women friends about this simple concept, everyone can immediately identify with either Earth Mother or Star Woman as their dominant personality archetype.

This book is written for both Star Women and Earth Mothers who are balancing their innate talents with their roles in life. Strong women no longer have to think of themselves as anomalies (something that deviates from the norm, something strange and difficult to classify). We can stop trying to hide our gifts. We can stop pretending to be less than our true selves and be proud of all that we really are.

We can stop pretending to be less than our true selves and be proud of all that we really are.

Strong Star Women archetypes are in the minority among the general population. Only about one in five women are Star Woman leaders and this is probably a good balance. We are all leaders in specific spheres of life, and we need people to follow us!

Star Women need to identify themselves as such and accept the fact that they may be a little short in the nurturing and empathy departments. They have to make an effort to develop their Earth Mother talents. A large part of the Star Woman's energy is masculine and action-oriented, and without some softer, more receptive feminine energy to balance it, this talented, energetic woman can come across as cold or standoffish.

A woman who projects this kind of persona is often mystified by her lack of success with men. She will complain, "Men just don't know how to handle a strong woman." An emotionally mature man is attracted to a woman's softer, more feminine qualities such as kindness and compassion. While he may admire and initially be attracted to her intelligence, toughness, or talent, those qualities don't make a connection to his heart. He is looking for that heart connection and a woman who has lost or rejected her connection to her own heart cannot connect with his. That is why it is so important that a Star Woman find the Earth Mother part of herself. When her personality is better balanced, she can let her softer side show, and thus become attractive to the kind of man she wants to attract.

Conversely, a woman who is heavily identified with the Earth Mother, but out of touch with her Star Woman is in danger of becoming too much of a people pleaser. Constantly looking outside herself for approval from others makes her seem weak and insecure. Often she has trouble saying, "no" to others' unreasonable requests because she is afraid of their disapproval. She is easy prey for a domineering man who is more than happy to run her life for her. This woman needs to develop her Star Woman aspect to give her the ability to stand up for herself. As she becomes better balanced, she can protect herself from those who would take advantage of her generous and giving nature.

Maternal? Not me!

My mother used to worry about me when I was growing up because I had no interest in children or motherhood, and little apparent talent for nurturing. My favorite toys were building blocks, not dolls. My lack in these areas was especially evident when we visited my Dad's Italian side of the family on Sundays. Family was the most important thing to them. Every son and daughter (all ten of them) was expected to bring their spouse and children every single Sunday to Grandma and Grandpa's house to check in and show their respects. Serious illness and death were about the only acceptable excuses for not showing up.

In such a big family, one or more of my aunties was always pregnant and a baby was always on the scene. I was the oldest female grandchild, but my younger cousins had much more interest in babies than me. They would be thrilled when an aunt handed them her latest bundle of joy, and let them hold and cuddle the baby. My aunts would push the baby into my arms. I'd hold it awkwardly out in front of me, hoping and praying that I wouldn't drop the little creature. I had no idea what to do with a baby and no interest in finding out. Cuddling was not in my vocabulary. I'd just hand the baby off to one of my cousins and run out to play. I know this embarrassed my parents. What kind of Italian girl doesn't love babies? The Star Woman kind, that's who!

I was repulsed by the idea of having children. It looked like way too much drudgery and responsibility to me. My Nonnie (grandmother on my mother's side) sometimes took me on her neighborhood rounds when she would help young mothers who were struggling with their little ones. They all seemed so miserable and worn out. She would charge in there, change diapers, clean up their kids and their kitchens, and get their laundry going. By the time Nonnie was done, those women had regained some hope of making it through another day. They were so grateful for my grandmother's visits.

This is a great example of how an Earth Mother uses her power and leadership abilities. She sees a need (especially where children are concerned) and takes the initiative to change the situation. Nonnie's strength and energy were a shining example to those young mothers. She was a model of how to combine heartfelt caring with a no-nonsense, practical way of helping others. She never belittled them for their failings. She simply lent them her strength and showed them the way.

One day we went to see a woman who had four kids all under five years old. The smell of dirty diapers in that house was unbelievable. It was a scene right out of a Victor Hugo novel – crying babies, dirty diapers, messy house, and that poor mother just sitting in despair on the floor in the middle of it all, shell-shocked and unable to move. That picture of motherhood was burned into my psyche forever. I decided I would never let myself end up like that.

As a young adult, my relationships with men were volatile and unstable, mostly because I was so self-centered. I knew that if I married and had kids, I was going to end up divorced and struggling to rear those kids on my own. So I chose not to have children. My mother would have liked grandchildren, but it was not to be.

Looking for Earth Mother

When I was in my late thirties, I started doing some soul-searching and realized that I needed to find the softer, nurturing side of myself. Now I understand that I was looking for the Earth Mother part of me.

I volunteered to be a Big Sister and that was a great experience. I was matched up with a beautiful, smart little seven-year-old girl and we got together every week. Sometimes we would go to a museum or a play. Other times we would just hang out at my home and do arts and crafts projects or dance. I really enjoyed being with her and giving her experiences that expanded her horizons.

My mother came out to visit me in California and met my little sister. She was so relieved to see that I did have mothering instincts after all, and she was proud of the way I nurtured and doted on that little girl. Although my dominant personality is definitely that of a Star Woman, acknowledging and expressing the Earth Mother in me helped me develop into a much better balanced, more loving, and more lovable person.

If you identify primarily with the Earth Mother image, it means your dominant energy is different from that of a Star Woman. You may not want or need to be as much of an outspoken leader in your marriage as a Star Woman might. However, your Star Woman qualities can undoubtedly help you exert a tremendous influence over your family. Every woman is a unique combination of all the feminine archetypes we are discussing here. And every woman needs to use each facet of her personality in an appropriate way to achieve the level of leadership that she desires in her household.

Every woman needs to use each facet of her personality in an appropriate way to achieve the level of leadership that she desires in her household.

Women have endless opportunities to affect the integrity, awareness, and values held by their husband and children. To do that with integrity and effectiveness requires that you develop your consciousness and awaken to your feminine power. Consciousness is what changes the world. Earth Mothers are every bit as powerful as their sister Star Women. The world needs Earth Mothers' power as well as that of Star Women, to help shape a balanced culture that both cares and achieves.

A Star Woman is a natural leader who usually ends up being the leader in her home as well as in her community. Until she learns how to lead her man gently and gracefully, she may just attempt to run roughshod over him and end up in a power struggle. She needs to learn how to handle her man with more compassion and sensitivity, so he will be happy and eager to provide the support she needs from him.

Because an Earth Mother often prefers not to engage in head-to-head battles with her partner, she may find herself giving in on important issues just to keep the peace. She needs to find her inner center of power so she will have the will and emotional strength to see that her partner takes her needs and opinions seriously.

A Balancing Act

A great many of us are born with a strong proclivity to either the Earth Mother or Star Woman archetype, and remain predominantly that type throughout the years. Others shift the emphasis in response to the ups and downs of life. As part of the maturing process, a woman usually discovers and accepts all parts of her nature and finds a comfortable balance suited to her personality. Princess Diana is a great example of this growing and balancing process. As her life was played out on the public stage, she underwent a fascinating transformation from all Earth Mother to an intelligently and deliberately balanced combination of both Earth Mother and Star Woman right before our eyes.

Princess Diana Finds Balance

Who can forget the sweet, innocent face and shy smile of Diana on her wedding day? She was all Earth Mother to Prince Charles in the early years of their marriage, bearing his heirs and trying valiantly to fit into the royal family and learn her duties as Princess. Then she was plunged into despair when the Prince's infidelities made the papers and she could no longer pretend everything was rosy at the castle. The tabloids informed us that she alternated between fits of anger and fits of depression. Crazy Woman and Volcano Woman were unleashed and sometimes raging out of control. Her innocence gone, she went through a dark period in her life before she found her footing again. By using her Earth Mother strengths, she put together a new life for herself and her sons. It was not easy for her to go through such a painful time in her life in the glare of the public eye, but she bravely carried on and developed herself into a sophisticated, strong woman. For Diana developing her Star Woman side is probably what saved her.

Toward the end of her life, Diana had completely turned the tables on the press, whose constant attention had made her life a living hell for a good portion of her adult life. Calling on her Star Woman qualities, she learned how to use her fame and popularity in the service of causes in which she believed. Of course, her Earth Mother traits were the impetus that set her sights on improving the lives of children the world over.

I remember seeing a television interview with her in which she described – with great satisfaction – how she had directed her staff to set up photo opportunities in places where landmines left from wartime were killing and maiming children. She wanted to bring world attention to the problem. The press would ordinarily ignore such issues; they would rather try to catch her scurrying out of some nightclub with her latest beau. But now, if they wanted to photograph her, they had to do it on her terms and report on the issues she valued. She was really in the driver's seat of her own life. Before her tragic and untimely death, she had learned how to be a first-class Star Woman when in pursuit of her world-class goals.

No matter which type of womanly traits you stress (at this moment), you need to learn how to choose a good man and how to lead him to your shared vision of a quality life together, once he is yours.

Initiating Change

A leader is a person who inspires and influences. Because we are not yet living in a truly egalitarian society and because both sexes have much cultural conditioning to overcome, women need to be the leaders and initiators of this change in the power balance.

Those who are primarily Earth Mothers need to exercise some leadership in their relationships with men, in order to achieve equality with their partners. Those who are primarily Star Women need to partner with men who appreciate their leadership abilities and support the full exercise of those abilities both in and out of the home.

All of us need to strive for the right balance between these archetypes for our own individual personality and current lifestyle. Some of the ideas and strategies for dealing with men in the pages ahead may seem extreme to you. Just keep these concepts in your back pocket and remember them. You can modify these ideas to suit your own style. But when your "old way" doesn't work, you can call on your new understanding of your four powerful inner archetypes to get the job done!

Observations on Balance

Here are a few observations about some well-known women and how the balance of Earth Mother and Star Woman appears in their life. Although without knowing any of them personally (yet), I can only go on what is generally known about their public images. Yet, it is valuable to look at those public images and see the evidence of the archetypes expressed in their lives.

Entertainment Personalities

Oprah Winfrey — An accomplished, high-achieving Star Woman nicely tempered with Earth Mother-type caring treatment of her guests. She uses her power and wealth in a selfless way to influence people to improve and change their lives.

Madonna — A gung-ho Star Woman who never lets anything get in her way. Looks like she finally found the right kind of man in her current husband, Guy Ritchie, and motherhood has helped her get into better balance with her Earth Mother side.

Barbra Streisand — An extremely gifted Star Woman who focused on developing her enormous talents, but who was nevertheless shy and nervous about performing. She seems to have found the perfect partner in James Brolin, and is softer and more relaxed (Earth Mother qualities) now than she ever was in her younger days.

Sharon Osbourne — Undoubtedly, pure Star Woman when it comes to managing the career of her rock star husband, Ozzie. She commands great respect (some say fear) in the music business, yet there is no doubting the Earth Mother love and concern she showers on her husband and children (and pets!).

Miss Piggy — The Muppet character (created by a man, incidentally) that personifies the extreme far end of the Star Woman spectrum in hilarious fashion. We love to laugh at her totally self-absorbed arrogant ways and her blatant manipulations of hapless Kermit the Frog. No real woman could be so completely lacking in Earth Mother sensibilities…could she?

Business Leaders

Carly Fiorina — As the CEO of Hewlett-Packard she is widely respected and admired by both men and women for her leadership and business acumen. In television interviews her intelligence, warmth and femininity shine through in equal measure, making her an excellent example of a perfect Star Woman/Earth Mother combination– powerful, successful and gracious.

Anita Roddick — Founder of The Body Shop, a large chain of cosmetic stores, this Star Woman was one of the first to create a business that is as concerned with the ethics of the products it sells as its customers are. She showed the business world that a company could act with Earth Mother-like caring to the environment and people of the countries where the products are made and make a profit as well.

Visionaries and Spiritual Leaders

Jean Houston — A Star Woman of imposing intellect and far-flung vision who is also a humorous, highly entertaining speaker and a loving wife and mother. She uses her Star Woman abilities to influence world leaders for the ultimate Earth Mother goal: saving our planet.

Marianne Williamson — Former leader of a New Thought church with thousands of members, this Star Woman is known for her passionate and persuasive speaking and writing. Her books chronicle her own inner journey as a woman, urging us to embrace our Earth Mother natures and pursue both spiritual transformation and political activism as she herself does.

Mother Teresa — The supreme Earth Mother whose simple goal of loving and serving the poorest and the most needy resulted in her becoming a global icon of pure love and selfless service. Yet she was shrewd enough to use her Star Woman aspect during public appearances with world leaders to get media attention and monetary support for her life's work.

Armed with the knowledge of your predominant personality type – Earth Mother or Star Woman – you have a new way to better understand yourself, as well as other women. Perhaps you have a daughter who is a budding Star Woman. The concepts in this chapter will help you to help her understand who she is.

For the next step on our journey we'll take a trip into the distant past of humankind to see how women's lives and roles in society were once very different from ours. Here is the surprising and disturbing story of how the power women once owned was lost and how we are now regaining it.

Chapter 4

Return of The Goddess

Finally we learn the Mystery – that unless we find the Goddess within ourselves we will never find Her without. She is both internal and external; as solid as a rock, as changeable as our own internal image of Her. She is manifest within each of us – so where else should we look?"
— Starhawk, author of The Spiral Dance: A Rebirth of the Ancient Religion of the Great Goddess

Modern women have been busy trying to emulate the worst traits of the male of the species (bullying, coercion, one-upmanship, winning at all costs, climbing to the top, etc.) because we thought it would make us more powerful and more in control. The problem is that these are the traits of the powerful as defined by males.

Our society does little to help women discover the true power of being female. So if you're feeling angry, frustrated, and worn out from the battle of the sexes, you've got lots of company. For the last 5,000 years or so, our mainstream Western culture has treated women as inferior beings whose main purpose in life is to bear children and tend to domestic duties. But wait – it wasn't always like that!

Early Ancestors

Scholars of prehistory generally agree that our ancestors, the first Homo sapiens, appeared around 40,000 BCE (Before the Common Era). Take a look at the following timeline:

Period	*Cultures & Events*	*Religion*
40,000 BCE	•First appearance of Homo Sapiens	Unknown
30,000 BCE	•Widespread distribution of goddess figurines & images	Great Goddess
20,000 BCE	•Possible predominance of matriarchal cultures	Great Goddess
10,000 BCE	•Cave paintings in Europe •End of the Ice Age •Domestication of plants and animals, beginnings of agriculture	Great Goddess
7,000-3,500 BCE	•Continued development of agriculture	Great Goddess
3,500-2,000 BCE	•Sumerians settle Mesopotamia •Indo-European invasions begin •Invention of writing (c.3,000 BCE) •Minoan culture develops on Crete (c.3000 BCE) •First pyramids built in Egypt (c.2,650 BCE) •Stonehenge built in England (c. 2,000 BCE)	Male-centered mythologies begin to dominate Fragmentation of goddess worship Great Goddess supreme in Crete
2,000-1,700 BCE	•Large-scale invasions of patriarchal peoples from the East into Greece	Great Goddess supreme in Crete
1,700-1,100 BCE	•Peak of Minoan civilization •Cataclysm in Eastern Mediterranean and destruction of Minoan culture on Crete (c.1,470 BCE) •Hebrews begin conquest of Canaan (1250-1200 BCE)	Male-centered mythologies begin to dominate in Greece
1,100-1 BCE	•High Classical Period in Greece (480-323 BCE) •Roman Empire begins (31 BCE) •The Buddha (564-483 BCE)	Male-centered mythologies dominate Europe
1-2,000+ CE	•Jesus Christ (5-30 CE) •End of slavery (1861) •Women's Suffrage (1920)	Patriarchal religions dominate the Western world

For about 35,000 years or more, humans lived in small groups and tribes where both women and men were shaman and leaders. The earliest known sculptures such as the *Venus of Willendorf* (around 25,000–30,000 BCE) are thought to be depictions of the "Great Goddess."

The mysterious power of women as the vessels of new life was worshiped throughout prehistoric times.

The mysterious power of women as the vessels of new life was worshiped throughout prehistoric times. In fact for many thousands of years women were respected as important members of their communities, as priestesses and shaman in cultures all over the world.

Woman as the Great Goddess

In the earliest of these societies the cause and effect relationship of sex to the birth of children was not understood. It seemed utterly magical that women brought forth the children. Women were seen as having powers of creation equal to nature itself. They were respected for their power and the center of their power resided in their wombs. The earliest works of art depict woman as the Great Goddess and are full of symbols of nature and creation. These works are devoid of the battle scenes of later periods when males dominated the culture.

Minoan Culture on Crete

The last great civilization in which women participated in all aspects of society on an equal footing with men was the Minoan culture on the island of Crete in the Mediterranean. From 3,500 BCE to about 1,400 BCE the Minoans developed a way of life where art and physical sports flourished for all people. Men and women alike took part in the dangerous but thrilling game of bull riding. Women proudly showed off their bare breasts in the popular fashions of this island culture.

On Crete the Great Goddess was worshiped in the form of a snake goddess. From the beginnings of the Great Goddess religion, coiled and winding snakes represented power. The snake symbolized life energy and regeneration. It was a positive force, often expressed in abstract form as a spiral.

> ***"I think of women who gain a sense of their own power and authority as 'reclaiming the power of the snake,' which was lost by feminine deities and human women when the patriarchal religions stripped the goddesses of their power and influence, cast the snake as the evil element in the Garden of Eden, and made women the lesser sex."***
>
> ***— Jean Shinoda Bolen, M.D.***

Some archeologists believe that a great earthquake shook the island of Crete around 1470 BCE, destroying many buildings and homes. Others think a volcanic eruption destroying a nearby island was the beginning of the end for the Minoans. Whatever the real cause, invaders soon conquered and destroyed what was left. By this time, male-centered mythologies dominated Europe and the Middle East. The one Great Goddess was fractured into many goddesses who came to represent individual aspects of the feminine in many different cultures. The female goddesses were the wives, daughters, and lovers of the dominant male gods. If they ruled, they rarely ruled alone. More likely, they ruled as a wife or queen of a male god.

The one Great Goddess was fractured into many goddesses who came to represent individual aspects of the feminine in many different cultures.

Decline of the Great Goddess

The Great Goddess still survived – even during the rise of the male gods. For centuries, pockets of pagan worshipers kept the cult of the Great Goddess alive outside the pantheons of first the Greek gods, and later the Romans. The early Christian Church did everything it could to stamp out the old Pagan rites and belief in the Great Goddess.

The dates of many Christian holidays were set to coincide with Pagan holidays so people could still celebrate at the same time of year. Christmas was declared to be December 25th so it would fall right in the middle of the pagan Winter Solstice celebration – a drunken bacchanal that could go on for eight days. The Church would not be seen as the religious authority over people if this kind of behavior was allowed to continue. To establish its authority over every aspect of people's lives, especially the sexual aspect, the church and its priests positioned themselves as intermediaries between God and human beings. People could not be allowed to think for themselves, have direct knowledge of God, or believe that sexual pleasure could be sacred.

People who are in the habit of experiencing pleasure, love, and peace are very difficult to control. They will resist attempts to make them feel bad or guilty about feeling good. By keeping people in poverty and declaring carnal pleasure a sin, upper class lords, ruling noblemen, and church leaders did a thorough job of keeping people miserable, powerless, and therefore, controllable. When toiling in the nobleman's fields was the only means of survival people considered themselves lucky to receive a pittance and a share of the grain. They had little chance of changing their destiny and fear ruled their lives. Church leaders eventually succeeded in replacing most of the important holidays of the old Goddess religion with their own, and the Great Goddess beliefs faded from the memories of the majority.

How Can We Know the Truth?

The science of archaeology is only about 100 years old and until quite recently, was relegated completely to men. Their interpretations of their findings were, of course, filtered through their cultural backgrounds as men in a male dominated society.

Archaeological evidence is dependent on knowing the precise location where each bone or pottery fragment was found. The meaning of symbols and images, the uses of objects, and how they came to be at the site are all open to conjecture and influenced by individual bias. Once a site is disturbed, unless careful photographic records are made and each object accurately tagged, a great deal of factual evidence is lost forever. So many, if not all, of the early archeological finds are of little use for us today.

One of the first and most influential female archeologists, Marija Gimbutas, collected evidence of the earth-centered Great Goddess beliefs in Europe and the Middle East, and reported that these societies were remarkably peaceful. Little evidence of warlike behavior was found until Indo-European invaders swept in from the East around 3,500 BCE bringing their male "sky gods" with them.

We are all products of the culture in which we live. The beliefs we have absorbed from our Western race consciousness about how to be a woman are not necessarily the only way to live. They are just ideas and traditions. Studying ancient and prehistoric societies shows us that these ideas promulgated by a male-dominated culture have been around for a mere 5,000 years or so. The time when women were respected and considered equal with men, when all people worshiped feminine qualities and feminine power, is a period of some 35,000 years—about seven times longer!

The time when women were respected and considered equal with men, when all people worshiped feminine qualities and feminine power, is a period of some 35,000 years—about seven times longer!

Back to the Great Goddess?

Does this mean we should go back to worshiping the Great Mother Goddess? Well, some women (and men) are doing just that.

I believe that what we really need is to understand that God is not exclusively male nor exclusively female, but one power that embodies both. A concept of God as the one source of creative intelligence and energy that creates our physical world would serve us all better. Male and female are simply different expressions of the same divine energy.

Male and female are simply different expressions of the same divine energy.

Women can and should explore Goddess mythology and use Goddess stories, symbols, and images to regain our connection with the divine femininity that lives within each of us. To this end, many women are joining informal groups that meet regularly to talk and share, dance and drum – and of course – eat and drink. Magic happens when women gather in a group to support and encourage one another.

Honor Your Womanhood

Whether you aspire to be in a woman-led marriage or an egalitarian partnership, you must learn to respect your uniquely feminine qualities and allow them their fullest expression. You cannot expect your man to honor your womanhood if you do not honor it yourself. This does not give us license to become arrogant and bitchy. It does mean that we have to develop a solid sense of self-respect and we have to expect, develop, and require respectful behavior from all men.

You cannot expect your man to honor your womanhood if you do not honor it yourself.

> ***"In my ballets, woman is first. Men are consorts. God made men to sing the praises of women. They are not equal to men: They are better."***
>
> ***— George Balanchine***

Man as Consort

Women will benefit richly from cultivating a different attitude about our relationships with men. Think of a man as your consort, your chosen companion, just as the priestesses and Goddesses of the old religions did. It was a privilege for a man to be selected as consort to a powerful woman, a privilege that could be revoked with swift and terrible punishment, should he displease his Goddess. The story of "Inanna's Descent" is a great inspiration for the aspiring Modern Goddess.

Inanna's Descent

One of the oldest stories we humans have is that of the Goddess Inanna from ancient Sumeria, which is our present day Iraq. Her story has the power to reach across the millennia and speak to women of all ages. Here is the story of Inanna's descent into the underworld and her return as told by Patrice Hawkwood Schanck, edited and reprinted with permission from *Caravan Trails, A Journal for Tribal Bellydance*

> Inanna, later known as Astarte and Ishtar (among other names), was not just a fertility goddess. She was Queen of Heaven and Earth. She was the source of life and ordering principle. Inanna presided over all aspects of life, from beer making to lovemaking; from the art of war to the art of poetry; from the ordering of a household to the ordering of the cosmos. We know about Inanna partly through hymns, which tell her stories, which were written down around 5,000 years ago. However, her stories and worship had been told for thousands of years before that.
>
> The hymn of Inanna's descent begins when the goddess is in the prime of her life. At this point in her story, Inanna has conquered her fears, gained power and knowledge, become queen, and been initiated sexually. She is married to her consort, Dumuzi, a shepherd, whom she wed after a sensual courtship. Their union has made the land fruitful and content.
>
> Yet in the midst of her power and fulfillment, Inanna "hears the call of the great below:" She is called to visit the underworld. From the depths of the earth she hears the call in the depths of her soul.

She prepares for her journey and arrays herself in finery. She is adorned as the goddess of love and power that she is, and she is ready. She does one more thing. Inanna summons Ninshubar, her faithful servant, who has divine and magical powers in her own right. Inanna tells Ninshubar to wait by the gate in the underworld for three days. If Inanna does not return in that time, Ninshubar must seek help from the gods.

Inanna's twin sister, Erishkagal, rules the underworld. While Inanna rules the lovely upperworld of light and life, her twin sister Erishkagal rules the underworld of darkness and death. As such, her main task is to "eat the dead" so that the cycle of life may continue. Inanna passes through seven gates and at each one she is required to surrender a piece of clothing or jewelry, which carries her magical powers. The original text says that when Inanna finally reaches the court of Erishkagal, she is brought in "naked and low."

Without a word of greeting, Erishkagal commands Inanna to be judged as all who come to the underworld are judged. And then Erishkagal touches Inanna. In an instant, Inanna is transformed into a corpse hanging on a hook on the wall.

After three days pass, and Inanna does not return to the world of life, Ninshubar goes first to one god, then another for aid in rescuing Inanna. They are deaf to Ninshubar's pleas for help. Finally the third god who hears Ninshubar's appeal, the god of wisdom, tells her that he will help; he cannot let the bright and beautiful Inanna languish in the underworld. The god of wisdom summons two beings, neither male nor female in form. He gives them the shape of flies, some magical tools, and instruction on how to save Inanna. The little beings do not go through the seven gates to the underworld; instead they descend discreetly through the cracks in the earth.

When they arrive at Erishkagal's court, the goddess of the underworld lies on the floor, "writhing like a woman in labor." She is naked and her hair is uncombed, coiling out from her head "like leeks." She is moaning in terrible pain. The little beings begin to comfort Erishkagal. When she moans, "O, my back," the little fly beings say to her, "O, your back." When Erishkagal says "O, my front," they say, "O, your front." When the dark goddess moans, "O, my liver," the beings reply, "O, your liver."

After struggling alone in the dark with her pain, Erishkagal is comforted by this sympathetic chorus. Now calmed and soothed by the little beings, Erishkagal sits up and asks them, "Who are you, what boon can I give you in return for your great service?" She offers them many treasures, all of which are refused. The little beings point to the rotting corpse and say, "We'll take that."

Inanna's corpse is taken down off the wall and laid before the beings. They sprinkle the Water of Life and the Food of Life into Inanna's lips and she is revived. Inanna goes back up through the gates, emerging into the light in all her royal glory, clothing, jewels, and magical powers restored. Yet she does not come back alone. Accompanying Inanna are two demons from the underworld. They are grim balance keepers, immune to bribery, appeal, or appeasement. Someone has left the realm of the underworld; someone must take Inanna's place.

The demons accompany Inanna on her journey back home and first attempt to take Ninshubar, then Inanna's two sons who have been grieving deeply for their mother, but Inanna stays the demons. Lastly, they come to Dumuzi, Inanna's consort, and where is he? Has he too been weeping, throwing dust on his hair, rending his clothes in grief for his goddess and wife? No. Instead, Inanna finds Dumuzi on her throne, in all his finery, ruling in her stead.

Inanna points at Dumuzi, fixes him with her eye, and says to the demons, "Take him." The demons lay their hands on Dumuzi, but before he can be taken to the underworld, he escapes. Exhausted, he lays down to rest and has a terrible dream. In this dream, the milk buckets are overturned and broken. The sheepfold is empty; the land is sterile and withered.

Dumuzi's sister, Geshtinanna finds her brother. He tells her his dream and she tells him the dream means that he must accept his fate. There is no escape; his life on earth has ended. So Dumuzi goes to the underworld, taking Inanna's place.

After a time, Inanna begins to miss Dumuzi; she grieves for him. Geshtinanna comes to Inanna and offers to take Dumuzi's place in the underworld. They decide she will go for half the year, allowing Dumuzi to return to the world of life and Inanna. Then after six months, Geshtinanna will return to the land of the living, and Dumuzi will go back to the underworld. Thus the world does not return to the way it was before Inanna made her descent, but a new balance is achieved and the cycle of life continues.

Similarities

This story is the earliest of many myths from different cultures that attempt to explain the changing of the seasons. Many elements of the story are like our familiar fairy tales: a queen with magical powers, a dangerous journey, an imprisoned heroine, obstacles to overcome, and a brave rescue.

The description of Inanna being turned into a corpse and hung up on the wall is rather gruesome, but it is a fitting act for an angry, jealous, underworld Goddess to inflict upon her more fortunate upperworld-dwelling sister. Any armchair psychologist would recognize sibling rivalry at work in this ancient tale—just like in our Cinderella story.

Differences

However, other elements highlight the differences between this peaceful woman-friendly culture and our own. All of the main characters in the story are women – not a king or warrior prince in sight. Inanna's faithful servant turns to the male gods for help, but their aid comes in a decidedly non-violent form. They create Inanna's little saviors as neuter-beings, neither male nor female. Inanna is saved by the compassionate attentions of the fly creatures to Erishkagal's pain, and not by any kind of fighting or killing, which is so common in our culture's myths and stories.

The relationship of Inanna and Dumuzi is nothing like any of the fairy tales we grew up with. Here the man is chosen by the queen to be her consort. A consort does not have quite the same status as a husband, even though she marries him. The marriage does not make him king or give him ruling power over her. He is simply her companion and lover.

When Inanna finds that her consort has overstepped his bounds and overtaken her throne, she does not hesitate to send him to the underworld. Can you imagine Snow White or Cinderella giving their prince the bum's rush if he misbehaved? Even the Little Mermaid, plucky as she was, would probably have difficulty banishing her precious prince, no matter what he did to offend her.

However Inanna is not lacking in mercy. After a cooling off period she is able to forgive Dumuzi enough to allow him to come back for half the year. This shows that Inanna not only has the strength and fortitude to make a decision, but also the compassion and flexibility to amend that decision. Her ability to see and use both the masculine and feminine viewpoint on issues made her a highly respected leader.

Distorting the Goddess

As the earliest Goddess-worshiping civilizations were taken over by Indo-European invaders from the North and East, societies became male-dominated. These societies proceeded to stamp out the old Great Goddess religion and replace her with their male deities. The Great Goddess was renamed and reduced to the role of wife of the male deity. New myths were created which cast women as the evil seductress, witch, or sorceress who was to be feared and destroyed.

In the earliest Hebrew writings, Lilith was the first female created by God to be with Adam in the Garden of Eden. She had a mind of her own and considered herself equal to Adam because God made her from the same dust as Adam. When Adam tried to force her to lie with him in the male-above female-below missionary position, she became enraged and fled from the garden.[1] Subsequently God made Eve from Adam's rib. Eve was more compliant, but she still made trouble for Adam by convincing him to eat the forbidden fruit.

Most of the old symbols of the Great Goddess, such as the serpent and the horns of the bull, were transformed into symbols of evil in the new stories. The serpent tempted Eve to disobey. The bullhorns became the devil's horns. Lilith was turned into the Destroyer, a treacherous woman whose capacity for evil knew no bounds.

Controlling Women Through Religion

Slowly but surely, the Goddess religions retreated before the onslaught of the male-dominated new social order. New religions were established to put women in a position where they could be intimidated and controlled. Most of the major religions in the world today (Christianity, Islam, Hinduism, Buddhism, Judaism) began during the next few thousand years – all started by men. It was men who conceived both of God as a superior male, and of women as being inferior. It was men who received "divine inspiration" directly from their male God, and who wrote down the scriptures that put women in their place.

Religion served a human master and that master was the power and property-hungry male sex. Males had to find a way to insure that their sons were legitimate so they could pass on the family wealth to a son. And in order to do so they had to control a woman's sexuality and freedom. They used brute force and fear to accomplish their aims.

---

[1] *Hebrew Myths* by Robert Graves and Raphael Patai (New York: Doubleday, 1964), pp 65-69

> ***"The relationship between men and women is a relationship between a victorious and a defeated group."***
> ***— Erich Fromm***

When the first Hebrews conquered the land of Canaan, it was a peaceful place where the people worshiped the Great Goddess. The Hebrews slaughtered nearly the entire population. Only young virgin girls were spared and given to the males to take as brides. After seeing their families slain before their eyes, those poor girls were completely at the mercy of their captors. Their fear was most likely enough to dissuade them from ever attempting to practice the religion of their mothers.[2] One after another, the temples and cities of the Great Goddess were either destroyed or forgotten.

The Goddess Goes Underground

The Great Goddess went underground, but was such a strong archetype in the collective unconscious of the human race that this powerful woman-image emerged in altered form within the new patriarchal religions. In the Catholic faith she is venerated as the Virgin Mary. In some Latin American countries she is called the Virgin of Guadalupe and the people pray to her more often than to Jesus himself. In Spain she is known as the Black Madonna.

The church had to make sex sinful and guilt-ridden. The old ideas about sex being a sacrament and women being revered as carriers of the mystical powers of creation just had to go. How else could they get control of the masses, but to make anything pleasurable into a sin? This is the legacy we were all born into. We find it nearly impossible to put the words "sacred" and "pleasurable" together in the same sentence.

---

[2] *When God Was A Woman* by Merlin Stone (Orlando, Florida: Harcourt, Brace & Co. 1976), pp 171-172

Sacred Pleasure

Our ancient and prehistoric ancestors did not separate the sacred from the pleasurable. They worshiped the Great Goddess as the creator and destroyer of life, and believed that she was responsible for both the fertility and the destructiveness of nature. Priestesses acted as representatives of the Great Goddess in sexual rites centered in their temples, which they performed with men selected by them for that purpose. To them the pleasure of sex was a natural way to connect to the Great Goddess and the mystery of creation.

There was a time – a long time – when men did not dominate the world and its cultures, when women's power of creation was honored, when feminine values were respected.

When I learned about how different life was for women for the first 35,000 years of our ancestors' evolution, I was first shocked and then outraged. There was a time – a long time – when men did not dominate the world and its cultures, when women's power of creation was honored, when feminine values were respected.

The following table compares various attributes of cultures that are female-centered (matriarchal) to those that are male-centered (patriarchal). It's easy to recognize all the main attitudes of Western culture in the column under patriarchy. What would our world and our lives be like if the attitudes of both patriarchy and matriarchy were given equal weight?

What would our world and our lives be like if the attitudes under both patriarchy and matriarchy were given equal weight?

Aspect	Matriarchy	Patriarchy
Orientation	Being	Doing
Attitude	Receptive	Aggressive
Love	Unconditional love, given freely	Conditional love, must be earned
Thought Process	Intuitive	Logical
Organization	Egalitarian, less structured	Hierarchical, more structured
Communication	Networking	Chain of command
Social Order	Compassion, cooperation	Manmade laws of State and Nation
Inheritance	Through mother	Through father
Legitimacy	Through mother all children are legitimate; there is no such thing as a bastard.	Through marriage only; a child born out of wedlock is considered illegitimate, a bastard
Legal System	Mercy	Justice
Material Resources	Universal, shared by all	Restrictive, controlled by few
Highest Values	Emotional and spiritual fulfillment	Fulfillment of duty and success

This comparison should help you to see how the deck has been stacked against women for thousands of years. When farming became a major source of food, the group that gained control and stayed in control of fertile land was the group that prospered. The concept of territory and ownership developed and men gained power through physical dominance and fear. But, times they are a changin'.

Today the collection, control, and dissemination of information are becoming the basis of our economy. Brute force is less important. Intelligence, education, management skills, and creativity are important and these qualities women possess in abundance.

> ***"Knowledge—not land, not capital, not machines—now determines the core value of every kind of enterprise, as the capacity to innovate becomes the primary determinant of success."***
>
> ***— Sally Helgesen***

We need to learn the complete story of human development, not just the story of the last 5,000 years, not just the story created and told by men. Let us learn the story of the other 35,000 years and use it as a foundation from which to be inspired and to grow. I am saddened when I think of how much human potential of the female kind has been repressed and destroyed in those 5,000 years.

However, I choose not to be angry with men just because they belong to the sex that did it to us. Physical dominance is what worked in the past and men, being the efficiency-minded creatures they are, simply did what worked. The old ways no longer work, and every day more men – and women – are coming to that realization.

I hope the information in this chapter helps you to see how most, if not all, of your beliefs and assumptions about who you are and how you should live have been shaped by male-centered ideas. These same ideas restrict and negatively affect men, too. Have compassion for them and don't let anger at the male sex, however justified it may seem, rule your thoughts. Our past does not determine our future.

Our past does not determine our future.

If you want to learn more about the Great Goddess religion and life in prehistoric times, there are a number of good books on the subject listed in the bibliography.

You can see how the history and heritage of women has been conveniently presented to us as an incomplete picture. Through the efforts of pioneering women archaeologists like Marija Gimbutas the full picture is at last emerging. Never forget that for the first 35,000 years of human existence the power of women was a recognized essential force in daily life. Men have dominated society for a mere 5,000 years and now the balance of power is shifting yet again.

We can make the shift happen sooner by coming to a new understanding of men and a different way of relating to them which is all coming up in the next section, *Understanding Men*.

I will show you how to choose the right type of man to love for your personality type, how to handle men and sex, and why the three Platinum Rules for great sex are the foundation for a happy marriage.

Venus ON TOP

SECTION TWO:

Understanding Men

Chapter 5

Loving The Right Man

If you are single you need to learn how to choose the right type of man for your personality type. If you are already married, you need to learn about different types of men and their character traits, so you can accurately gauge the best way to strengthen the loving relationship with your partner.

The Right Dating Attitude

Most of us were never taught how to date productively. The more sure you are of your ability to take care of yourself, the more objective you can be about the men you meet and date. The better you know yourself, the easier it is to determine if a man has the potential to make you happy. The best dating attitude is to be an observer. Watch for the signs and clues that a man gives out continually that reveal his character. Your job is to refrain from falling madly in love until you are sure that he is a good match for you.

The best dating attitude is to be an observer.

You will be so much more attractive and intriguing to the men you date if you keep things light for as long as you possibly can. Dating is not about you trying to please him; it's about letting him try to please you. Let him audition for the plum role of co-starring with you in your life.

Dating is not about you trying to please him; it's about letting him try to please you.

Never act aggressively toward a man to whom you are attracted, especially if you don't know him very well. He must be attracted enough to you to make the first move. All you need do in any social setting is give off some signal that you would be receptive to him. If you simply catch him looking at you and smile, that tells him he is welcome to approach you. If he doesn't come to you, the attraction is not strong enough.

There must be enough chemistry between the two of you to make him want to pursue you. This may require some restraint for a Star Woman. We are accustomed to going after what we want in our working world, but this kind of behavior is counterproductive when it comes to romance. You may run after a man and seduce him into a romantic relationship with you—but your chances of ending up with a man who is a user are very high.

You need to look for a man's motivation and willingness to please you. You cannot do this if you are focused on winning him over and pleasing him.

So give up the cute pick-up lines, the little notes, the intrigue with his friends, and any other elaborate games you dream up to get his attention. Give him a smile and act receptive. That's all. If he doesn't respond to your receptiveness, just assume that there is not enough of a spark between

You deserve a man who is absolutely thrilled at the prospect of courting you.

you to start a fire, and move on. Keep your dignity at all times. You deserve a man who is absolutely thrilled at the prospect of courting you.

Just watch a few of those nature programs on television showing the mating habits of animals. A female peahen has higher standards than most human females these days. She makes those peacocks put on a show, strutting around with their tail feathers spread wide. She lets them fight it out over her and then picks the one who best meets her criteria for a mate. She wouldn't dream of chasing a male. They have to prove their worth to her and then she makes her choice. You should be at least as choosey as a peahen.

Deal-Killers—Your ABC's

Make up your mind firmly about which traits or habits are deal-killers for you. A deal-killer is something that you absolutely cannot tolerate and could not live with. My deal-killers were simple and practical. Any man who exhibited any of the following was out of the game immediately (or never reached the starting line):

A. Smoking or addictive behavior of any kind

B. Poor health habits

C. Incompatible religious or spiritual beliefs

A. Addictions

This list of the three ABCs is a good basic starting place for any woman. Addictions are listed first as Item A because no one can have a good relationship with someone who is addicted. Their substance of choice will always be more important than their partner, and who wants to contend with that? If you don't smoke, don't even consider going out with a man who does.

Other kinds of addictions can be hidden from your view when you first start dating. It's fairly easy for him to conceal heavy drinking or drug use when you are only spending a few hours at a time with a man. When you start spending more time with him and get to know him better, keep your eyes and ears open for clues. If a man has addictions, they will show up over time. Don't ignore your intuition in this area either. If something feels wrong to you about a man, there is a reason for it.

B. Poor Health Habits

I take care of my health because I intend to live a healthy, active life for a long time. My goal was to marry a man who had good prospects of being with me for many years. So a man who had allowed himself to go downhill physically was not a good match for me. A man who is overweight, out of shape, and doesn't take care of his health exhibits a lack of self-discipline that is a turn-off for me. Both items A and B can often be determined before you even accept a first date, unless it's a blind date.

C. Spiritual Compatibility

I learned through bitter experience that Item C was extremely important to me. Husband number three was a fundamentalist Christian. I was interested in metaphysical philosophy. How I ever thought we could make a marriage work is beyond me. Can you picture what it is like being married to a man who believes you are going straight to hell? And all the while, you don't even believe there is such a place as hell. What insanity!

If your spiritual life is important to you, then your man should have a similar philosophy toward life. His beliefs must be at least compatible and on the same page as yours, or you will be missing the opportunity to have real spiritual depth in your relationship.

I enjoy being involved in my church; my husband only comes to church occasionally. However, we both agree on the basic spiritual principles that we live by. We speak the same spiritual language and look at life the same way. We can talk about things that happen and how we feel. We can open up to each other completely on any subject without fear of being rejected or ridiculed. I never had this level of spiritual compatibility with any of my other spouses.

When I look back with the knowledge I now have, I know that none of those other marriages ever stood a chance of succeeding. None of those men met even two out of three of the very basic ABC criteria for dating—much less marrying! But when you are desperate for a relationship – as I was in those days – you don't make good choices.

Weed Them Out

Armed with your relationship deal-killer list, you can weed out a lot of men on the first date or two. It's easy to refuse any further dates when you know this is not the kind of man you want.

However, once you get past that point, you need to understand the two types of good men and which type is best for you.

For our purposes, we need a clear and simple set of criteria by which to evaluate potential partners. One of the reasons that women have trouble in relationships is that we get involved with men who just don't possess the necessary ingredients in their character to be successful partners for our personality type.

First we must know what to look for in a man, and then we must know how to test him to make sure he is truly compatible for us. Otherwise, we date – or worse, marry – men who don't have what it takes to make us happy and never will. Once you are armed with a practical way to choose a compatible mate for yourself, there is no reason for you to end up hurt and disappointed ever again.

Dark Stars (Bad Guys)

This kind of male operates from a very low state of consciousness and a big, fearful ego. He is basically selfish and uncaring. At first he can be a real charmer. He seduces you with promises and romantic gestures until you fall for him. Once he knows you're hooked, he counts on your kindness and sympathy, as he plays you for all you're worth.

This is the true bad guy who uses and abuses women and then drops them without a thought. Or he tells you he loves you and then hurts you over and over. Or he is addicted to something: alcohol, drugs, gambling, or other women. Or he physically or verbally abuses people, then apologizes and promises never to do it again. And, of course, he always does it again.

If a man you have just met seems utterly dashing and romantic, a yellow warning flag should be waving furiously in your head. If he oozes with charm and tries to sweep you off your feet, keep them firmly planted on the floor. You might be one of the few lucky women whose romantic and charming guy is also a good man. But there's a very high probability that the oozing charm is a mere façade.

Only time will tell if a charmer has real heart and substance beneath the attractive exterior. This man's "best foot forward" is easy to observe, but it is important to also watch carefully for signs that he might be "all hat and no cattle" as a smart sister from Texas would put it.

Dark Stars should be simply wiped off your radar screen and never even given a chance to get near you. If you don't yet have enough self-respect to boot this kind of man unceremoniously out of your life the minute you discover his defects, then you need more help than any book can provide.

Please do yourself a favor, get away from a bad guy and heal those destructive patterns before you even think of trying to meet someone new. Bad Guys have no place in your life, ever!

If you are married to a Bad Guy, you must get away from him before you can even begin to think clearly. Once you heal the emotional issues that are attracting these Bad Guys to you, then you'll be able to attract a Good Man.

The Good Man

What is our definition of a good man, meaning a man who is a good prospect for a long-term relationship? Here are the key points that define a good man:

1. **He respects women in general and his partner in particular**
2. **His primary goal in the relationship is to please his woman**
3. **He allows his woman to influence him**
4. **He supports her dreams**

Respects You

Respect is the bottom-line bedrock of any good relationship. If a man doesn't have fundamental respect for you as a woman, nothing else he may have will make up for it.

> ***"Ask a man what he thinks of his mother, and he will show you how he treats his wife."***
>
> ***—Carl G. Jung***

Look at his relationship with his mother. If he is respectful and polite to her – chances are he will be the same with you. I have run into some exceptional men whose mothers were poor parents, yet they were able to overcome that handicap. They gave respect to their partners and developed a good relationship despite their childhoods.

Respect is a ground floor, basic, foundational element on which there is no compromise, because all positive relationships depend upon it.

> ***"What women want is what men want. They want respect."***
>
> ***— Marilyn Vos Savant***

You and your man will likely have a few personality quirks that annoy each other. You may have some issues that you will never agree upon. If you keep your respect for each other, you can tolerate each other's quirks and agree to disagree. But if you lose respect for your partner, it's a warning sign that your relationship is on shaky ground. People who love each other respect each other as well.

Desires to Please You

The right man for you must have a real desire to please you. His main goal in life should be to make you happy. When the woman of the house is happy, the whole household is happy. When the woman of the house is unhappy, nobody is happy. The smart man knows this and makes it his business to please his woman. He either has the pleasing gene embedded in his personality or he doesn't. If he doesn't already have this attitude, no amount of begging, crying, or pleading on your part can create it in him. Pleasing his woman must be his prime directive or he is not worth your time.

Accepts Your Influence

The ability and willingness of a man to accept your influence is utterly crucial for your future happiness. Women have been taught to accept the influence of men. Most women have little resistance to listening to our partner's opinions and considering them when we make a decision. A man who cannot – or will not – do the same for you is not a good bet for marriage. A Star Woman will never be happy if she cannot influence her mate. An Earth Mother may bear the situation more patiently, but she too will be much happier in the long run with a man who is considerate of her opinions.

> ***"We have found that...men who allow their wives to influence them have happier marriages and are less likely to divorce than men who resist their wives' influence. Statistically speaking, when a man is not willing to share power with his partner, there is an 81 percent chance that his marriage will self-destruct."***
>
> ***—Dr. John Gottman***

Supports Your Dreams

It isn't necessary that your man has the same dreams as you, but he does need to be supportive of you reaching your dreams. If the two of you have dreams that are not compatible, it means somebody may have to give up their dream to keep the relationship going. And that damages your chances for a long-term marriage.

If your most cherished dream is to have children and he waffles around when you bring up the subject—yellow flag! If he wants to risk everything on starting a business and you can't stand the thought of not having a regular paycheck coming in—yellow flag! Get these things out in the open and discuss them before making a commitment. The partner whose dream goes unsupported is likely to build up a case of resentment, often irreparably damaging the relationship.

> ***"For any woman to succeed in American life she must first do two things: Prepare herself for a profession, and marry a man who wants her to succeed as much as she does."***
>
> ***—Cathleen Douglas***

What About Money?

Money is a touchy subject between men and women these days. A responsible woman normally wants to develop the skills to be financially self-sufficient, even if she intends to spend some years making child-rearing her main focus. Yet most of us still cling to the Prince Charming fantasy, hoping that once we find the Prince he will take care of us financially forevermore. So a man is still likely to be judged by his occupation and its moneymaking potential. You must learn to accept the fact that the Prince is not coming (even if you look like Cinderella)!

Many good men are never given a chance by women, because they do not meet our financial expectations. As a woman earns more money, she may get a taste of what men have been suffering for years. She wonders if he loves her for herself or for her money. Some high-earning women insist that their partner must make as much as she does. This attitude can greatly limit your chance for happiness. If this high-earning woman is a Star Woman she does not realize that a man who is just as hard driving as she is may not be the best match for her. She would be happier with a man who is more playful and can help her relax and enjoy life with him.

It is fair and reasonable to expect that your man is responsible with money and has the means to support himself. Money is important to the point that you need enough to be comfortable—whatever that means to you. For some it might mean a little house in the suburbs, two kids, and two cars. For others it might mean a co-op apartment in a city high rise and a weekend place in the country. Once you have enough money to meet your definition of comfortable, more money does not necessarily increase happiness.

Be as flexible as possible when it comes to a man's financial situation and you will widen the playing field of potential partners considerably.

What About Kids and Ex-Wives?

Some well-known relationship experts flatly discourage people from dating and remarrying when they have children to raise from a previous marriage. If you start dating a man who is divorced with children you need to take a good long hard look at what your life will be like if you marry him. Does he have a vindictive ex-wife who will make things difficult for you whenever she gets the chance? Don't start auditioning for the role of step-mom too soon. It's a painful adjustment for children to see their Dad with another woman. Some kids never lose their resentment no matter how hard you try.

"Look before you leap" has to be your motto in this situation. Give it plenty of time before you consider getting married. If you want to have babies with this man, it can cause even more hurt and resentment to his other children. Living in the midst of this emotional stew proves to be much more difficult than most women want to believe. Be careful of getting involved in this kind of relationship unless you are sure you have the emotional maturity and strength to deal with the complexities of a "blended family."

If you are the one with kids, the same cautions apply. Take plenty of time to know a man's character and to gauge whether he is a good match for you and your kids. If he paints a picture of his former life with his ex-wife as though she were the wicked witch and he the long-suffering innocent victim—yellow flag! Any man who cannot admit his part in the problems of a past relationship is likely to be too immature or dense or stubborn to create a better relationship this time around. However, if his ex-wife is a difficult person to deal with, but he exercises a good deal of restraint and patience in the process, you might well have a winner!

Asteroids

All men start out in the Asteroid Belt. They travel in a pack in an endless circle, hanging out with their buddy asteroids, making the rounds but going nowhere. They have no direction until they meet a woman who puts a fire under them. Then they leave their comfortable routine and get motivated to pursue the woman that attracts them.

> ***"A man in love is incomplete until he has married. Then he's finished."***
>
> ***—Zsa Zsa Gabor***

Some men catch fire for a short while – until they win you over – and then they get lazy and return to their old asteroid belt routine. These men are not Bad Guys, but they don't have a very strong desire to please you. They won't deliberately hurt you or treat you badly, but they are lazy and will take the easy way out of most situations. Some foolish women take on a guy like this and make a project out of him. Trying to make this lump into something worthwhile is an exercise in futility.

When it comes to men—what you see is what you get. If you don't like what you see or what you're getting, cut your losses and move on!

Does this all sound too cold and calculating for you? All I'm advocating here is that you engage your brain before you open your heart. This is how a woman of power conducts herself.

Power Dating

A woman who respects and values herself does not waste time on a man who will not be able to meet her needs. She uses her head to look at the facts about a man's character and behavior. When all signals are a go, then she allows her heart to open and lead the way—investing her life in their life together.

Engage your brain before you open your heart.

The wise woman also understands how critical it is to refrain from sexual involvement until you know a man well enough to objectively evaluate his potential for you.

Refrain from sexual involvement until you know a man well enough to objectively evaluate his potential for you.

I'm not against sexual pleasure – far from it. However, if you have sex with a man, all your objectivity vanishes and you can't help forming an attachment to him. You become infatuated and start falling in love too soon. This clouds your judgment and makes it easier for you to ignore warning signs about his behavior that you would have noticed had you kept a clear head.

When you take a stand of abstinence in the early stages of your dating life, your chances of meeting the right man shoot way up. That's because you are not spending precious time getting entangled with the wrong man. Instead, you are available when Mr. Right shows up. You must have the patience, strength of character, and consciousness to keep yourself open for the right man.

Keep your self-confidence high and your rational mind at the forefront.

Dating two or three men at the same time is an excellent way to keep your self-confidence high and your rational mind at the forefront. You are unlikely to get involved with any one of them too quickly. You'll derive a great deal of enjoyment in comparing and contrasting their behavior and sharpening your skills of observation.

If you've learned to be a gracious receiver, you'll no doubt experience an especially delicious little thrill when one of your suitors comes to pick you up for a date and notices that gorgeous bouquet of flowers given to you by another man. Men thrive on a hint of competition. Don't feel guilty! Remember the peacock and the peahen!

Two Types of Good Men

There are two kinds of good men. Both Star Women and Earth Mothers can have a good marriage with either type, but if you want to have a really great marriage, one type is a better match for you than the other.

Meteor Men

The first and more plentiful of the two is the Meteor Man. This is a good man who is capable of being influenced and inspired by his woman – but only so far. He heads toward Earth because he wants to come home and put his feet up. His concept of marriage is one where the man is supposed to be in charge. He is apt to be a loyal partner with a single-minded devotion to his woman once he aims himself in her direction.

Meteor Man and Star Woman

With proper handling, a Meteor Man can be developed into a good partner for an Earth Mother, but he is not as good a match for a Star Woman.

The Meteor Man may be initially fascinated by a Star Woman's sparkle, but over the long run they are likely to find themselves in a power struggle. He wants things his way and she wants things her way. He is too much work for her and she is too demanding for him.

Meteor Man and Earth Mother

The Meteor Man prefers to be the leader in his marriage and is generally a kind and fair-minded fellow who likes to see his partner happy. Earth Mothers are comfortable with this kind of man as leader, as long as their opinions are respected and incorporated into family decisions. The woman needs to be alert for signs of her man backsliding into macho attitudes or lazy relationship habits. If he becomes overbearing or inattentive to her, she has to nip that in the bud. As long as she is vigilant about being considered a full partner in the marriage at all times, her chances of having a long and satisfying relationship with a Meteor Man are good.

> ***"In my house I'm the boss, my wife is just the decision maker."***
>
> ***—Woody Allen.***

Comet Men

The Comet Man is an ideal partner for the Star Woman. Her energy and zeal light his fire and propel him in her direction. He will follow her just about anywhere. He does not merely accept her influence, but welcomes it. He is not intimidated or threatened by her leadership abilities. He is secure in his own masculinity and truly admires and values her strength and competence.

> ***"The most attractive thing a woman can do for a man is to give him a way to serve her."***
>
> ***—Regena Thomashauer***

Comet Man and Star Woman

The Comet Man enjoys being a Star Woman's best friend and head cheerleader—and delights in her accomplishments as much as his own. He is willing to go the extra mile for her. She is his own personal goddess whom he enjoys serving. He is a master at consideration and cooperation. The only problem she might have in the relationship is seeing out how much love and admiration she is capable of accepting from this man. And learning how to relax into her role as leader in the marriage.

Does this sound too good to be true? I assure you it is not. As a matter of fact there are more Comet Men out there than you would think. Some of them are quite powerful and successful in the outside world – lawyers, senators, CEO's, and the like. Some Comet Men are blue-collar men who are the picture of sexy masculine charm – construction workers, policemen, and firemen.

The Comet Man has a deep desire to surrender himself to a woman. It brings him joy to leave his workday role behind and pamper you instead.

A smart Star Woman who is savvy and self-confident enough to let her dominant side shine can easily capture the heart of a Comet Man. You must be strong and determined enough to overcome the old ideas ingrained in your subconscious about how women are supposed to be. You must be willing to discard the need for anyone else's approval.

Being your outrageously wonderful true self with a man who loves you as you really are is a Star Woman's well-deserved reward. When a Comet Man finds a Star Woman who gives him ample opportunity to serve her needs, he feels that he has hit the jackpot in the game of love.

Be your outrageously wonderful, true self.

Comet Man and Earth Mother

The pairing of an Earth Mother with a Comet Man is not as good a match for either of them. The woman in this case will always be hoping that he will take the reins of leadership because she doesn't always want to.

Meanwhile he will always be hoping that she will be more aggressive and more willing to exercise control. The leadership role in this marriage can be like a hot potato tossed back and forth causing disappointment for both partners.

"Man has his will – but woman has her way."
—Oliver Wendell Holmes, Sr. (1809-94)

If you are an Earth Mother who is already married to a Comet Man that you want to keep, you can improve your relationship by developing your inner Star Woman and taking charge in more areas. If you're willing to be adventurous sexually, you can use the sexual techniques in the next chapter to motivate your Comet Man to be more of a leader for you, just because it pleases you when he does so. You cannot turn a Comet into a Meteor, but you can help him develop a broader range of relationship skills with the right training and motivation.

Testing Him

As I mentioned earlier, there is a way to test a man's potential for making you happy. This is a simple way to see if pleasing you is really important to him.

No matter how wonderful he seems when you first start dating, before you let yourself fall in love, and certainly before you have sex with him, you must give him the Venus On Top Litmus Test of Pleasuring Potential – the Toilet Seat Test.

In my house, the toilet seat is always down. Oh, I'm physically capable of putting it down if it was left up, but practicality is not the point here. The point is that it honors me that my man makes the effort to leave the toilet seat down for me just because it pleases me. It makes me feel respected and cared for. It is daily proof that he is considerate of me. If you think I'm being silly or petty about this, here is the opinion of one of our foremost relationship experts:

> ***"For many women a raised toilet seat is symbolic of the male's sense of entitlement. So a man can score major points with his wife just by putting the seat down. The wise husband smiles at how smart he is as he drops the lid."***
>
> ***—Dr. John Gottman***

The Toilet Seat Test

This is the kind of simple, daily behavior on which to test your man's long term potential as a mate. If he is not willing to make it his sworn duty and daily habit to always put the toilet seat down for you, then he is probably too selfish and stubborn to warrant any more of your attention. Never, ever marry a man who won't put the toilet seat down for you! Flush that lump out of your life immediately!

Never, ever marry a man who won't put the toilet seat down for you!

The issue here is that women can instill respectful treatment by drawing the line and insisting upon it. If you are insistent on being treated with respect you stand a good chance of winning them over—as long as you treat men with respect and good humor in the process. If a man refuses to make small gestures of respect for you, then you need to choose a better type of man!

In my guest bathroom, I keep a little sign to remind male guests of my Number One House Rule: "Gentlemen: Please leave the toilet seat down! The Goddess thanks you!"

"Gentlemen: Please leave the toilet seat down! The Goddess thanks you!"

During the early dating period, men are on their best behavior, trying to win your love and approval. You must date a man long enough to get past the initial infatuation to see his true character. Start early – the initial dating period is the time to start testing a man's willingness to please you. Don't wait until you are engaged. By then your head is full of wedding fantasies and your ability to be objective is out the window.

> ***"I married beneath me. All women do."***
> ***– Lady Nancy Astor (1879-1964),***
> ***English politician,***
> ***first female member of the British Parliament***

The Toilet Seat Test is a must for every woman to administer to any man she dates on a regular basis. If he passes this first, most basic test, you should devise more of your own tests to check your compatibility and his motivation to please you.

You are looking for a demonstration of his sincere desire to please you, even if your request makes no sense to him. He will be eager to do practical things for you, like fix your car or weed your garden. You should come up with a few off-the-wall requests to really test his mettle.

"Women are made to be loved, not understood."
—Oscar Wilde

Man on a Mission

For example, when I was decorating my house I found some cute red plaid stadium blankets on sale at the local K-Mart, the lone department store on our mountain. I used them to create curtains for my living room, but I needed two more to complete all the windows. I asked the man I was dating at the time, who lived down the mountain, if he would stop by his local K-Mart store and see if they had any left. Well, he went to not just one, but *six* different stores in order to find two of those blankets just for me!

You know how men hate shopping. Yet he went charging forth with the determination of Sir Lancelot to succeed in his quest or die trying. Wow, did he ever earn bonus points from me on that one! I was duly impressed and I marveled at his dedication and perseverance. I also made sure to tell everyone at my housewarming party the story of his brave and successful quest. The only thing that pleases a man more than you telling him in private how grateful you are is you telling the story of his prowess to all your friends in public. (P.S. I still didn't go to bed with him!)

Star Women, especially, need a man with a high level of desire and willingness to please. Without a large dose of this motivation in her mate, a Star Woman's marriage is doomed from the start. And she needs a finely tuned reward system to make a man feel it's worth his investment. All women need to get into the habit of noticing when a man does something to please her, and being lavish with praise for him in private and in public. Men love being our heroes!

The Mother-in-law Mandate

You may be dating a man who passes your initial tests with flying colors. He appears to be a man who loves to please women. Yet some of these men have a fatal flaw that you must watch out for. They learned to respect and love women from their mothers. However, if their mother is a Volcano Woman at heart, she does not want to ever let her little boy go. If he is too attached to her, he will never be able to make you the number one woman in his life. Be on the lookout for signs that his mother's opinions are too influential over him.

A woman who marries a man who is still a Mamma's boy is practically guaranteed a life of misery. Both of you will be at war over lover boy, and he will always play the innocent victim. You will be incensed when he follows his mother's recommendations instead of yours. You can never win against such a strong hold; so don't even try.

A woman who marries a man who is still a Mamma's boy is practically guaranteed a life of misery.

For some months I dated a man who was as macho as you can get on the outside. He had quite a high-ranking position in law enforcement, a well-muscled body, and a comfortable retirement package waiting for him. He appeared to be a great catch. We talked about my moving in with him and getting engaged. He had an ugly, old flowered sofa in his living room and I had a nicer, newer one. He refused to let me put my sofa in his house! After a series of quarrels about the subject, I finally got the truth out of him. That old sofa once belonged to his now deceased grandmother. It had a lot of sentimental value to his mother and she would be devastated if he tried to get rid of it. He was so afraid of displeasing her that he would rather displease me!

I did not marry that man, thank Goddess! He was not a bad man. He was actually a very decent guy, kind and generous. He even put the toilet seat down. But I thought about what my life would be like with a Volcano Woman for a mother-in-law and knew I had to bail out. He retired a few years ago and built a beautiful custom home not far from where I live. The old flowered sofa was moved in to the living room of the new house. He later got married to a very nice woman. I went over and peeked in the front window one day when they weren't home. The sofa was still there. Good luck, sister!

For Married Women

If you are married, I hope your husband meets the four basic requirements for marital happiness and passes the Toilet Seat Test.

If you are a Star Woman and you know your husband is a Meteor Man, you can still have a reasonably happy marriage. If you use some or all of the sexual techniques outlined in the next chapter, you stand a very good chance of increasing your husband's desire to please you and willingness to accept your influence. It will just take more work on your part to develop and train him to be a good husband to you. If you really love him and want to stay with him, you can be even happier than you already are.

If your current relationship is not satisfying, only you can decide if it's worth working on, or if you would be better off without this man.

A man is usually not worth keeping as your mate unless he meets at the very least, the first three basic requirements of the good man:

- He respects women in general and his partner in particular
- His primary goal in the relationship is to please his woman
- He allows his woman to influence him

A man is usually not worth keeping unless he meets, at the very least, the first three basic requirements of the good man.

Working on your own character and issues will certainly help, but if your man will not make any effort to improve your relationship, you may have to face the situation you dread most: being single again.

Oh, No, Single Again!

When I separated from husband number three, I was 47 years old and plenty scared that I would never find a good man to love. I read all those stories about how a woman over 40 has a better chance of being hit by lightning than getting married again. It's all nonsense. Your life is determined by the state of your consciousness.

Your life is determined by the state of your consciousness.

When you end an unhappy chapter of your life, it means you've got some soul-searching and spiritual work to do. If you are willing to do the work required to heal your emotional hurts and resentments, you can write a new chapter with a very different ending. I went through a real "Dark Night of the Soul" following my third divorce, but I had such a big, stubborn ego that the only way I was going to learn the lessons I needed to learn was to be completely humbled.

I didn't really find my own spiritual truth until I lost everything else. It took some time, but I eventually turned my life around completely on every front—health, finances, work, and relationships.

Poster Child for New Thought

I was so motivated to get out of all the pain I was in that I absorbed information like a sponge. I studied a spiritual principle in the evening and put it to work the next day. My minister dubbed me her "Poster Child for New Thought" because of the way I was able to soak up truth and then use my new expanded state of consciousness to demonstrate incredible changes in my life with amazing speed.

I don't claim that my life is perfect now or that I no longer have any problems. Elevating your consciousness does not guarantee you a problem-free life. However, it does help you cope a whole lot better when life throws you a curve ball. I can honestly say that I'm satisfied and content with the state of my life these days. I have regained my health, cleaned up my finances, expanded my business – and most important of all – married a good man who is a perfect match for me. None of that seemed remotely possible back in the dark days. I made it through to the other side and so can you.

> ***"Love and respect woman. Look to her not only for comfort, but also for strength and inspiration and the doubling of your intellectual and moral powers. Blot out from your mind any idea of superiority; you have none."***
> ***— Giuseppe Mazzini (1805-72).***

If you are a Star Woman who is thinking about getting out of a relationship with a man who is wrong for you, your future is brighter than you think. Star Women who are willing to let themselves be the strong, take-charge women they were born to be are precious gems. There are lots of men out there who are dreaming of a woman like you, and you don't have to be young, thin, or pretty to attract them. These men want a woman who is not afraid to take control. The world is yours. You just don't know it yet.

Finding Your Man

There are so many good books and articles written on how to meet men that we don't need to cover that subject in-depth here. However, I do want to tell you about how I met my current husband – through the Internet!

As you get older, it becomes more difficult to meet eligible men. More and more people of every age are using the Internet to find their special someone. My story should give you lots of confidence that you can meet the right man for you, no matter what your age or geographical location.

If anyone had a good reason to complain about how hard it was to meet a good man, it was me. I was over 50, living in a very small mountain town where most people in my age group were married couples. It's a community of pickup trucks and blue jeans. The local joke is: "If you find a guy in Big Bear who is still single, he's either in recovery or on parole." In nearly three years of living here I met a few single men, but no one that I wanted to date. Most of them flunked all three of my ABC standards so they never even made it to the starting gate! My prospects were looking mighty dim. But the solution was never outside of myself.

The Secret to Meeting Your Match

Most of us put lots of time and attention into making a list of all the wonderful qualities we want in our ideal soul mate. The secret is to BECOME that person yourself. Relationships are a mirror.

You can only attract a person who is on the same level of spiritual development as you are. So, if you want a great man, you've got to be an equally great woman. Developing yourself spiritually – so you have total faith and trust in God or a Higher Power – is the best thing you can do

If you want a great man, you've got to be an equally great woman.

for yourself in this situation. It takes that kind of faith to get you through those seemingly endless stretches of months or even years when your soul mate is nowhere in sight. Use that time to develop yourself into a woman of strength.

I studied, and meditated, and prayed—and grew stronger emotionally. Although the relationship door of my life seemed to be closed to me for the time being, other doors opened easily, so I walked through them. Success in work, making new friends, becoming part of a supportive spiritual community – all these situations blossomed in my life – but the longed-for love relationship still eluded me.

At some point I realized that putting so much of my attention on what I perceived was missing, was actually creating more of the same lack. I knew I was ready to be a great partner, but I had absolutely no control over how or when it would happen for me. I surrendered all my ideas about how I thought my life was supposed to be. I accepted the idea that only God knew how and when I would meet the right man for me.

In those days my surrender process was a lot more emotionally charged than it is today. I decided I had to get my attention off what appeared to be a lack in my life.

Demanding Your Good

I was at the end of my rope over the situation and on one of my daily hikes I held a shouting match with God right there in the forest. "OK, so you're not ready to send my soul mate right now, God. I accept that. But I demand that you send me someone to just date and have fun with. I'm ready for some kind of relationship NOW. So send me someone NOW!" I screamed and cajoled and demanded. I had been reading some spiritual books that said it was okay to demand that the universe bring forth your good.

Passionately demanding your good will make it manifest itself sooner in your life.

These spiritual authors said that passionately demanding your good will make it manifest itself sooner in your life, so I decided to put this theory into action for myself.

Sure enough, within a week I met a man who was interesting enough to date. He lived some distance away, so we didn't see each other very often. But seeing him once or twice a month and having someone of the opposite sex to talk to in between, was enough to eradicate my sense of lack. We enjoyed each other's company and had fun together, and I felt satisfied that my demand had been answered. No longer did I feel there was something missing in my life.

My minister came to my home one day to drop off a church project and I invited her in. When she saw my crowded little apartment and tiny bedroom with my Spartan single bed, she commented, "Barbara, you've been doing all this work to attract your soul mate, but look at this place; there's no space for him in your life. To manifest our dreams we need to make space for them before they can appear."

I had to admit she was right. I thought I was all mentally and spiritually prepared for a great new relationship, but I certainly wasn't prepared physically. If my life was truly going to expand, I had to demonstrate my faith and belief by expanding my physical environment. I was ready and able to pull it off financially.

To manifest our dreams we need to make space for them before they can appear.

I put all my attention and energy into building a new house so I could move out of my cramped quarters into a home that would be comfortable for two people. I kept my loving energy flowing into family and friends and work. I put my trust in God to guide and direct me and concentrated on being the kind of person I wanted to attract.

I moved into my new home and had a wonderful time decorating it just the way I wanted. I bought a whole bedroom set with a real bed for the first time in my adult life. It was not just a mattress and spring perched atop one of those cheap metal frames. I now had a beautiful sturdy queen-size pine sleigh bed just like I always wanted. I was surprised at how different it felt sleeping in that bed. It felt solid, secure, and permanent. I never realized how insecure and temporary my other bed felt. I was very proud of my new house and furniture. I felt like a real adult at last, instead of a scared child pretending to be an adult.

Meeting My Soul Mate

Two weeks after my housewarming party I met my soul mate. It all started several months before, when a woman I knew showed up at church one Sunday with a nice looking, neatly dressed guy in tow. In a sport coat and slacks, not blue jeans – wow!

"He's not from around here, is he?" I asked, "Where did you meet him?"

"On the Internet!" she replied.

"Are you serious?" I gasped! She told me there were lots of nice men in our age group on Internet dating sites and encouraged me to try the one where they met.

I put my profile and picture on the website and a whole new world opened up to me. Quite a few men contacted me, and this gave me the opportunity to practice and hone my skills at determining whether they were worth the time and trouble to actually meet in person. I was very specific about my basic requirements in my profile and it amazed me to see how many guys seemed to just ignore what they read. I stated that I did not want a long distance relationship. He must live close enough geographically so we could see each other at least twice a week. I'd get e-mails from New York, Florida, Texas.

I stated flatly "no smokers." Then I'd find out in a phone conversation that the guy smoked! What were they thinking? Couldn't they read?

I did meet several good men and dated them for a period of weeks or months, but no one really clicked with me. That was all right. It was fun checking the Internet site to see who contacted me, then writing and talking to lots of different men. Sure, a few were losers or idiots, but most were just decent men who wanted to meet their special woman and fall in love. The whole experience restored my faith in the male of the species. I saw that most men want someone to love just as much as we women do. They touched my heart and strengthened my resolve to keep the faith. I believed with all my heart that my soul mate was out there looking for me and wanting me as much as I wanted him.

Most men want someone to love just as much as we women do.

I read some of the success stories posted on the site and noticed that in many cases, the woman had made the initial contact. It gave me the confidence to try my own search instead of just responding to those who contacted me. I wondered if there might be anyone interesting who lived anywhere nearby. My search turned up dozens of men who lived within an hour's drive.

Something immediately drew me to Stephen's profile. He lived in a nearby town right at the bottom of the mountain. His face was blurry in his photo but he was wearing a sleeveless tee shirt, which revealed his muscular upper arms. I'm a sucker for a great pair of biceps, so I contacted him by e-mail. In his profile he said he liked to write poetry so in the subject line I wrote: *"Your muse awaits."*

He was intrigued by my message. He wasn't quite sure what a muse was and had to look it up in the dictionary. (A muse is someone who is an inspiration to an artist, especially a poet). He told me later that my clever, romantic line made his day.

We wrote back and forth a few times, and then talked on the phone for several weeks. He sounded rather casual on the phone and I wasn't sure I wanted to meet him. He was persistent though, and convinced me to meet him at a coffee house called *Grounds for Enjoyment* – little did I know how prophetic that would turn out to be!

I still didn't know what his face looked like. Oh, but there was no mistake about those biceps! I assumed his looks would be nothing special because of the blurry photo. I kept my expectations low and my mind open, so I wouldn't be disappointed, no matter what happened.

I was waiting outside when he pulled up in his purple Explorer. He got out and walked toward me and my heart nearly stopped! He was tall, slim, and extremely good looking, half-Italian with dark hair and eyes, an aquiline nose, and strong jaw line. He was wearing a black leather jacket that immediately reminded me of my old high school swains back in New Jersey.

We said hello, and then he impulsively gave me a hug. It caught me off guard but I liked it, and it was okay with me that he did it.

We hit it off immediately. We talked for hours that first night and before I drove back up the mountain I told him that he felt like family to me. He reminded me so much of my Italian family back east. Being with him was easy and comfortable.

We dated, got engaged, and then married a year and three months later. Needless to say, he is the quintessential Comet Man. So, of course, he wanted a woman who was gutsy enough to make the initial contact. I understand that completely now.

If I had not done all that spiritual work before I met him, none of this would have come to be. He is so grateful to have a woman in his life who enjoys being in charge. And I am so grateful to have a man in my life who accepts and loves me for being the complete Star Woman that I am.

Great relationships are created through your consciousness.

Great relationships are created through your consciousness (as is everything else in your life). That's what I know to be true through my own experience. Great love is possible for every one of us, so don't give up!

This marriage has really challenged me to live the spiritual principles I profess to believe in. Like not judging other people no matter how different they seem to be. Like totally accepting and loving another human being exactly as he is. What's important is to love and accept each other unconditionally.

What's important is to love and accept each other unconditionally.

When I envisioned my soul mate, I asked God to send me the right man to love, the right man to help me grow spiritually. I didn't have any preconceived ideas of what he looked like or what kind of work he did.

I realized that I really didn't know *what* I needed, so I left it completely in God's hands. I didn't know all the information about men and relationships I am sharing with you now. My new understanding and experience were hard-won and I'm happy to be able to share it with you, so you won't have to make all the mistakes I made!

From Relationship Hell to Relationship Heaven

Now there's one last piece of this puzzle that I want to tell you about. It is about the process of going from relationship hell to relationship heaven. It was a very long and painful journey for me, but it doesn't have to be that bad for you!

These are my personal observations about the process. Being raised Catholic I cannot resist the temptation to use some of my childhood religious terminology to describe the stages of the process. How much time you spend in each stage is a very individual matter. It depends totally on your consciousness and God's will. Here are the stages as I see them:

I. Relationship Hell

II. Relationship Purgatory

III. Relationship Limbo

IV. Relationship Heaven

I. Relationship Hell

The Time of Ignorance: This is the time period when you do not know how to have a good relationship with a man. Your ego is running your life and you suffer through disappointments and disasters in your attempts to love and be loved. If you don't learn your lessons through mildly painful experiences, you progress to more and more painful experiences. When you are finally willing to do whatever it takes to change your ways and change your life, you move on to purgatory.

II. Relationship Purgatory

The Time of Healing: Your time in Purgatory is spent cleansing and healing the emotional hurts that created your Hell. Here you develop your spiritual philosophy and your personal connection to your God or Higher Power. You educate yourself to understand how the universe works. You learn the laws and principles that you can use to better your life. You learn forgiveness and compassion. You graduate from Purgatory armed with the basic tools and a new way of thinking, which you need to attract your good and create the life you desire.

III. Relationship Limbo

The Time of Surrender: Limbo is a state of suspension, a time of waiting, when you must learn to be patient. You know what you want to create in your life now. You have healed your old hurts. You have let go of the past. Yet your desired new mate has not yet appeared.

You can create your desired result in your mind in an instant, but it can take days, weeks, or even years for it to appear in physical form. There is no way to rush God. This is when you learn to surrender your will to God's will and let go of your expectations. Your soul mate appears according to God's timetable, not yours.

Your soul mate appears according to God's timetable, not yours.

In some ways, Limbo is the most difficult period. In Hell there is lots of action and drama to occupy you. In Purgatory there is new knowledge and skills to acquire, and changes to institute. In Limbo your life settles into a relatively quiet, less exciting routine that can lead to frustration because things aren't happening fast enough for you. It can feel like an endless trek through a parched desert. You must have faith and live out your time in Limbo with grace and equanimity.

As I went through these four stages, I found the Limbo stage was the hardest because the excitement of making big breakthroughs in thought and dramatic changes in my life had passed. For protracted periods of time, life sailed along smoothly without any big problems. I wasn't used to this!

Frankly, this stage seemed a bit dull to me, but it did make me learn to surrender my will to God's. It was either surrender or drive my friends and myself crazy with my complaints about not yet having the right man in my life.

During this time I listened to Caroline Myss's audiotape of a workshop she did called *Spiritual Madness*. Her message convinced me that surrender was the only thing I could do, so surrender I did. And eventually I made it out of Limbo into the wonderful marriage I now have.

IV. Relationship Heaven

The Time of Gratitude: Your long-awaited soul mate appears at last. Now it's time for you to learn how to love him and how to create a relationship that fulfills both your needs. Learning this is a joyful experience and you are continually thankful to God for sending you the right person to love. This is the time to appreciate daily all the good you are receiving.

> ***"For one human being to love another: that is perhaps the most difficult of our tasks; the ultimate, the last test and proof, the work for which all other work is but preparation."***
>
> ***—Rainer Maria Rilke***

Now you know how to choose the right kind of man for your personality type. You will never look at men and dating the same way once you have absorbed the material in this chapter. You also know what to expect as you progress from Relationship Hell to Relationship Heaven. You should be feeling a lot more confident that you can attract a good man, then observe and test him to make sure he's the right man for you.

The next question is: how do you treat him once he is yours? We will now delve into the secrets of how to create a great satisfying sex life with your man.

Chapter 6

Men And Sex

"God gave us all a penis and a brain but only enough blood to run one at a time."

—Robin Williams

Women have known for eons that sex to a man is like candy to a baby. He wants it, and he wants it right now. You know that already. So men should not be in charge of sex. That's like putting the cookie monster in charge of the cookies!

Don't get me wrong. I absolutely love men and I find the differences between the sexes fascinating and delightful. Men are blessed with a natural aptitude for focusing on one thing at a time and achieving their goal. When he is focused on sex (which any man will tell you is a good deal of the time) he can't think about anything else. We've already established how much men need our guidance in many areas of life and sex is one of those areas.

If you have the guts to take charge of sex in your relationship, your life will be so pleasant and satisfying, you'll wonder why you ever lived any other way. What I am about to tell you in this chapter goes against how "nice girls" are supposed to behave. But you've tried being the nice girl and it hasn't gotten you what you want, has it?

If you want great romance and sex – plus a way to get your man to do his share of the domestic chores (or all of them – why not?), this chapter is required reading.

If you are a true Star Woman, you are a visionary who is able to look toward the future and see the big picture. You are more likely to be open to new ideas and willing to try new things. That is just what I'm asking you to do now with regard to your sex life.

I don't expect you to put the entire program into action in one fell swoop. Just try whatever intrigues you and whatever feels most comfortable right now. As you begin to try the techniques described and see that they work, you'll gain confidence and get bolder. Star Women always do!

If you are an Earth Mother you may not want to use these techniques all the time, but you need to activate your Star Woman aspect now and then to take charge of sex with your man. It is the best way to insure a good balance of power in all areas of your partnership. Your man needs to see and feel your feminine power unleashed on his body to remind him why he loves you and why his top priority is to please you.

Your man needs to see and feel your feminine power unleashed on his body to remind him why he loves you and why his top priority is to please you.

So when I speak to Star Women in this chapter I'm speaking to the Star Woman in every woman.

Who Should Be in Charge?

This new sexual model of Venus On Top -- the woman in charge – could well be the missing ingredient of the relationship recipe for your romantic life.

Being a follower at the workplace would eventually frustrate and bore the natural leader – the Star Woman. Why would the bedroom be any different? Leaders are more assertive in general than the average person. We are likely to be more assertive – or even aggressive – in the bedroom, too. Being in the "clutches" of such a woman is something most men only dream about. Does that surprise you?

One of the major complaints of married men is that they wish their partners would initiate sex more. If you have a pretty high sex drive already, your partner no doubt appreciates it. If your interest in sex has waned over the years, these techniques may be just the ticket to kick you back into high gear.

> ***"If love and sex are such natural phenomenons, how come there are so many books on how to?"***
>
> ***—Bette Midler***

Congratulations to all the Earth Mothers who are still with us! You've got an adventurous spirit that I admire. Don't get discouraged if some of this information seems too extreme for you at first. Just try some of the milder ideas on your partner. And don't be surprised if he asks for more!

The Slippery Sliding Scale

Before we discuss the Venus on Top approach to sex, there's something we need to clear up. Despite the so-called sexual revolution, and despite the proliferation of sexual images in the media, most Americans are still very uptight about sex. If you want to have a woman-led marriage – or to experiment with woman-led lovemaking

– you've got to get past those old puritan attitudes about sex in which only certain practices are considered proper.

Each of us has our own slippery sliding scale of what's acceptable for us. I call it the slippery sliding scale because that's just what it is. The "OK" marker keeps sliding further down the line as you go along in life. What was unacceptable yesterday becomes acceptable today for society in general – and for individuals in particular.

Remember when you first learned there was such a thing as French kissing? As a pubescent girl you probably thought it was "yucky" – something you wouldn't be caught dead doing. Yet sooner or later you found yourself French kissing some boy and enjoying it. You started down your very own slippery sliding scale.

There is no such thing as absolute right and wrong. Even the Pope takes a slide down the scale now and then. Remember when Catholics were not allowed to eat meat on Fridays and Catholic women had to cover their heads in church? Both of those rules are ancient history now. Times change, people change— and we each need to consciously choose and adopt our own set of values about what is acceptable for us.

"Vanilla" Sex

The typical marriage consists of a basic diet of vanilla sex. This is the kind of sexual activity (like intercourse and oral sex) that the majority of people in our culture believe is acceptable "normal" sexual behavior between husband and wife. The man initiates (or begs, or whines, or makes you feel guilty) and you give in to keep the peace. The man makes love to the woman, so you feel like sex is something that is done to you. The man is always satisfied – the woman is sometimes satisfied.

It is rare when you can really communicate to each other about what turns you on, how you like to be touched, or what your deepest, darkest fantasies are. Maybe you spice things up now and then and get adventurous with videos, sex toys, or bondage games.

If you're lucky and manage to keep the spark of your early romance alive, you sometimes have great sex with your long-term partner. But, most likely, you settle down into a routine and accept it because "that's how it is when you're married."

The woman can lead in the bedroom, too. And it is actually better when she does.

It doesn't have to be like that. In a woman-led marriage, the woman can lead in the bedroom, too. And it is actually better when she does.

Star Women like to be in control most of the time. Being in control in the bedroom is a great way to give free rein to all your diva fantasies. Be your most haughty, demanding self. Let the bitch in you come out to play. Push your man down on the bed, get on top, and tell him he is now in your power and you mean to have your way with him. This is nearly every man's secret fantasy and he will absolutely love it.

The Three Platinum Rules for Satisfying Sex

Remember that sex to a man is like candy to a baby. He wants it, and he wants it right now. You know that. What you don't know is that it is your privilege, your right, and yes, your duty, to take control of the sex in your relationship.

It is your privilege, your right, and yes, your duty, to take control of the sex in your relationship.

You will of course need to first talk over these rules with your man and get his agreement on them. Men like clear-cut rules. They like to know where they stand and exactly what is expected of them. Here are the three simple rules for sex guaranteed to keep you and your man happy:

The Three Platinum Rules

Rule #1. The primary goal of sex is the woman's pleasure.

Rule #2. The woman decides if, when, where, and how.

Rule #3. When you forget Rule #2, refer to Rule #1.

Rule #1 should be ironclad in any marriage. Rule #2 is an individual preference. Some couples make it their everyday style with an occasional exception when the woman is in a particularly magnanimous mood. Some couples make it a sometime, or most-of-the-time, thing. You need to experiment to find the right amount of control for you and your partner. This is your relationship so have it your way.

These rules are really very simple. You may be a little shocked because you've never heard of anything so outrageous as these three little rules. I was shocked, too, when I first discovered them.

Powerful women like Cleopatra and priestesses of the Great Goddess have used these rules throughout the ages to keep their men intrigued, enthralled, and hungering for more.

I was curious enough and brave enough to give these audacious, time-tested rules a try and they are now the cornerstones of my marriage. My husband is as happy with these rules as I am. Trust me. They work.

Rule #1: The primary goal of sex is the woman's pleasure.

Women are very sensitive to their surroundings and circumstances — especially when making love. Most like having a relaxing physical setting and plenty of uninterrupted time available for that special time. Women require more romance, more foreplay, more stimulation, and more time to reach orgasm than men. Women need to be "in the mood" to have a really good sexual experience.

Rarely does a man have a problem reaching orgasm. When isn't he "in the mood?" A man can have sex at the drop of a hat, and reach a climax before it hits the floor if he's not careful.

We women just don't operate like that. So it makes logical sense that the one with the special needs should be the one calling the shots.

"If it's true that men are such beasts, this must account for the fact that most women are animal lovers."
—Doris Day

Men Are Sluts

Let's face it. Men are sluts. They will do practically anything for you if they think it means getting laid. This is a good thing for us. It gives us lots of leverage. Don't forget we're talking about the good men here – the ones who sincerely want to please us. The other ones are sluts, too, but they don't have the desire to please. We don't give those types the privilege of our company.

We stick with the good guys who want to give us pleasure and total satisfaction in bed, but they don't always know how. A good man feels successful and proud of himself when he has done something that pleases his woman.

If you don't believe me, then listen to someone who is an expert on relationships, the best-selling author of the Venus and Mars series, and a happily married man:

"When a man loves a woman his primary goal is to make her happy."
–John Gray

Making his woman happy is a good man's prime directive, his reason for living and loving. A man who truly loves you and wants to make you happy will have no problem with this rule.

A good man feels successful and proud of himself when he has done something that pleases his woman.

No Guessing For Him

When you tell your man that sex is now first and foremost initiated/managed by you for your pleasure and his responsibility is secondary, he will be relieved. Up to this point he's been guessing and hoping that he's pleasing you sexually. When you take charge it means no guessing for him. He will be happy to give you carte blanche to do whatever pleases you in bed, because it takes the performance pressure off him.

As a woman of power you take responsibility for everything in your life. That includes your sexual pleasure. You are responsible only for yours, not his. You must wipe any thought or concern about his pleasure out of your mind entirely. He will have his pleasure easily enough without any extra effort on your part. You come first (literally!).

As a woman of power you take responsibility for everything in your life. That includes your sexual pleasure.

I bet no one ever told you this before! Now you see why learning to receive is so important. Putting your own pleasure before your man's goes against everything we were taught about how a woman is supposed to behave.

The first time you put your pleasure first, it may feel a little strange, but don't worry, you will learn to really enjoy it. And you will see the wisdom of this method. It frees you to focus on doing what gives you pleasure. Your man wants you to have that pleasure! He is your consort — eager to please his exotic goddess. It gives him untold pleasure seeing you enjoy yourself. When you are happy his prime directive is fulfilled and then he's happy.

> ***"When I'm good I'm very, very good but when I'm bad I'm better."***
>
> ***—Mae West***

Treat Him Like Your Sex Toy

Be totally selfish when you make love to your man. Men love to be used, so use him for all he's worth. Show him or tell him in graphic terms what you want him to do. Time has no meaning when you are making love this way. Be ruthless and don't give a single thought to how long it may take you to reach a climax. Treat him like your sex toy. Don't allow him to climax until you are satisfied. An aroused – but unsatisfied – man is highly motivated to pleasure you. Once he has an orgasm, that high level of enthusiasm can disappear.

Some of you will talk about these ideas with your man and get a positive reaction immediately. Perhaps your man even gave you this book. In that case you don't even need to ask what he thinks— you already know. What are you waiting for, girl? Go for it!

Asking Permission

Once you and your partner agree on Rule #1 (the primary goal of sex is the woman's pleasure) you will see that there is a natural corollary to this rule:

Corollary to Rule #1: The man must always ask permission from the woman to climax.

Men who are exceptionally sensitive to a woman's feelings and eager to please her may well have developed this gallant habit on their own. They wouldn't dream of taking their pleasure unless they are sure it is alright with their woman. And the only way for them to be really sure is to ask. Some men find it exquisitely arousing to give control of their orgasm to their woman. For this kind of man it can actually turn him on more if you tell him he may not come until you say so.

If your man isn't asking permission from you already but agrees that your pleasure comes first, then it shouldn't be difficult to get him in the habit of asking you. Nearly all women experience times when sexual activity has been very pleasurable, but for one reason or another she's not sure she really needs or wants to have an orgasm. At times like these when a man asks permission it gives you an opportunity to assess your feelings and make a clear decision about whether you want to keep going or not.

Because you are the one making the decision you will have no resentment if you allow him to climax while you do not. And your man will have no reason to feel guilty about it because you have told him straight out that this is your choice. If a man thinks he has not done his job of pleasing you unless you have an orgasm, he will feel like a failure when you do not climax. When asking permission becomes a normal part of sex for him, he will be happy to do it because he won't have to guess about it or feel bad or guilty ever again. And you won't have to fake it ever again!

Premature Ejaculation

Only a man who has learned some self-control can be successful at asking permission and following your desire. Many men are able to learn to delay their orgasm on their own, but many are not. If your man ejaculates prematurely encourage him (or insist, if necessary) to educate himself in techniques that enable him to control or at least delay his climax.

The ancients knew these techniques and today you can learn them through the many sex educational videos, books, and classes available. This problem can easily cause anger and resentment to build up in you over time – but it is entirely avoidable. Your man will be so happy and proud of himself when he uses his new self-control skills to produce more pleasure for you.

Just For Tonight, Honey

If you're unsure and not ready to talk about the rules yet, there's a slower approach you can use. You take one baby step at a time and then see how you both feel about it before taking another. I call it the Just For Tonight, Honey method. You tell him you want to try something a little different in bed. All he has to do is what he is told to do. You want to be in charge but it's just for tonight. That way there is no pressure on either of you. It's just for tonight and if one of you doesn't like it, no one is under any obligation to do it ever again.

Most men will fall all over themselves saying yes! to this. Have him lie on his back with you on top. Kiss, touch, and do whatever else feels good to get yourself very aroused before you have intercourse. Take your time. Don't worry about him because whatever you do for yourself will get him aroused, too.

Put Him in the "Zone"

Then, sometime during intercourse, take his hands in yours and hold them down firmly over his head as you keep going until you climax. This will give you both a little taste of sex with the woman in charge. Tell him his job is to hold off climaxing until you are through with him.

Have a little pity on him; take a break and stop moving if he gets too close to orgasm. If you are not too far gone yourself by this time, open your eyes and look into his. If you see a glazed look in his eyes and he seems to be off into another dimension and can't even speak, you have sent him into the zone.

A man who reacts this way to your small gesture of control is a man who has a submissive streak that you may utilize to your mutual benefit. Being under your control and in the zone is such an incredibly pleasurable sensation to him that he will crave it more and more. As he learns that pleasing you outside the bedroom can put you in the mood to put him in the zone, he becomes more eager to please. It's a lovely pattern of behavior to create.

If you enjoy it, you can play more of these kinds of games with him from time to time. He will probably ask for more if he enjoyed being put in the zone.

Don't feel obligated to do anything for him unless you want to and you enjoy it. Personally, I get a kick out of putting my man into the zone. It gives me a feeling of power and control that's just a natural high for a Star Woman.

As he learns that pleasing you outside the bedroom can put you in the mood to put him in the zone, he becomes more eager to please. It's a lovely pattern of behavior to create.

Once you see how fun and fulfilling it is for you to be in control, you can talk about putting Rule #1 into place permanently. Or you can make it your prerogative to invoke Rule #1 only when you are in the mood for it and have vanilla sex when you're not. If your man has a fairly deep submissive streak, he may welcome the structure of having all three rules in place even sooner than you will.

Rule #2: The woman decides if, when, where, and how.

This rule probably seems even more preposterous than Rule #1. But let me remind you that as a Star Woman leader and visionary, you have quite a dominant personality. Chances are, the man who loves you has a submissive streak in him. You are attracted to each other because you balance each other out. This is exactly the right kind of man for women like us. He enjoys your dominant personality and likes it when you take control. You know that you enjoy being in control, so why fight it?

If you are a Star Woman like me you don't like anyone telling you what to do in the bedroom, the boardroom, or anywhere else. So relax, accept, and love yourself the way you are. Your man sure does.

> ***"I'm tough, I'm ambitious, and I know exactly what I want. If that makes me a bitch, okay."***
>
> ***—Madonna***

Rule #2 works only if you really love your man. When he agrees to this rule he is really putting his fate in your hands. He is trusting that you have such a high level of integrity that you will see that his need for sex is met. Yes, we know that men are sluts and will do anything for sex. The hunger for sex is hard-wired into his brain and you can't change it, so you might as well accept and enjoy it.

> ***"Imagine what will happen to this nation if large numbers of American women start using the Wonderbra. It will be catastrophic. The male half of the population will be nothing but mindless drooling Zombies of Lust. Granted, this is also true now, but it will be even worse."***
>
> ***—Dave Barry***

Men are very driven by their hormones to attempt to propagate the species every chance they get. But we have to understand that men, especially the good ones, have a tender place in them as well. To him, your attention to his sexual needs is evidence of your love for him. Your man needs sex like a plant needs water. His love for you won't survive without it. Physical closeness and sexual activity with you are his way of being close and intimate with you. If he doesn't get some at least now and then he may well conclude that you don't love him anymore.

To him, your attention to his sexual needs is evidence of your love for him.

This doesn't mean that you give him all the sex he wants whenever he wants it. That would be foolish and take up way too much time. No, the key is to keep him on low boil most of the time with occasional full-blown sexual escapades that end with one or more orgasms for you and sometimes (but not always) one for him.

When you are in control of if, when, where, and how the sexual activities happen, you are never bored with sex and neither is he. I only make love when I feel like it. However, when my husband and I do make love he gets a woman who is totally in the moment with him. He knows I'm enjoying myself (remember Rule #1?) and he knows that I really want to do this with him (or to him as the case may be).

I can be my naturally whimsical and capricious self and it works to the advantage of our relationship. He is often off-balance wondering what's coming next and when. He never knows when I'll be in the mood. Frankly, neither do I! I'm free to be myself and express myself sexually exactly as I choose, when I choose.

Rule #3: If you forget Rule #2, refer to Rule #1.

This last rule is important, especially for couples that do not use Rule #2 all the time. Even though the man may be allowed to initiate or ask for sex, he must never be allowed to forget Rule #1.

If you let him slide on this, your whole relationship will slide downhill, too. Before you know it, his burning desire to please you will deteriorate into a feeble flicker. He may start to get the unholy idea that his pleasure is more important than yours. You must never allow this to happen.

I think you will see that once Rule #1 is in place, you will have little problem putting Rule #2 and Rule #3 in place. Do it and your romantic happiness is secured.

Since I am well past menopause, my level of sexual desire is not as high as it used to be. I have to pay more attention to myself and make sure my sensuous side doesn't get neglected or lost in the shuffle of everyday routine. My husband is always doing nice things to entice that part of me out to play, like making candlelit dinners for us and having a drink and a spotless house ready for me when I come home. We are always very affectionate to each other every day.

Because I love him, I want to meet his needs for sex. But those needs can be met any number of ways. Sex doesn't always have to mean intercourse. Some men find it a real turn on if you order them to masturbate for you, or if you do it for them. You being in control of his orgasm can be a really fun experience and a terrific turn-on for both of you. Seeing your man utterly vulnerable and helpless with pleasure in front of you is so gratifying and amusing. If you have never done this to your man, you are missing a great experience. It's time to start!

Seeing your man utterly vulnerable and helpless with pleasure in front of you is so gratifying and amusing.

There are endless ways to be creative in the exercise of Rule #2. Here are just a few to get you started. I'm sure you're very creative and will come up with other ideas that are just perfect for you and your partner. We'll break it down into creative ideas for each of the four parts of Rule #2 (i.e., If, When, Where, and How).

If

Making your man guess about whether he is going to get some is about the oldest woman's game in the world. Never underestimate the power of the tease.

Never underestimate the power of the tease.

Never feel guilty about arousing him into a rock hard erection, and then telling him you have to go make a phone call. He'll live.

When

Tease him with a promise of things to come (maybe). Start thinking of an orgasm as a "treat" for him and tell him you might give him a treat tonight. Call him at work and tell him you have a treat waiting for him after work today. Don't get into the habit of having sex at the same time of the day. Wake him up in the morning and give him a treat before work. Keep shifting the times around so neither of you gets into a rut.

Where

For women like me who work at home, home can seem like a very unsexy place. Home is where I work, so I tend to think a great deal about work when I'm at home. Many days I'm home all day and the only time I go out is to walk the dog.

Get me away from my workplace into a different environment and I perk right up and start thinking about other things! Weekend getaways to anywhere are great. Don't forget the great outdoors either. Some people find that a setting with some danger of being caught makes them as horny as a high schooler. At the very least, don't always make love in your bedroom.

How

Sex can be anything that gives you pleasure. It doesn't have to always end in orgasm for one or both partners. Massage each other, feed each other, play with vibrators, and other sex toys, try something a little bit kinky. Your man would probably go bonkers if you tied him to a chair and teased him unmercifully, or if you made him watch you masturbate.

You were probably a big tease in high school. I know I was. Bring that mischievous girl back and give her free rein to drive your man crazy! He will love it.

But What if He is Really Kinky?

The kind of man who is attracted to a powerful woman may have a submissive streak in him. Submissive in this context does not mean weak or wimpy; it means that he finds it sexually arousing to give up control to a woman. But what if he is really kinky? Women need to be aware of the fact that we might well attract a man whose sexual desires are considered extreme or outside the norm.

Your soul mate may want you to do more than lead or guide; he may want you to actually dominate him in bed and out. He may have a fetish for high heels and nylons, leather, or rubber. He might be masochistic and want you to spank or whip him or humiliate him verbally. He might want to be tied up and gagged or be "forced" to wear feminine articles of clothing.

This all sounds rather shocking, but there are some people who make these activities a regular part of their sex lives. A great many look just like the couple next door and lead lives no different than the average except for their sexual activities.

> ***"I truly feel that there are as many ways of loving as there are people in the world and as there are days in the lives of those people."***
>
> ***—Mary Steichen Calderone***

About 5 percent to 10 percent of the general population are turned on by these kinds of things and are what we would consider "kinky." Every woman needs to discover whether her man falls into this category well before she ever considers marrying him.

Many a man hides his kinkiness from his girlfriends and later, his wife. Then years later, he decides he can't lie about it anymore or she discovers his little secret. This is potentially a terrible blow when they have already created a family together. Most women would feel like they had been betrayed or had been living a lie. You deserve to know exactly what you are signing on for before you tie the knot.

You deserve to know exactly what you are signing on for before you tie the knot.

Star Women are usually pretty sexually adventurous. You might find that you enjoy indulging your lover in his fantasies now and then. Some women discover that they have a sadistic streak and enjoy play-acting at being cruel and inflicting a little bit of pain on this more than willing victim – within reason, of course. Before you try any kind of sexual activities involving possible pain for either partner, you must educate yourself about how to do these activities safely. See the bibliography for the best books on this subject for beginners!

Role-playing fantasies can be a lot of fun. You can be the Amazon Queen and he, your captive sex slave (most men would jump at the chance to be a sex slave!). It's a way of letting your shadow side out to play and some people find this liberating. People who have strong dominance/submission fantasies and desires are never completely satisfied with a steady diet of vanilla sex.

People who have strong dominance/submission fantasies and desires are never completely satisfied with a steady diet of vanilla sex.

> ***"You don't appreciate a lot of stuff in school until you get older. Little things like being spanked every day by a middle aged woman: Stuff you pay good money for in later life."***
>
> ***—Emo Philips***

Responsible people who regularly participate in these kinds of activities advocate a simple motto: "Safe, Sane, and Consensual." This means partners discuss beforehand which activities are acceptable for each one and which are not. No one initiates an activity unless their partner has consented to it in advance. Partners agree to a "safe word" so they can immediately halt the action or "scene" by saying that word. Responsible partners do not engage in an unsafe or dangerous practice even if their partner desires it. If you want to explore this subject more, there are good, informative books listed in the bibliography.

Responsible partners do not engage in an unsafe or dangerous practice even if their partner desires it.

I feel that it is my responsibility to include the subject of non-traditional sexual behaviors because, if your future mate has these tendencies, you will want to know sooner, rather than later. You don't want to find out after you've had a couple of children that he's going to a professional dominatrix or is addicted to kinky porn sites or magazines.

If a man has a deep need for things like bondage, physical discipline, humiliation, or cross-dressing, it will not go away no matter how hard he tries to deny it. Earn his trust and get it out in the open fairly early on in the relationship.

Do some research and reading so you understand what it is that he wants and needs. Kinky men are rarely molesters or rapists. They simply become highly sexually aroused by objects or activities that other people do not find arousing in the same way.

No matter how much you think you love him, if you cannot accept a man's kinkiness, don't marry him.

You cannot have a relationship of true intimacy if you cannot be honest with each other about sex. Lots of couples experiment with kinky sex activities as an added turn-on or for variety, but only as a prelude to the usual forms of vanilla sex. This might be something that arouses your curiosity. There is nothing wrong with experimenting to experience it for yourself and to enrich your romantic life together.

You cannot have a relationship of true intimacy if you cannot be honest with each other about sex.

The vast majority of women who enjoy kinky sex are first introduced to it by their partner and find that they like it. Some men report that it can be like opening Pandora's box – they pry open the lid for her and then end up with more than they bargained for! Now they've got a woman who is kinkier than they are, although I doubt any of them are really complaining about this!

But if kinky activities are not your thing, don't try to pretend they are just to keep your man. Do him and yourself a favor by ending the relationship if you know you don't want to engage in these activities. Never forget Rule #1 – your pleasure comes first. You are not obligated to do anything for him that you don't want to do.

You are not obligated to do anything for him that you don't want to do.

Be a woman of integrity. If your man trusts you enough to tell you about his most secret sexual fantasies, that information is not to be shared with anyone without his consent. Be happy that he thinks that you are compassionate enough that he can open up to you. Don't judge him or punish him for being honest with you. Be a woman of integrity.

Can I Live With This?

Make your own determination: "Can I live with this?" If you can't live with it, your relationship has no future. It is best for both of you to recognize that fact and part amicably.

Men often have trouble talking about these things because they fear being judged and they fear losing you. As a powerful woman who is now aware of these possibilities, you must insist on getting the whole truth before you commit yourself to him. If you suspect his submissive streak is as deep as a canyon, tie him up and interrogate him like a strict schoolmistress – I guarantee he'll confess!

If you are married and among those wives whose husband has finally confessed his little secret to you, I hope you will find it in your heart to have compassion for him. He has probably tried every way he can to bury and deny that part of him. He would prefer to be "normal" if he had a choice, but he does not have a choice. That is the way he is made.

Real love is being willing to accept another person with all their virtues as well as all their faults.

If you are confronted with this situation you will have to search within yourself for the true definition of love. Real love is being willing to accept another person with all their virtues as well as all their faults.

It is easy to love the good parts of anyone. The real test comes when we see something in our beloved that we cannot understand.

It is easy to love the good parts of anyone. The real test comes when we see something in our beloved that we cannot understand. The true meaning of love is to find it in your heart to accept your partner's sexual nature, no matter how strange it may seem to you.

"I love you not only for what you are, but for what I am when I am with you. I love you not only for what you have made of yourself, but for what you are making of me. I love you for the part of me that you bring out."
—Elizabeth Barrett Browning

The following is a beautiful message found on an Internet discussion group, reprinted anonymously with the author's permission. It was posted in response to a man's question about how he could get his wife to accept his submissive desires. What an eloquent, deep expression of this woman's love and compassion for her husband.

To: DOMestic
Subject line: Looking for help
From: John A.

Can anyone advise me how I can get my wife to be more dominant? She refuses to try even the most mild things like giving me a light spanking. I love my wife but my fantasies and desires just won't go away, and seem to be getting stronger.

To: DOMestic
Subject line: Responding to your request for help
From: Anonymous

My husband has a submissive side which I was not expecting to see, nor was I experienced or familiar with it at all. At first I was even frightened and alarmed by what he was sharing with me.

At times I was annoyed, really, for one example, I am not turned on seeing people get spanked or by receiving spankings (it pisses me off) or giving them–to me this is not sexual at all. But time has passed and I am learning and growing in this area because I LOVE MY HUSBAND. I ACCEPT HIM–ALL OF HIM–WITHOUT RESERVATION.

Everyone has a secret place in their mind they go to when reaching orgasm. I have a place, you have a place, my husband has a place. My place, the place that seems most erotic and naughty to me and always sends me over the edge is not as intricate, or highly developed or even physically as practiced as the place my husband has. But it is the same essential concept.

The place where he experiences fulfillment is not HIM. It is the "place" just like the "place" I use or you use or the man down the street uses.

My husband is the most wonderful person in the world. He is separate and different from that place he uses to climax sexually. Just as me, the mother, employee, grandmother, volunteer, daughter, sister am different from the place I visit to climax sexually.

My sexual place is a small part of my life. His sexual place is but one facet of his life and activity. His place is different than mine. I, at times, do not relate to his place. Most of the time, his place and the way he uses it, would not serve as a sexual turn on for me.

I love that my husband trusts me to even know of this– he shares this with me and it makes us very close. I love that my husband wants me with him in his place and needs me there. I love that he shares my place with me because he loves me and I think he loves that I share his place with him because I love him.

I have discovered there are facets of his place that I can enter into that do serve to turn me on and we both now can enjoy, at times, what it is that he needs.

I have discovered there are facets of his place that I cannot relate to, that do not turn me on and that annoy me actually. Those parts or times are times when I participate or just be with him because I love him and he deserves to have what he perceives as pleasure in his life whether I perceive this as pleasure or not or even understand it or not–it doesn't matter–it works for him and he deserves to have something that works for him.

My husband is responsible, manly, capable, a good citizen, a most excellent father, and he is the best husband I could ever hope to find in every way. However, his place would be perceived by the mainstream as odd and gay or fem or weird. I value my husband and I value his honesty and I value his trust of me and I value that he desires to share as much of his heart and life with me as is possible and he desires to be real with me.

I hope your wife, even if she feels stupid participating and even if she thinks it is stupid of you to have these ideas, begins to try and find a way to join you in your place–if just for your occasional pleasure alone–or hopefully for mutual satisfaction some day.

I hope she recognizes the courage, the faith, the trust, the hope, you have placed in her and her love for you by sharing what is true and real for you. I hope she learns to value you and accept you–all of you–not just the public you or the readily understandable you.

My heart would just break, to know my husband was so sad. I would stand on my head–do almost whatever–to help him. She needs to stop rejecting you in my opinion. You need and deserve to be accepted by your wife.

Of all the people in the world she should be your closest and best friend and truly a part of you–and in my opinion if she truly LOVES YOU she will accept you–all sides of you–both interesting and not so interesting facets of you, both the sides she understands and relates to and the sides of you she doesn't.

If she loves you she will make the effort. If she does not love you I don't think she will care enough about you to do so.

I hope you work it out–life is short.

—Anonymous

If that message is not a perfect example of unconditional love in action, then I don't know what is.

But what about Rule #1, you're asking? I thought that my pleasure comes first and I don't have to do anything that doesn't please me. Yes, that is the rule. But consider this: this woman's husband is a good husband and father and she truly loves him and values having him in her life. She wants to give him pleasure. She sometimes participates in things with her husband that she doesn't understand or really enjoy. This she does consciously and willingly because she wants to meet his needs. This is the ultimate gift of love — to care as much about your partner's needs as your own.

"This is the miracle that happens every time to those who really love; the more they give, the more they possess." —Rainer Maria Rilke

Having an intimate, loving relationship with that special person is something all of us desire deep in our hearts. We give lip service to how much we want to love and be loved, but achieving true intimacy requires courage and commitment. The big rewards go to grown-ups who are willing to see and be seen from the grunge to the glory and everything in between.

Achieving true intimacy requires courage and commitment.

The information and insights about men and sex you've learned here take most women decades to discover. Some of us stumble onto this knowledge one little piece at a time. Some of us never discover any of it and just keep on suffering. You now have the tools and techniques to take as much control as you need to have a satisfying and romantic sex life with your man.

You may be wondering how a real life Comet Man thinks and feels about being married to a Star Woman. In the next chapter you'll find out as I give you the highlights of my interviews with some estimable Comet Men who love and adore their powerful Star Women partners, and wouldn't have it any other way.

Chapter 7

The Man's Perspective - Why She Leads

"The bravest thing that men do is love women."
—Mort Sahl

This chapter reveals the inner workings of the minds of three men who are proud partners in women-led marriages. I interviewed each of them to give you some insight and tangible proof that there are, indeed, men out there who enjoy being married to a powerful woman.

I deliberately chose not to interview any stay-at-home dads because many of them have been pushed into that choice by economic factors. The men I interviewed all have grown children from their first marriage and no children in their current marriage. I wanted to speak with men whose only motivation to be in a woman-led marriage is that they are happy and satisfied in it.

One, of course, is my own husband, Stephen, a musician. We also have Robert, a graphic design consultant whose wife is an editor. And Alex, a retired electrician who is now his minister wife's right hand man. All three men are in second marriages now after being divorced from long-term (average 20+ years) first marriages. The complete text of the interviews can be found in Appendix A. Here I'll summarize my findings about the male viewpoint from these three formal interviews and from informal conversations I have had with other Comet Men who are married to Star Women.

Before I met my husband I had been living in the little mountain town of Big Bear Lake for about three years. As I got acquainted with more of the people in my community I came to be friends with many more married couples than I had ever socialized with when I lived in Los Angeles. I began to notice that many of the strong dynamic women who were business owners and leaders in local organizations had really great husbands. I observed these couples and made them my mental models for the kind of relationship I wanted to have.

The husbands of these women intrigued me because each and every one of them exhibited such a respectful, proud, almost worshipful attitude whenever he talked about his wife. He openly admired her talents and accomplishments and was happy to do whatever was needed to support her with her work or with the family. These relationships seemed to be quite harmonious – without competitiveness or power struggles.

Yet these admirable husbands were not weak, wimpy, or dependent men. They were strong and masculine, yet kind and caring at the same time.

These were solid, enduring partnerships between people who obviously loved each other. Rather than being jealous and resentful that I didn't have that kind of marriage yet, I looked at them and said, "That's the club I want to join!"

A Different Form of Partnership

I believe the initial idea for this book was born out of my observations of this different form of partnership – although it took a few more years for me to attract my partner and develop that kind of relationship for myself.

So who are these men and how do they think? Are they really an unusual and rare type of personality, or are they simply human beings who happen to be male, but have refused to buy into the cultural stereotype of how a man is supposed to behave?

Are they simply human beings who happen to be male, but have refused to buy into the cultural stereotype of how a man is supposed to behave?

Unaware of Their Needs

One of the main insights I gained after talking to these men was that they had not been fully aware that a strong leader-type woman was the perfect partner for them. None of them made a conscious choice to look for this kind of woman for a partner. They were powerfully drawn to a strong woman—and the roles of leader and follower emerged gradually as the relationship developed. Most likely this is because, until now, we have not had a positive model for a woman-led marriage, or complimentary rather than derogatory names for the personality types suited to this kind of marriage.

Until now, the typical reference our culture had for this kind of marriage was something like the snide remark, "She wears the pants in that family." People assumed that if the woman had the upper hand, the man was weak and deserved the epithet of "henpecked" or worse, "pussy-whipped." No man would ever say, "Oh, yes, I want to marry a ball-buster of a woman and be henpecked for the rest of my life!"

In the past if a man and woman developed a woman-led marriage and found that both partners were happy that way, they couldn't admit it to anyone else – maybe not even to themselves. There have probably been many women-led marriages that were concealed from public view by both partners to avoid social disapproval.

Thank Goddess things are changing! Still, it takes a man who is strong, self-confident – and maybe a bit of a rebel – to stand up against society's prescribed formulas for acceptable masculine and feminine behavior.

There are probably more men than we think who would be happy in a woman-led marriage. They often don't discover the truth about themselves until they find a woman who brings it out in them...which is one of the powerful secret techniques of Star-womanhood shared in this book.

The old rigid definitions of what is masculine and what is feminine are slowly crumbling.

The old rigid definitions of what is masculine and what is feminine are slowly crumbling. We can speed up the process by living openly and proudly in a woman-led marriage, and by respecting and celebrating the fine men who make these partnerships possible.

Attraction

A woman's self-confidence is an important factor in her attractiveness to these men. Her intelligence and leadership abilities also attracted them. The men in these successful marriages were all notably non-competitive when it came to their partner's accomplishments, and had no concern that their wives might "outshine" them. On the contrary, they were proud of the fact that such outstanding women were attracted to them.

"Men's minds are raised to the level of the women with whom they associate."

—Alexandre Dumas

Compatibility

In interviewing three of these happy men, I found that in all three relationships the men are easy and comfortable within their marriages because the partners are extremely compatible with each other. They don't necessarily have the same interests or hobbies as their partner – but when it comes to living everyday life, the men felt there were no big differences in opinion or huge obstacles that could cause difficulties between them.

"It's Not a Problem"

These Comet Men are very aware that they are in the minority in the kind of marriage they have in common. When asked how they feel about the woman being the leader, taking care of the finances, or making all the plans, they all had a similar response: "It's not a problem for me," which implies that for other men it could or would be a problem. However, these men have found real happiness with their Star Women, and they accept living outside the norm with apparent ease.

Finances

All three men responded very positively when asked about who handled the finances in their marriages—"She does and I'm fine with that!" Two readily admitted that financial matters were not their strong suit. One said he was capable in that area, but thought his wife was more capable so he was glad to let her handle those responsibilities.

All three men said they discussed financial matters with their partners, so the men's ideas and opinions were heard and considered, but they left the details to the women, and were happy to do so.

Decisions

The women are collaborative leaders, not dictators.

All three men said that decision making was a mutual process, and that their wives always discussed any major decisions with them; the women are collaborative leaders, not dictators. The men all placed high value on their partners' ability to think carefully and weigh all factors when a decision must be made. They all respected and admired their woman's brainpower.

They all respected and admired their woman's brainpower.

Handling Conflict

All the men maintained that there was very little conflict in their relationships. And when it did happen, they all claimed that the great majority of the fault was theirs. Now these guys may or may not be telling the truth on this subject, but their responses show that they are all very astute about how to get along with a woman!

Housework

None of the men thought that housework was inherently a woman's job. They saw it as a set of regular, common tasks that needed to be done for the family. One has outside help with housecleaning, but all of them take care of many household jobs and consider it part of their responsibility in the partnership.

Advantages

When asked about the advantages of being married to a powerful woman, the men enthusiastically reported that they were living a better lifestyle than they would be able to attain if they were still single. They were doing more interesting things, going to more places, and living in a nicer home because of their wives' financial management and planning abilities. Another advantage they mentioned was that they didn't have the pressure of a spouse who was overly dependent on them. They thought it was great to have a self-sufficient woman as a partner.

Disadvantages

The men found few or no disadvantages to being married to a powerful woman. They all had attitudes similar to Robert, who said, "Well, if I go to a party I can't say that I'm the man of the house – big deal. Who cares?"

Conclusion

None of the men felt their manhood was threatened because their woman was the leader or because they did housework.

These men are comfortable being who they are and confident within themselves. They do not subscribe to the old standards for themselves or their women. They are reaping the benefits of loving and living with a powerful, successful woman partner who loves them for being who they really are. They feel appreciated and validated for their supportive qualities. They are not a strange breed. They are merely another expression of what a man can be.

These men are comfortable being who they are and confident within themselves.

Every human being is a unique personality with an individual combination of talents, abilities, strengths, and weaknesses, as well as a unique balance of what are termed feminine and masculine qualities. When a society approves of only certain models of behavior and disparages all others, it creates unnecessary suffering for those who can't fit into the few favored models. And it loses the productive contributions that the "misfits" never make because of the arbitrary limitations placed on them.

A woman who recognizes that she is a Star Woman can stop trying to fit into the old standard relationship mold that will never work for her. What she needs is a Comet Man who appreciates her leadership, supports her vision, and harmonizes with her personality.

A woman who recognizes that she is a Star Woman can stop trying to fit into the old standard relationship mold that will never work for her.

We need to help the Comet Men of the world recognize who they are and help them realize that Star Women are stimulating, satisfying partners for them.

Star Women and Comet Men may always be minority percentages of the human population, but when both groups are recognized, respected, and accepted as they really are, they are free to create happy and fulfilling relationships in their unique ways. As that happens, a tremendous amount of positive energy is released to do good on our planet.

At this point in our exploration of the woman-led marriage, you have been introduced to some new and expanded understandings about men and women. You have a good idea of whether you are stronger as an Earth Mother or a Star Woman, and you know what kind of man (Meteor Man or Comet Man) is a good match for you.

The next section of the book gives you the tools you need to transform your life into a strong springboard for attaining your dreams, and a step-by-step plan for becoming a woman of power. You will also learn how to train your man to please you both inside and outside the bedroom! Sound exciting?

Venus ON TOP

SECTION THREE:

Creating A Better Life

Chapter 8

Tools For Transformation

"Breakthroughs come not primarily by changing what we do, but by changing first and foremost how we think about what we do."
—Jim Collins, author of Good to Great

In Chapter 9 we will outline a vision and a plan to take you from your current life to the life you want to live. The plan requires that you challenge and change some of your fundamental beliefs about life and about being a woman.

In order to identify and meet those challenges, you need the basic tools for transformation provided in this chapter. This is information about how the universe works, and about the spiritual laws and principles that you can use to make the changes you desire. If this information is new to you, you will need to read and absorb this chapter carefully. Think of it as a mini *Spiritual Quickstart Course* to give you a very basic understanding of how to effect change in your life. If you are already familiar with these principles, you can skim over this chapter and consider it a spiritual refresher course.

These principles are not something I arbitrarily made up. They have been known and used for thousands of years by people of many different faiths and traditions. They are found in sacred scripture and teachings all over the world. This wisdom has survived for one simple reason: it works.

A spiritual truth is a principle that works the same way every time for anyone who uses it.

The definition of a spiritual truth is a principle that works the same way every time for anyone who uses it. Some of these principles may seem contrary to the religious faith in which you grew up.

Remember what we learned earlier about the Great Goddess religion and how it was obliterated for political reasons so one group could gain power over another? Every one of our current major religions has its roots in those times and events. Every religion has been distorted through the ages to serve the purposes of those in power. Yet every religious tradition retains kernels of truth, love, and compassion within it – along with some untruths.

Science is now confirming what the sages have been trying to tell us all along: we are all one. Our planet and indeed our whole universe is a single living system, and everything in it is composed of energy vibrating at different frequencies. Our universe is constantly creating itself and everything in it.

We are all one.

The unseen source of our world – and life itself – is a limitless creative intelligent energy which is called by many names: God, Allah, Jehovah, Buddha, The Force, The Tao, Spirit, Higher Power, etc.

The vast majority of people on earth believe in some kind of God, often thought of as a superior being separate from human beings. Today more and more people are coming to believe that we are not separate from God. They are looking within themselves to find God.

If you are willing to consider the possibility that there is a spark of the Divine at the core of your being, then you are no longer at the mercy of what some human so-called "authority" tries to make you believe about your true nature and about God.

Six Basic Spiritual Principles

You can have your own personal relationship with God, and you can decide what is true based on your own personal experience. Truth and spiritual principle can be tested and proven in your life. If you are ready to try this grand experiment, here are six basic spiritual principles to use for transforming your beliefs. Of course, there are more principles beyond these six. You will learn about others later on, but just knowing and using these six will take you a long way down the road to a better life.

1. You Are Spirit

You are a spiritual being having a human experience. You are an eternal being, a part of the Divine Intelligence that created you. You are not your body or even your mind. These are the vehicles we use to navigate our way through the physical world. The thing that is *you* does not die with the body. You are a child of a loving Creator that does not punish or condemn anyone. There is no hell and no heaven except for the hell or heaven that you create for yourself in your life right here on earth.

2. God is Your Source

God takes care of your needs. Everything you need comes from God in sometimes mysterious and sometimes miraculous ways. The good of God can flow to you like a big, wide river or a tiny trickle. It all depends on the state of your consciousness. I remember when I was working on my money consciousness—I would affirm daily, "A mighty Mississippi River of cash flows into my life easily and effortlessly." And indeed more cash did start flowing to me as repetition etched this thought permanently into my brain. Today cash does come to me easily and effortlessly. I always have more than enough. This is an abundant universe and there is more than enough of everything for all of us.

3. Thought Creates

God — the universal life energy — is in, around, and through everything in our world. This is a holographic universe where the physical objects that we perceive as solid actually have more space between their bits of matter than matter itself. Everything that we detect with our senses started as a thought in the universal mind. Our thoughts actually create our reality. If we don't like what we perceive to be our reality, we can change it by changing our thinking.

> ***"If you do not learn to control your thought, thought will control you."***
>
> ***—Ernest Holmes, founder of Religious Science***

4. You Don't Need to Know the "How"

This concept of *"not needing to know the how"* amazed me when I first heard it. I was used to trying to figure out everything and do everything my own way. It was difficult to believe that I didn't have to know exactly how to accomplish my goals or fulfill my desires. Yet I found it to be true.

I learned to quit worrying about *how* anything would come to pass. If you focus on the "what" and believe you can have it, God takes care of the "how," often in ways that you never would have imagined.

5. Conceive, Believe, Receive

This is the natural cycle of creation that we use every day whether we know it or not. Everything starts as an idea in our mind, and then it is filtered through our belief system. Our beliefs create a kind of mental mold for the idea. Suppose the thought is "I want to pass this test." If we believe we have the ability and knowledge to pass, the mold reads, "Pass." If we believe we are not smart enough and can't do it, the mold reads, "Fail." Although we wanted very much to pass, if we don't really believe we can, then that belief is what determines the final result.

The subconscious mind works in the background to create what we are thinking according to what we believe. It pours energy into our mental molds until the thing or situation manifests into the physical world. It has no judgment about what we give it to create. It goes about the business of creation in a rather mechanical fashion; it simply follows instructions blindly. What we receive in the process is a manifestation created by our thoughts through the subconscious.

The subconscious mind works in the background to create what we are thinking according to what we believe.

6. The Law of Cause and Effect

To change the results we are getting in our life, it does no good to merely wish and hope for something different to happen. We have to find the cause of that result and change it.

The cause is always rooted in our belief – not necessarily our actions – about the desire or thought. To change the result, change the belief. This entails being willing to look at what we believe to see if it really serves us, or if it limits us and keeps us from attaining our desires. What we see happening in the physical world is the effect of our beliefs. Beliefs are always the cause.

Think a New Thought

Ernest Holmes, author of *The Science of Mind,* was fond of saying, "Change your thinking, change your life." He, along with a number of other scholars and philosophers like Ralph Waldo Emerson and Thomas Troward, studied the great scriptures and literature of the world's religions for years. Looking for the common denominators in the collected wisdom of humankind, they found that nearly all of the great spiritual masters taught that what we think and believe has a direct effect on us and the physical world we inhabit.

> ***"As thou hast believed, so be it done unto thee."***
> ***—Jesus of Nazareth (Matthew 8:13)***

These thinkers were interested in metaphysics (study of the ultimate nature of existence, reality, and experience) and how to put the power of the mind to practical use in daily living. Today there are many spiritual communities and religious organizations that are in agreement about the power of the mind and our ability to use that power. We can change the circumstances and direction of our lives by learning how to think a new thought. Thus these groups are known as the "New Thought" movement.

Carl Jung, a very influential 20th Century psychoanalyst, theorized that the power of our mind is not limited to the individual, but also extends to a great collective mind of humankind, which he called the "collective unconscious." This mind holds the images and symbols, which we all know on a subconscious level. Holmes refined this idea further as "race consciousness," which holds generalized human ideas that are passed from one generation to the next. These ideas are believed to be the truth and are not easily changed.

For example, in the early 1600's Galileo narrowly escaped imprisonment when he claimed that the earth revolved around the sun. Everyone believed that the sun revolved around the earth, and this idea was so imbedded in the "race consciousness" of that era that it took many years before Galileo's theory was finally accepted. Today we know that the earth is not the center of the universe and we send telescopes out in unmanned spacecraft to photograph distant galaxies. Only four hundred years ago you might have lost your life for merely suggesting such a thing was possible.

The human race is made up of individuals who have the free will to choose how and what they think. As more and more people begin to think a different way, the thoughts contained in our race consciousness are affected and changed slowly and gradually. Individuals can choose to change their way of thinking and change what happens in their lives relatively quickly. They only need the courage and the awareness to question the ideas that have been handed down to them through the race consciousness.

Individuals can choose to change their way of thinking and change what happens in their lives relatively quickly.

The ideas and beliefs of any culture are transmitted and handed down from one generation to the next through songs, stories, and poems called myths. Before the invention of writing this oral tradition was the only way that knowledge could be kept and passed on. Myths are powerful because they portray in grand, fanciful, and memorable imagery the ideals, beliefs, and fears upon which the people of that culture base their lives.

The Power of Myth

Myths are not merely fairy tales or amusing children's stories. Our cultural myths are rooted deeply in the subconscious mind of every individual. They are rooted so deeply that we don't even recognize these beliefs as myths that were handed down to us. We think they are truth. Some might be true; many are not.

Your mother, father, and other family members planted these beliefs deep in your mind. They were then solidified by the media and the culture in which we live. We have all been led to assume that there is such a thing as "race" because we are in the habit of judging people by their appearance. Now scientists who study DNA are startling the world with their discovery that "race" is an erroneous concept. They can show that people who appear to be very different in skin color can actually be very much alike genetically.

Professor Brian Sykes, a leading world authority on DNA and human evolution, conducted extensive studies tracing our human ancestors back in time through DNA evidence. He produced a complete maternal genealogy for the whole of humanity, which converged on a single woman in Africa some one hundred and fifty thousand years ago. In his fascinating book *The Seven Daughters of Eve* he says, "She lies at the root of all the maternal ancestries of every one of the six billion people in the world. We are all her direct maternal descendants."

We now have scientific evidence that there is only one race: the human race.

We now have scientific evidence that there is only one race: the human race. Our differences in appearance are only superficial. But ideas about racial superiority and inferiority are still quite deeply imbedded in the collective unconscious of mankind. Some people will have a very difficult time with these new ideas about race; it may take generations before this new truth is accepted by most of the world. Some will cling to their old "truth" despite the evidence that proves it wrong.

This new way of viewing our world can be as significant as the transforming vision that changed perception of the world as flat into one of a globe!

We didn't make a conscious decision to believe these old, established ideas, but we've been made to feel that they are true. If we bring them out into the light of our conscious mind, we can make a choice about whether these precepts serve us and are worth keeping. So let's examine some of our Western culture's commonly held beliefs about relationships between men and women.

You may protest that many of these myths have been dismantled and are no longer held to be the truth. We have laws in place that directly oppose some of these ideas, but that doesn't make the ideas go away. Instead, we live in conflict.

We know that an idea like "A woman needs a man to take care of her" is not true in our world, but that doesn't stop us from wishing that some knight in a white BMW would sweep us away from our mundane life and solve all our problems.

> ***"It's easier to live life through someone else than to become complete yourself."***
>
> ***—Betty Friedan***

Look Deeply

If you are willing to look deeply and be honest with yourself, how many of the following ideas can you find lurking down in the dusty basement of your mind?

- The man should be the head of the household.
- A woman needs a man to take care of her.
- Women are not good at math or managing money.
- A woman should learn how to please her man.
- Men should initiate sex.
- Men give love to get sex, women give sex to get love.

- Women should get married and have babies.
- Women should take care of the children.
- Men should work and bring home the money.

I'm sure you could add many more to this list. The point here is to encourage you to dig up these beliefs and bring them out into the light of your awareness. When you are aware of an old belief starting to raise your anxiety or anger, you have the ability to stop that thought and choose a different response.

Looking deeply within yourself to bring all your limiting beliefs into the light of awareness is a good first step. But it is not enough to merely become aware of the unconscious beliefs that are running your life. In order to change a belief you must *replace* it with a different and better one.

Changing a Belief

If you just say, "I won't believe that anymore," your subconscious mind will only pay attention to the "believe that" part of the sentence. Your instructions to your subconscious are most effective when worded in positive terms – not negatives – because your subconscious will go right on believing and acting on the thing you want to get rid of. Why? Because you're giving your attention to it.

In order to change a belief you must replace it with a different and better one.

In some ways the mind is like a computer program. You can hit the delete key and words disappear from the screen—but until your computer actually writes over those words, they remain embedded on your hard disk. Your mind will keep carrying out the actions caused by a belief until you overwrite and replace it.

Does this make it sound like there's some work ahead of you? Yes. But isn't it wonderful to know that you do not have to be stuck with your old programming for your entire life!

We are free to change what we think and what we believe. There are lots of ways to accomplish this and lots of people who can help you when you want to make changes in your life. But it is up to you to find what works for you.

Old Belief Into New Belief

Here is a simple, effective technique that has worked for me. I call it the "Old Belief Into New Belief" method.

Get a notebook and divide several pages into two columns. Label the first one "Old Belief" and the second one "New Belief." Write down one of your beliefs about relationships in the first column. Then imagine for a moment that you are now the highest version of your best self whose life is centered in the Divine and whose faith is unshakeable. Let your Higher Self speak and compose a new belief that serves you better in the second column.

Words Are Powerful

Your words have power whether written or spoken. Writing down your words this way is a clear, unmistakable directive to the universe that you are ready and willing to change your life for good.

> ***"Writing is medicine...It is an appropriate companion for any difficult change...Writing allows us to rewrite our lives."***
>
> ***—Julia Cameron***

When you give the universe clear instructions and put the emotional power of your desire behind those instructions, it must respond to you. *That is a proven spiritual law.* You don't have to understand how

Everything is created on the mental plane first. Then it appears on the physical plane.

the change happens. Everything is created on the mental plane first. Then it appears on the physical plane.

Your life will not change just because you wish it to. You must work with your mind to change what you think and believe before the results of your effort appear in physical form.

You must police both your thoughts and your spoken words. Changing your beliefs requires mental vigilance and may seem like a lot of work at first. Every time you catch yourself thinking or saying something that you don't want to see in your life anymore, you must stop and replace it with a positive.

You must police both your thoughts and your spoken words.

For example, if you are in the habit of thinking and saying, "There's never enough time. I'm always late," your subconscious will go right to work for you to keep you in the habit of being late. To change that belief and that condition in your life you must affirm instead, "There's always enough time for me and I am always on time."

Statements to the universe that begin with "I am" are the most powerful statements you can make.

Statements to the universe that begin with "I am" are the most powerful statements you can make. You have to stop giving your energy and attention to anything you don't want, and start affirming to yourself that you are now believing and receiving what you do want.

These new positive, affirming statements must be precise and must be in the present tense, not in the future. If you say, "I will get better about being on time," your directions to your subconscious are vague (what does "get better" mean?) and off in the future ("I will"). For the subconscious this statement means nothing and has no effect because it can only create in the moment. It knows only "now" not past or future.

> ***"You have to believe it before you see it."***
>
> ***—Wayne Dyer***

You have to make a leap of faith to consistently affirm something that has not yet appeared in the physical world, but that is the only way to effect real change.

Four Steps to Affirming a New Life

You can change your life with this simple four-step procedure:

1. **Become aware of the old belief**

2. **Be sincerely willing to change the old belief**

3. **Create and write down a new belief to replace the old**

4. **Continually affirm the new belief**

Sample List

I wrote the following list of beliefs and affirmations a few years ago when I was single. These are some of my old beliefs about relationships that ran my life and kept me miserable for decades. Alongside the old are the new beliefs that I created to replace them. Some of the new beliefs took root and bore fruit in the physical world more quickly and easily than others. Today, however, I can read down the New Belief list with complete conviction that these are my truths.

The ones I selected to include here are those that are typical for many women. Some will hit home for you, others will not. This is a just a sample list to give you an idea of how to do your own.

I gave myself a goal of writing down 100 beliefs that were holding me back from being happy with my life and myself. It took me about a month to accomplish my goal. Some days I wrote just one or two; some days, none. Other days I wrote a dozen or more.

You don't have to be that ambitious. Take it at your own pace, but DO IT! Read over your list and add to it on a regular basis (daily is best if you can manage it). Lock up your fear-filled ego in the trunk and imagine your higher self in the driver's seat cruising down the road of life, knowing that these new beliefs are absolutely true for you. Let yourself feel what it is like to be relaxed, optimistic, and full of self-confidence.

When you first start this process you may only be able to get into that higher feeling state for a few minutes at a time before your ego breaks out and tricks your mind back into its old worry and fear routines. I sometimes felt like I was in the middle of an old Disney cartoon with an angel on one shoulder and a devil on the other fighting for control of my mind. I was determined to change my thinking habits and all those old beliefs that had made me unhappy for so many years.

Many times I would just rewrite my list of new beliefs because the physical action of writing them out over and over helps to anchor these ideas in your consciousness. Gradually but steadily I literally overwrote the old mental programming, and now my higher self is firmly planted in the driver's seat of my life.

When I read over this list now some years after writing it, I am so grateful for the way my life is today. My old unsatisfactory life created by those old beliefs seems like a distant bad dream. Do you want to live a happier life? Toss out those old hand-me-down beliefs and think a better thought!

Beliefs About Being Single

Let's start with some of my old beliefs about being single. With the vision I created with my beliefs about what it is like to be a single person, it's no wonder I felt so unhappy being single. With every belief I had reinforced the idea that "married is better," and that being single was an inferior way of life. I certainly don't believe that anymore!

Old Belief	*New Belief*
If I get too comfortable with being single, I'll never get married again.	This is insane thinking! It's no problem for me to adjust to being married again.
People feel sorry for single people.	Self-pity has no place in my life. I release these thoughts and rejoice in the fact that I'm alive. No one needs to feel sorry for me!
Nobody is really happy being single.	Happiness comes from within me and does not require any particular set of outward appearances.
Single people are sad cases.	I am footloose and carefree when I am single.
Since I am a strong woman only weak men are attracted to me. Who wants a wimp!	Strong men who are secure within themselves love to be with women like me. I now have the patience to discover a man's character before I get too involved with him.

Beliefs of the Ego

My ego certainly held some rigid and arrogant beliefs. The conflicts between how my ego thought about me and what my Higher Self knew was the truth is very evident in these statements. No wonder I couldn't seem to get anywhere with my life until I got rid of all the demands on God and the attempts to control everything and everyone else but me! Now I know that once you learn to control the ego, there is no need to control anything else.

Once you learn to control the ego, there is no need to control anything else.

Old Belief	*New Belief*
Life is supposed to proceed in an orderly fashion according to my plan.	Life is what happens while I'm busy making plans. God's plan for me is always bigger, better, and more wonderful than any thing my puny ego can conceive.
Freedom is one of my highest values. I love being free to do what I want to do.	I now release all these useless, false ideas and declare that I'm free from them. I'm free to live in whatever way suits me best.
I am open-minded.	I cannot claim to be open-minded when I hold all these rigid ideas about what relation ships are supposed to be. I now release the hold these false beliefs had on me.
I can influence my family members to be the way I think they should be.	I have no control over other people. I release them from my expectations and accept them just as they are.
I've got to understand why my ego's demands are not being met and figure out how to fix it.	I may never understand the why of my life and it is not important that I do. I simply accept my life as it is.

Beliefs About Feelings

For much of my adult life, I was hostage to my feelings. They seemed to have the upper hand and I wasn't able to put them in their proper place until I developed my spiritual side. Being constantly overwhelmed by feelings is a difficult way to live. Now I know that my identity does not depend on my feelings. Feelings come and go. I stay anchored in my spiritual center.

Old Belief	*New Belief*
When I'm disappointed, I get depressed.	When I'm disappointed, I'm just disappointed. I do not get depressed.
If I were just prettier, thinner, and/or younger, I'd have no problem attracting men.	I'm fine just as I am. The kind of man that is attracted to me is attracted by my character and my soul, not my body.
I am what I feel and I have no control over my feelings.	My feelings do not dictate who I am. Feelings are temporary and always changing. I can choose a different emotional response to any situation.
Certain situations and certain people always trigger bad feelings in me so I have to be careful to stay away from them.	Reacting to a situation the same way every time is just a bad habit, one that I can change by choosing to respond differently.
I'm worried about my future.	God is my source of supply, so I do not worry about my future. All the love and all the money I need are always there for me. I only have to be aware of it and be grateful for it.

Beliefs About Happiness

Oh, how elusive happiness becomes when you make it your goal and then set up all kinds of restrictions and conditions that must be met in order for you to be happy. Happiness is a natural by-product of living a good life, being your authentic self, and fulfilling your highest purpose.

Old Belief	*New Belief*
I missed out on having children and I'll never know the joy of being a mother.	Motherhood is not required for my happiness. I enjoy and love all children. I don't need to have my own.
I can't be completely happy unless I'm married.	My happiness has nothing to do with whether or not I'm married.
If I'm not happy every minute something is wrong.	I don't need to be happy every minute. I accept that I experi ence a full range of emotions. Emotions come and go, but I am not my emotions! I have no need to be happy every moment. I release that childish thinking and replace it with acceptance.
I'll never be happy if I don't get what I want.	Life does not have to meet my expectations for me to be happy and content.

Complaining About Life

One of the quickest ways to make yourself unhappy is to refuse to accept your life the way it is right now. Whining about the conditions of your life only serves to create more of what you don't want because you are giving your attention to it. The more you resist, the more it persists.

Learning to accept life as it is was a big step for me. I stopped whining and complaining and surprise! – Life got better! One of the mysterious paradoxes of life is that you have to accept circumstances as they are, while at the same time mentally envisioning and creating something better.

Old Belief	*New Belief*
Life is boring without a boyfriend.	Life is whatever I make it.
I have to understand why my life is the way it is.	I don't need to understand everything about my life—just be grateful for it.
It's not fair that other people have what I want and I don't.	Life is not fair and I accept that.
My life was not supposed to be like this. I should be rich, successful, and married.	My life is perfect the way it is. It does not have to be any particular way for me to be happy.
It will be a miracle if I ever get married again.	Miracles are everyday occurrences. They happen to me all the time and there's no reason for me not to meet a good man, fall in love and get married.
I'll feel that my life has been wasted if I never experience what it's like to have a good marriage.	If I never have that experience it simply means that it was not in God's plan for me. My task is to be loving and to stay centered in God no matter what is going on in my life. No life is a waste.

Beliefs About Loneliness

Being alone and being lonely are two different states of mind. Lonely can be a passing feeling or you can hang on to it and keep yourself in a state of constant misery. We have to feel our feelings and not deny them. But we don't have to be a prisoner to them. Here again acceptance is the key to attaining some serenity and peace. Focusing on what we think we are missing only prolongs the pain.

Looking for what is good in our life and appreciating it gets us off the pity-pot and into a better frame of mind. An easy cure for loneliness is to find someone who could use a kind word or a helping hand and give it to them. Stop thinking about the love that you believe you are missing. Reverse the flow and give some love instead. Works every time!

Old Belief	*New Belief*
It's just my fate and my bad luck to be isolated and lonely.	I accept a life full of love, joy, and belonging. My fate is what I create.
I can't stand being alone without somebody to love.	It would be nice to have a lover, but I don't need a lover or anything else. I always have whatever it is that is perfect for me.
If I go out by myself no one will talk to me.	I go out by myself with a friendly smile and a receptive attitude and the nicest people talk to me.
Living alone is terrible. I've done this long enough.	Living alone is peaceful and serene. I could do this forever.
I'm afraid of being alone. I'm afraid there will be no one to care for me when I get old.	There is nothing to fear. I am not alone. God is always with me. When I allow God to direct my life and love to lead it, I always have more than enough of everything I need.

Beliefs About Love

My beliefs about love were mostly concerned with why I didn't have it and how things should be when I did. I was so concerned with what I wanted to get that I had barely any idea about what I could give! Focusing on giving was the antidote to these empty complaints and demands.

Old Belief	*New Belief*
I don't feel loved and my life isn't as good when I'm without a partner.	God always loves me and I can always feel love by giving love. Life is good with or without a partner.
I'm afraid of facing the rest of my life without ever knowing what it's like to really love a decent man.	I may never have a life that looks like what my ego wants, but I can give and receive love from other people in endless ways.
Love has to look and feel the way I imagine it.	I release my expectations about love. Love is whatever it is.
Love is too hard and too much work.	Love is easy when it's given with no strings attached.
Love means giving up who I really am so I can get a man to stay with me.	The right kind of man loves me for who I am. He supports me in becoming all that I can be, and I do the same for him.
Life seems empty without someone to love.	Empty is a perception. I choose to perceive a different idea. My life is full of people to love. I love whoever appears in my life!
If I tell my partner the truth, he will leave.	If I tell my partner the truth and he leaves, then he is not the right partner for me, and I'm glad I'm finding out now instead of later.

Beliefs About Marriage

Having a good marriage was a goal like winning the Relationship Super-Bowl to me. I wanted it but I had no idea how to get there from where I was. When I honestly looked at my old beliefs about marriage, I had to admit that my attitude really needed reworking. It was a relief to expose these immature and fruitless ideas to the light of my growing awareness.

I let my Higher Self write the new beliefs and then just prayed for acceptance of what I knew was the real truth. I had to accept the possibility that I might never have the great marriage that seemed so necessary to me. Surrendering the whole situation to the will of God was the only answer that gave me peace.

Old Belief	*New Belief*
Married is better.	Nonsense. Married is just one way to live out of many ways. No one way is better than another.
Being around happily married people makes me envious and uncomfortable.	I choose to soak up the consciousness of a loving partnership when I am around married people. I love being around people who are good at relationships.

Beliefs About Marriage (continued)

Old Belief	*New Belief*
My ideas about marriage are so deep-rooted they must be true. Mom believes them and so do I.	Mom used to tell me that all she wanted was to see me happily married. She doesn't even want that for herself any more! Just because a belief is old and deep doesn't mean I can't replace it with a belief that serves me better.
If I stop believing that I have to be married, I have no concept for what my life should be.	Exactly – and what a good thing this is. My life doesn't have to be any particular way. I can focus on "being" and let my life flow from my highest self instead of from the ego.
Marriage is a trap in which you lose your freedom and yourself.	I have experienced marriage as a trap because of my own ignorance and immaturity. I now view marriage as an adventure and an opportunity to love and grow.
Being in a relationship brings emotional upheaval and struggle all the time.	Being in a good relationship is relaxing and comfortable. Occasional instances of emotional upset happen in order to bring up old hurts to be released and healed with the help of your partner's love.

Beliefs About Men

My beliefs about men were mainly about getting one and keeping him, with no thought given about how to love him! No wonder I was having trouble! Men are not the enemy – they need love just as much as women do. As I grew spiritually, my relationships with men became interesting adventures instead of heartbreaking struggles. I knew I was on the right track when I began to think more about what I could give to a man instead of only what I could get.

Old Belief	*New Belief*
I'm too much of a challenge – that's why no man is interested in me.	There are lots of good men who are interested in women like me, and who are not afraid of the challenge.
If I don't find a man right away, I'll never be able to find one and I'll end up a lonely embittered old crone.	My well-being does not depend on having a man now or ever. I can be alone without being lonely.
All the good ones are already taken.	There are many good single men available. All the good ones are not taken.
The best way to experience love is with a man.	There is no one best way to experience love. I experience love in endless, limitless ways.
There's nobody out there who is a suitable match for me.	There are lots of good men who are a perfect match for me. I will meet one if and when it's right for me.
But I need a man NOW. I don't want to wait any longer.	I have no control over when I meet anyone. I can live the rest of my life without a man if that's what God plans for me.

Spring Cleaning for the Soul

Whew! What a list! It may seem like I did a lot of work here, but the process felt like spring-cleaning for the soul. Yes, it's work while you are doing it, but when it's done you feel great and it was worth every bit of effort. I cleared out and eradicated the old ideas that were holding me back. When I started dating again I looked at men and relationships with a clarity of mind that I never had before.

I encourage you to do your own soul level spring-cleaning and enjoy the benefits as I did. You'll then have a clear field from which you can easily progress. The method of replacing an old belief with a new one that your learned in this chapter is something you can use again and again any time you feel stuck.

It is also a method you can use as you work your way through the Eight Steps To Power that you'll find in the next chapter, which takes you step by step through the process of developing yourself into a real woman of power.

Chapter 9

The Vision and The Plan

"If you want to accomplish the goals of your life, you have to begin with the Spirit."

—Oprah Winfrey

To create a plan to accomplish anything, you must first create a vision of the end result you desire. Everything is created first in the mind – as thought – before it can take form in the physical world. So, before you can become a total woman of power you need a clear picture of what that looks like. Once your vision is clear, you can begin taking the first step toward it.

The Vision

I believe a woman of power is a woman who is:

- A whole person, a person who knows her strengths and weaknesses, who stands on her own two feet and takes responsibility for her life.

- A woman who has great respect for herself and always treats both herself and others with respect.
- A woman who has a spiritual foundation, who knows her values and lives according to them.
- A woman who is in touch with her erotic nature, who is just as good at receiving love as she is at giving it.
- A woman who knows who she really is and whose life is anchored in love, not fear.

This list may seem like a tall order at first. And some of these phrases may already describe you as you are today. Give yourself credit for the character you have already developed. Take the time to think about who you would be as a woman of power. If all your limitations dropped away and you could live without fear, what would you be like?

Write out a description of your own personal ideal and leave room to add to it as more ideas come to you. Make it very personal and make it yours alone.

Now you have a vision of the powerful woman you are already becoming. Simply writing down your vision has power to start moving you into your future. You have made the commitment to yourself to step into your power. No more will you look to anyone else to rescue you or protect you. You have everything you need within you.

> ***"I declare to you that woman must not depend upon the protection of man, but must be taught to protect herself, and there I take my stand."***
>
> ***—Susan B. Anthony (1820-1906)***

The Eight Steps to Power Plan

Here's the eight-step plan that will help you develop the attitudes and beliefs that will magnetize the right man to you. Once you have completed the work to heal and change attitudes and beliefs that are limiting you, your life will change in delightful and surprising ways.

The Eight Steps to Power

1. **Be open and willing to change**
2. **Create a spiritual foundation for your life**
3. **Accept total responsibility for your life**
4. **Release anger and resentment**
5. **Stop judging and stop blaming**
6. **Clean up your finances**
7. **Live a balanced, healthy life**
8. **Give and receive graciously**

The first three steps must be completed before you undertake any of the others. These three steps are essential because they help you create a strong foundation from which to work. Steps Four through Eight can be completed in any order that makes sense to you. Some people find that getting their finances in order becomes the last step because other issues need to be handled and healed before they feel capable of cleaning up their finances.

Some steps will be easier for you than others, but be aware that you can't skip or gloss over one or two. To truly be a woman of power, every one of these issues must be explored and healed, if necessary. The principles must be learned and held securely in your conscious awareness so you can put them to work in your daily life.

Whatever work it takes to complete the steps is well worth the effort. Your life will begin to change as soon as you start. As you make progress on each step, you will feel more confident and more serene. And you will be better prepared to experience a marriage or partnership with a man who will make you happy.

Step 1. Be Open and Willing to Change

All the following steps rest on a foundation of willingness to change. This willingness is a decision you must make for yourself. No amount of spiritual or psychological work is enough, in itself, to make a difference. You must be willing to be uncomfortable for some time while your old thinking and habits drop off and are replaced with new ones.

Many of us become open to change only when the pain of remaining the same becomes greater than the pain of changing. Why are we so afraid of change? It's our ego wanting to protect us and keep us safe in a familiar environment even if that requires being unhappy.

Many of us become open to change only when the pain of remaining the same becomes greater than the pain of changing.

I believe that everything in this world is temporary, except for our souls. Everything is always changing and there's nothing we can do to stop change except waste a lot of energy on trying to hold it back.

> ***"Change excites me. I am fifty years old. It's when the mind catches up with the body."***
>
> ***—Raquel Welch***

Embrace Change

So consider embracing change and welcoming it. It's going to happen anyway! The wise woman never forgets that whatever appears in her life, whether it be a physical object, a situation, or a relationship, is only temporary.

Willingness is a magical and necessary ingredient for manifesting your dreams.

When you combine acceptance of change with a sincere willingness to change, the universe goes to work on your behalf. Willingness is a magical and necessary ingredient for manifesting your dreams. Willingness allows you to influence positive changes to happen for yourself.

Step 2. Create a Spiritual Foundation for Your Life

Life is so much easier when you develop a personal connection with your Creator, whether you call it God, Great Spirit, Great Mother, Allah, Jehovah, Higher Power, or any one of the thousand names we human beings have given to the Divine Intelligence who gives us life. Without a spiritual philosophy and faith in something beyond the material world, you are living life the hard way, trying to do it all by yourself. This is not necessary. There are many, many paths to God because we are all individuals with different ways of perceiving and learning. If you become a sincere seeker, you will find the right path for you.

There are many, many paths to God because we are all individuals with different ways of perceiving and learning.

> ***"It isn't until you come to a spiritual understanding of who you are – not necessarily a religious feeling, but deep down, the spirit within – that you can begin to take control."***
>
> ***—Oprah Winfrey***

Questions and Answers

We have all wondered why we are here. If you believe in God you have asked, "Why did God make me?" God knows all, sees all and is All. God is eternal and infinite. God is the Oneness that can never be separated from Itself.

Now think for a moment. If you were God, might you not get a little bored? After all, you know everything and have everything. You are all-powerful. You are everything. There is nothing that is not you. So what are you going to do with yourself?

I've been asking those deep questions and trying to understand the nature of existence ever since I was a child. No organized religion ever provided an answer that satisfied me. Through fifty-plus years on the planet, lots of searching, studying, observing, and meditating; I've been blessed with some experiences, which gave me an immediate intuitive understanding about who we are and why we are here.

When I began living in the mountains, I developed the habit of hiking and exploring the forest every day with my dog. There were few trails in the area I hiked, but lots of rock formations. It was intriguing how some of the rocks looked liked sculptures of familiar things, so I gave them names like Beluga Whale, Megalith, Balcony Rock, Table Rock, etc. I used them as landmarks to guide me.

No two rocks, trees, or leaves were the same. The beauty of the places I discovered was so breathtaking that at times I would just stop and exclaim out loud, "Great job, God!" My appreciation for the endless creativity of God so evident in the natural world grew and grew.

Ordinary everyday experiences can often be the best way to find answers that make sense. Being aware and observant of my own life gives me all the faith and wisdom I need.

The Value of Forgetting

Another everyday insight happened when I was driving through the city of Los Angeles on an errand, and happened to pass a store I had designed a few years earlier. I decided to stop and check out the place since I did not have an opportunity to see the result of my design project when it was first completed.

I have been a professional interior designer for nearly twenty years, specializing in commercial design. When I design a shop or office, I start with an empty space and I envision just how it is going to look before drawing up a plan on paper. The design is fully formed in my mind, and then put on paper with all the information the contractor needs to build it.

This tangible design is created in my mind first, just like everything else in my life. Once the plans are completed I move on to the next project. I didn't remember much of anything about this store design since it had been completed quite some time before.

I walked in the door, and just stood and stared. The colors were stunning, the lighting sparkled, and the whole effect was a visual treat. "Wow, this is great!" I said to myself, "Did I do this?" The delight I experienced and the wonderful sense of surprise and appreciation was such a joyful experience. The intensity of the experience was caused by not remembering what I had designed in this particular case. It was new to me. It was as if someone else had created it. I could not have experienced these same feelings if I had remembered what I created. Forgetting gave me the opportunity to experience the joy of discovery, and to appreciate the gift of my own creativity in a way I had never felt before.

We are born in a state of forgetfulness about whom we really are, into a world and a life that makes it appear that we are separate from God and each other.

The Delight of Discovery

The next time I went hiking I had one of those "Aha" experiences that was so intense that I had to sit down and process it. I scrambled to the top of a huge boulder and there was a gorgeous view of the lake below. I was about to give God another "Way to go!" cheer, when, in a sudden flash of insight, I understood why we are here and why we are made the way we are. We are born in a state of forgetfulness about whom we really are, into a world and a life that makes it appear that we are separate from God and each other. The longing we feel for connection is our longing to get back to the Oneness from which we came.

God is already whole, complete, perfect, and totally aware of everything past, present, and future. So the only way God can experience the delight of discovery is to create offspring whose knowledge of the Oneness is veiled and hidden. In a way, we're like little bits of God playing a private game of hide-and-seek. Our forgotten memory of our Divine nature is the very thing that makes our existence a joy and an adventure. God can't discover anything – but *we can*!

***God can't discover anything – but* we can!**

Now, when I walk through the forest in awe and wonder at the beauty of it, I understand that God is having that experience through me. When I delight over discovering something new or inspiring, I realize God is experiencing that delight with me. When I create something or express myself through music or dance, my joy is God's joy. Our Higher Power cannot experience these things in its natural all-knowing state, so it created us in a form that can have those wonderful "aha" experiences.

God created us as an individualized expression of Itself, with a unique set of personality traits and talents. When we express ourselves creatively and when we appreciate our experiences on earth, we are fulfilling our highest purpose. We are not here to suffer. We are here to enjoy! We are here to explore, discover, experience, develop, and grow. Our Creator cannot have those experiences or feel the joy of them without us.

We are not here to suffer. We are here to enjoy!

When we reconnect with our source, we can experience our wholeness again and learn how to use the power of our own mind to consciously create what we desire. We learn to have faith in our God, and do not have to look outside ourselves to feel content. Having faith and having a spiritual philosophy that is forged through your own effort and experience gives you the foundation for a happy and successful life.

Having faith and having a spiritual philosophy that is forged through your own effort and experience gives you the foundation for a happy and successful life.

Step 3. Accept Total Responsibility for Your Life

> ***"As one goes through life one learns that if you don't paddle your own canoe, you don't move."***
>
> ***—Katharine Hepburn***

As you develop a spiritual foundation, you discover that you must confront a common concept that makes many of us uncomfortable. It is that little word, *responsibility*. For fun loving, free spirits like me that word can feel like a ball and chain. Many of us are afraid of that word because it sounds like a lot of work, a lot of stress and pressure. But the truth is that it merely means *to have the ability to respond*.

Respond or React

Life is all about the willingness to respond in a conscious, thoughtful way to situations rather than blindly reacting and creating a vortex of emotional drama.

> ***"The willingness to accept responsibility for one's own life is the source from which self-respect springs."***
>
> ***—Joan Didion***

When something happens, or someone says something to provoke us, we typically allow our ego to react before we think – unless we have learned how to respond. The key to responding instead of reacting is to recognize that split-second of awareness before the reaction occurs and take control in that moment. Take a breath, hold yourself back, and use those next few seconds to think before you do or say anything. To respond or to react – that is the question!

Until you learn to respond instead of react, your personal power is limited.

With determination and practice you can train yourself to automatically reject that initial reaction impulse from the ego. Reacting is the way of unconsciousness and immaturity. Responding is the way of consciousness and maturity. Until you learn to respond instead of react, your personal power is limited.

Responding rather than reacting is a quality that your friends and family really appreciate. A little experience I had over a birthday cake is a perfect example. I went to a board meeting at my church one evening and our minister led me to the kitchen where she proudly displayed a lovely birthday cake and a card for all of us to sign for our treasurer, whose birthday was that week. It was to be a surprise for her during our meeting break.

Reacting is the way of unconsciousness and immaturity. Responding is the way of consciousness and maturity.

My birthday was just a few days before our treasurer's birthday. What do you think my initial reaction was when I realized that my birthday had been ignored or overlooked? I was hurt, of course! I felt just as left out and sad as a five-year-old child would. But did I express those feelings to anyone or even let my disappointment show on my face? – NO! I had the presence of mind to keep those feelings to myself because I knew that they were coming from my ego, which can be very sensitive to any hint of rejection.

I signed the card with a smile and retreated to the meeting area to sort out my feelings and give my higher self a chance to decide what to do. Did anyone intentionally do this to hurt me? I know these people; they are my friends and colleagues. They would never do anything to hurt me intentionally. Would it help the situation for me to point out that they had forgotten my birthday? That would just make them all feel bad. So I decided in the space of just a few seconds that I would say nothing and just let it go.

When we surprised our treasurer with the cake at break time, she was delighted and happy. Then she said, "But isn't it Barbara's birthday this week too?" She remembered! I was touched. They all apologized to me and said they hadn't realized it was my birthday. I just brushed it off as "not a big deal" and the birthday girl insisted that I help her blow out the candles, which I did. And that was that.

Now I could have sulked and stayed hurt and made everyone feel guilty, but I chose a better way. And believe me they all appreciated it. Silly little incidents like this can turn into resentments, which can undermine your relationships with the people with whom you live and work.

Learning to rein in the reaction, even though we're feeling bad, is a huge step in the right direction.

It takes a person who is highly evolved spiritually to have an ego so tamed that reactions like this don't even happen in the first place. For the rest of us, learning to rein in the reaction, even though we're feeling bad, is a huge step in the right direction, one that brings big benefits to our daily life.

Here is the bad news and good news about responsibility:

The bad news is that you are totally responsible for your life. Your decisions and choices have brought you to this point in your life – exactly as it is today. All your experiences were necessary to get you here. There's no way to live your life "wrong."

And the good news is that you are totally responsible for your life! That means you do not need to look to anyone else to change your life. Look only to yourself. The more awareness and spiritual maturity you exercise in making decisions and choices, the better your life will be. The more gracefully you accept responsibility for your life, the freer you are. Your future is not constrained by anyone else; you determine it.

> ***"Never grow a wishbone, daughter, where a backbone ought to be."***
>
> ***—Clementine Paddleford***

I used to think that being responsible meant living a dull, boring life. I wanted to make somebody else responsible when things went wrong. If you think you can be powerful, but avoid responsibility and put the blame on someone else, you are very mistaken.

Responsibility Creates Freedom

Responsibility doesn't create limitations; it creates freedom. When you open your eyes and realize that you had a part in everything that has ever happened to you, you start to accept responsibility for yourself and your actions. You see that your response to any situation is a choice you make.

> ***"The price of greatness is responsibility."***
>
> ***—Winston Churchill***

The Price of Power

I say the price of power is responsibility. If you truly accept responsibility for what you do and say, it means that you don't expect anyone to rescue you from your own choices. Willingness to be responsible for our choices is the foundation of personal power.

Willingness to be responsible for our choices is the foundation of personal power.

Choices and Results

Accepting responsibility makes you more aware and more careful about the choices you make, because you know the buck stops right here with you. This is what gives you tremendous freedom to take calculated risks and reap the results and rewards.

Willingness to accept responsibility for your own life is powerful in and of itself. It is a necessary step you must take before you can successfully make the changes you desire.

Step 4. Release Anger and Resentment

When we hold onto negative emotions like anger and resentment, they become toxic and poisonous to us. When something or someone hurts you, the immediate reaction of your ego is to get angry and fight back. If we can just do that much and then let it go, it might not create long-term damage. But we don't let it go. We replay it over and over again in our mind, adding the more devastating remarks we wish we could have thought to say at the time. We build an ironclad case around the other person's fault and our own innocence. Soon a big patch of resentment takes root and begins to fester in our emotional body.

Emotional Clogs

If you've got this kind of anger and resentment playing on your mind and emotions, it acts just like a bad clog in a water pipe. The water cannot flow freely as long as the clog remains in place. In the same way, the good things that God wants to send you cannot flow freely to you when negative emotions are in your spiritual pipeline, stopping up the works. Healing and releasing negative beliefs is just like pouring spiritual Drano™ clog remover down the pipe. Dissolve the clog and good things start flowing your way.

It is essential to admit it to yourself when you are carrying around old hurts. "But he (she, they) did me wrong," you're saying. "My anger is completely justified." Your anger may well be completely justified and no one is trying to make a wrong into a right. However, the longer you hold onto resentment, the bigger it grows. The bigger it grows, the more it prevents good from coming into your life.

Letting anger and resentment churn within you is like digging yourself into a pit. The original hurt might have been equivalent to digging a foot-deep hole. Reliving the emotional feelings of that experience digs you in another foot deeper every time you run your mental instant replay. The only way out is to make a decision to stop this downward spiral and release your need for justice or revenge.

Understanding Emotions

Our emotions are like waves on the surface of the ocean. The surface can be turbulent and wild at times, but the storm always passes. While the surface is always changing, down at the depths the ocean is undisturbed by what goes on above. When you are not in touch with that deep reservoir of calm at your center, you become too tied into your emotions.

You are not your emotions. Emotions are powerful energies that can either carry you toward your dreams or send you down a dead end road. This is why it is so important to have a spiritual connection and to take responsibility for your actions and reactions.

Because we are these creative, complex, growing humans we can't avoid having feelings and reacting emotionally to people and events in our lives – nor should we. Emotions are like traffic signals. Positive emotions like love and joy give us the green light that says, "Go!" We know we are on the right road and it feels good. Negative emotions are like a yellow or red light. They are telling us, "Slow down, pay attention here!" or "Stop!" The more centered we are spiritually, the

The more centered we are spiritually, the easier it is to become the observer of our emotions.

easier it is to become the observer of our emotions. If we step back and observe what is going on within ourselves, we can stop ourselves from saying things that escalate a bad situation, or doing things that hurt ourselves or others.

Emotional Self-discipline

This self-monitoring discipline is an extremely important skill to develop in dealing with people. Once a hurtful remark has come out of your mouth, there is no way to take it back. A wise woman uses her emotions as an early warning system and rarely allows them to run wildly out of control.

It's Not Personal

A person with a strong spiritual center is less likely to react unconsciously when hurtful remarks are directed her way. You learn to not take anything like that as a personal attack. Most of the time hurtful communication comes from the scared and fearful ego of the other person projecting their own pain or confusion onto you. If you accept their attack as real, you start firing back and things can get ugly real fast. If you can identify the source of the problem and maintain your awareness that this is their stuff, you can diffuse the situation instead of making it worse. You can feel the waves of your emotions, observe them, and let them pass.

Toxic Anger

No one knows better than I the destructive consequences of holding onto anger. My divorce from husband number three was precipitated by his gambling addiction. As it was we were not doing well financially. Then he began staying out until all hours and making up lame excuses about where he was. I thought he was probably having an affair, but he was really at the local casino playing blackjack – and losing. By the time I discovered what was going on, all our cash was gone. After a period of tears and anguish I kicked him out and filed for divorce.

For three or four years I barely managed to survive financially in the hope that I'd get half of an insurance settlement from my husband's auto accident injury case, and be able to pay everything off. I paid our creditors just enough to keep them from taking legal action. When the accident case was finally settled, all the settlement money was given to my ex-husband even though I had been awarded half of it in the divorce decree.

Oh, did I ever seethe with my totally justifiable anger. He skipped out with all the money, leaving me with all the bills. I decided my only hope of getting some of that money back was to sue both my divorce attorney and the personal injury attorney. Since the claim was only $5,000, it was too small to interest any other lawyer in taking my case. I had to go to Small Claims Court. I won't bore you with the details of the misery I went through trying to maneuver through Small Claims Court by myself.

At the first hearing the judge sympathetically told me that I must get another attorney as an expert witness to testify about the incompetence of the two lawyers I was suing. Do you have any idea how hard it is to get any lawyer to testify against another lawyer? I spent hours on the phone trying to find just one lawyer with enough integrity and guts to help me. It was making me crazy. My flow of good slowed to a mere trickle.

I made enough money to survive, but not enough to really thrive. Since much of my mental and emotional energies were focused on thoughts of loss and lack, that is what I created for myself. My anger and resentment ebbed and flowed like an emotional undercurrent that never let me feel peaceful and positive for long. The times when

I was able to notice the good things I had and be grateful for them were in the minority.

I went to my minister, ranting and raving about the unfairness of it all. I was livid. How could God let people do this to me and get away with it? She had to tell me over and over again about the spiritual principles at work in this situation. Here in a nutshell is what I heard:

- **God is your source.** The court is not your source, nor the lawyers, nor the ex-husband, nor even your business. All good comes from God and you simply need to have faith that all your needs will be supplied with the right things at the right time.
- **Surrender the outcome to God.** You must be willing to give up the idea that you must win this money in court, and that you must get revenge for the wrong that was done to you. All the attention and the emotional energy you are putting into this is keeping you in a state of lack and limitation. If what you really want is peace, then surrender the whole situation to God and detach yourself from the outcome. Let God take care of it.
- **Be grateful for what you have.** Gratitude increases our good, so be grateful that you have enough of everything you need right now.

I finally reached the point of giving up.

How much longer did I want to make myself suffer? Yes, my ex was a creep and those two lawyers were idiots, but I was making myself more miserable than any of them ever knew or cared. I decided to admit my own part in creating this mess:

With the state my consciousness was in at the time, these were the kind of people I attracted into my life.

Could I forgive myself for my ignorance?

Could I find some way to forgive them as well?

Forgiving Means Letting Go

Forgiveness does not mean that we condone the actions of those who hurt us. It means releasing their hold on our consciousness and choosing peace instead. I weighed my choices – insist that I must have justice and the $5,000 and stay miserable, OR let it go and make peace with myself.

The thought of peace started to feel like a viable and appealing alternative to me.

How do you actually get to forgiveness? I didn't know how, but I remembered that when we really want something, we can ask God for help. We don't need to know how—God takes care of that in mysterious, sometimes unfathomable ways. So I didn't worry about how. To reach forgiveness I believe that sincere willingness on your part is all it takes for God to step in and take you the rest of the way. I had to turn the situation over and over in my mind until I got myself to a state of mind in which I was truly willing to forgive – to let go of all the emotional turmoil and accept whatever the outcome would be.

To reach forgiveness I believe that sincere willingness on your part is all it takes for God to step in and take you the rest of the way.

Show Me, God!

The process of getting to that place of willingness was neither pretty nor peaceful. As I drove up the mountain to my home one day, my frustration at being unable to find anyone to help boiled over and spewed out. I shouted, cried, and screamed at God. I couldn't take it anymore. "Show me a sign, Goddammit!" I screamed as I pounded the steering wheel. "Either send me the right person to help me or show me that I should give it up – I *swear* I will pay attention. I surrender! JUST SHOW ME, GOD!"

At the time I didn't know that one of the most powerful prayers you can send out is a "show me" prayer. By the time I got home I was completely exhausted emotionally, but a strange feeling slowly rose to the surface of my awareness. An unfamiliar sense of calm and peace came over me. I went to bed and slept for 14 hours straight.

Two days later, I received a call from a lawyer who listened to my story and said he was willing to appear as an expert witness for me. One of the dozens of lawyers I called had discussed my situation with him and given him my phone number. *He* called *me*! *Thank you, God!*

Releasing Resentments

I was extremely grateful, even hopeful, that I might win after all; but I knew better than to go back to my old thinking. I stayed calm and worked on remaining detached from the outcome. I had my day in court and did the best I could. I got the satisfaction of making both of those incompetent jerks sit in front of the judge and squirm because they knew they had screwed up. I was awarded enough money to pay my expert witness with just a small amount for me. By that time, the money didn't mean anything to me. I was so happy to let go of all those poisonous resentments and instead, focus on directing my energy into positive pursuits.

I learned that lesson. These days I don't allow myself to build up big blobs of resentment. I enjoy having good flowing to me freely and easily. The ocean of my emotions has its ups and downs, but the storms blow over quickly. Rarely am I disconnected for long from the peace of God that is at my center.

Are you holding onto anger and resentment from the past? Unless you find a way to release yourself from these blocks, you'll have a very difficult time having a good relationship with a man. A man worth having is smart enough to back away from a woman with left-over anger infecting her mind and soul. When you're free of it, you can handle upsets and disagreements with your partner in a way that doesn't inflict fatal injuries on your relationship.

The Magic of Detachment

To improve your relationships with the people close to you (and people in general) one of the best qualities to develop in yourself is detachment. Detachment doesn't mean that you don't care. It means that you don't take things personally. Many of us are emotionally thin-skinned and super-sensitive when another person does or says something that seems hurtful. This super-sensitivity can usually be traced to old emotional hurts that have never been healed. A small word or gesture from another can trigger an automatic reaction as if that person unwittingly reopened that old wound. We jump to conclusions, overreact, and get upset.

Detachment doesn't mean that you don't care. It means that you don't take things personally.

When you heal those hurts, you develop a thicker emotional skin. Now, those same words and gestures bounce off you. You are able to use your rational mind to observe what is going on and realize that the other person's upset probably has little or nothing to do with you and everything to do with them. This ability to stop yourself from having an emotional reaction and detach yourself from getting entangled in the other person's emotions is difficult, if not impossible, to practice when you are full of your own anger and resentment.

In our most intimate relationships, exercising the skill of detachment has huge benefits. It allows you to sidestep or shorten the time you and your partner spend quarreling about the little stuff. It gives you the courage and compassion to repair the hurts you may inflict on each other before they turn into deep emotional wounds.

Even on our best days, both Earth Mothers and Star Women can be impatient and sharp-tongued when things upset us. Don't let old hurts lessen your chances for happiness. No matter how bad it feels right now, those emotional potholes *can* be healed and sealed.

Remember, you don't have to know how to do it or even who should help you. Send a prayer of sincere willingness out into the universe, then pay attention and watch for signs. You will be led to whatever and whomever you need to help you heal. Your present (or future) partner will be thankful that you did.

Step 5. Stop Judging and Stop Blaming

We human beings have this thing called the ego, which loves to be right. It enjoys pointing out other people's flaws and foibles and telling them how wrong they are. It gets all puffed up with self-righteousness and is quick to place the blame on anyone but us.

You can almost laugh off this one-sided behavior when you see it in children, but it is most unattractive in an adult. Not only is it unattractive, it is also very destructive when it comes to relationships. Jesus himself cautioned against it in no uncertain terms: "Judge not, that ye be not judged." (Matthew 7:2)

The error we make when we are judgmental is that, as mere human beings, we can never know the whole truth about any situation.

The error we make when we are judgmental is that, as mere human beings, we can never know the whole truth about any situation. Only God knows that. Your mission on earth is not to be the judge and jury of everyone else's business. You have quite enough to occupy your mind if you just stick to your own business.

A Tough Lesson About Judgment

I learned a very tough lesson about being judgmental within my own family. My mother's brother, Uncle Fred, was married to Aunt Dot for many years. She was never a terribly sociable person and usually spent family gatherings sitting quietly, chain-smoking in a corner. She became more withdrawn as the years went on and then started having mental problems serious enough to land her in the hospital. She would stabilize temporarily for weeks or months, then get worse again and return to the hospital. Sometimes my aunts babysat her while my uncle was at work, because she couldn't be trusted to care for herself.

As the years dragged on, many family members became increasingly irritated with the situation. We'd make fun of her and wonder why my uncle didn't just put her in the hospital permanently and make a new life for himself. Uncle Fred never complained. He just kept on taking care of her as best he could. The doctors never figured out exactly what was wrong with her. They kept trying different drugs and treatments without any great improvement in her condition.

Finally she passed away and we were all relieved. Uncle Fred allowed the doctors to do an autopsy to see if they could find the cause of her illness. It turned out that there was a tumor deep in her brain that was intermittently pressing on blood vessels. Lack of oxygen to her brain for random periods of time caused her aberrant behavior.

When I learned this, I felt sick to my stomach. I had been making snide comments about my aunt and uncle for years. No one knew the whole story until after she died. My uncle didn't judge her. He promised to love and cherish her "in sickness and in health" and that's just what he did all those years.

Mental Self-discipline is a Must

Judging and blaming are just bad mental habits that we need to change. It takes mental self-discipline to hold your tongue when one of those thoughts begs to be expressed, but your relationships with other people are so much more pleasant when you refrain. You can learn to express your displeasure or disappointment without being accusatory.

Judging and blaming are just bad mental habits that we need to change.

Courtesy or Contempt?

Men are especially grateful when you overlook something they know they did wrong. It hurts them deeply when we criticize them (especially in front of others) and their hurt is often expressed as anger. Some of us are more polite when we talk to our employees than our mates.

Marriage expert, Dr. John Gottman, says he can predict with great accuracy whether a couple is headed for divorce by simply observing whether they treat each other with contempt or courtesy.

Harmony is the Reward

Giving up the ego's habit of judging and blaming is a small price to pay for harmony. Whenever I'm tempted to blame someone or something outside of myself, I make myself stop and think about what my part is in the situation. Were my expectations unclear to this person? Is this situation simply not within my control? I find the lesson to be learned, clean up or change whatever was my part in it, and let the rest go.

Giving up the ego's habit of judging and blaming is a small price to pay for harmony.

> ***"Freedom...is the outgrowth of our willingness to make conscious choices of our own free will and to live through the consequences of our choices without blame, shame, or guilt."***
>
> ***—Iyanla Vanzant***

Serenity is Alluring

Make up your mind to stop wasting your emotional energy on judgment and blame. Life is too short for that nonsense. Once you are well on your way to mastering Steps Four and Five, you will have an incredible advantage over other women on the dating scene, or you will begin to experience a whole new level of harmony and joy in your married life.

Do you know how difficult it is for single men to find a woman who is responsible, compassionate, and non-judgmental—who is quick to forgive and slow to criticize? You are a rare and desirable treasure, indeed!

Can you appreciate how grateful your husband will be if you hold your tongue instead of firing off one of your devastatingly clever critical remarks next time he messes up? A merciful wife is a precious jewel to her man.

Step 6. Clean Up Your Finances

Fear of taking responsibility for their finances can actually stop some women cold in their journey to power. This fear must be faced and conquered if you are ever to be the powerful woman you want to be. The numbers in that checkbook of yours are not your enemy. They are just numbers.

The numbers in that checkbook of yours are not your enemy.

Money and Consciousness

Money is a very emotional issue for everyone. The way we use (or misuse) money is a reflection of our consciousness. If you are overspending and mismanaging your money, superficial fixes like "making a budget" don't work. The place to do the work is in your consciousness. What beliefs do you have that are operating in the background and causing you to put yourself in a place of scarcity and lack? What beliefs do you have about yourself that cause you to accept a job that doesn't pay enough, or hold you back from starting that business you dream about?

Star Women and Money

Star Women are visionaries and leaders. Most don't like to get bogged down in gritty financial details. Star Women often run their own businesses or are self-employed because they like to be free to do things their own way. They are constantly envisioning the big picture and may not pay careful enough attention to the details of their financial picture. If we don't develop enough self-discipline to manage our money responsibly, nasty surprises and money disasters plague our lives and drain our energy.

If we don't develop enough self-discipline to manage our money responsibly, nasty surprises and money disasters plague our lives and drain our energy.

Star Women are often in a position to attract lots of money because they can be so results-oriented. They shine in fields like sales where aggressiveness is rewarded, but they can easily get caught up in overspending on luxuries and status symbols. When they learn to rein in their impulsiveness and exercise patience and prudence, Star Women can enjoy keeping and growing their money as much as spending it.

Earth Mothers and Money

Earth Mothers can be excellent stewards of money by using their aptitude for nurturing and growth if they are emotionally well balanced and mature. However, Earth Mothers can also be plagued with an apparent inability to manage their money and a tendency to overspend and create debt, if they allow emotional issues to affect their money consciousness. Some Earth Mothers marry and expect their husbands to take care of all the finances. Then they receive a rude wake-up call when divorce or death makes them realize that their ignorance of the family finances has left them in a precarious position.

Money Responsibility

Every woman, no matter what her personality type, must learn to handle money responsibly and learn the basics of personal finance, whether her man is a pauper or a prince. Most financial experts will tell you that it is not the amount of money you earn, but what you do with that money that makes the difference. Since women so often outlive their husbands, it is foolish and shortsighted to assume that a husband will always be there to take care of you and your money.

And don't think that if and when you have a large amount of money, you can simply hand it over to that nice man or woman at the big investment firm and they will take care of it for you. How many horror stories have you heard about people who did just that and lost their entire life savings by trusting someone with their money who turned out to be unscrupulous or just plain incompetent? No one will ever look out for your money as well as you do. Learn to do it yourself and no one will have the power or the opportunity to destroy you financially.

No one will ever look out for your money as well as you do.

Your Attitude About Money

Your attitude about money is just like the positive and negative poles of a magnet: it can attract or it can repulse.

If you have the attitude "I hate dealing with money," then guess what? Money runs away from you! Money is not bad or evil, but it doesn't like to hang around where it isn't appreciated. Your attitude about money is just like the positive and negative poles of a magnet: it can attract or it can repulse. I've been on both sides and, believe me, attraction is better.

In my younger days, my money consciousness was so negative that I had to declare bankruptcy not once, but *twice*. In fact, it would have been *three* times except that when husband number two declared bankruptcy during our separation before the divorce, I found out that legally I could not do it. It was too soon after my first bankruptcy! Imagine how scared I was that his creditors would come after me.

But even that wasn't enough to make me change my ways. Some of us have extremely strong, wily egos and mine was a real monster. I didn't learn my lesson after husband number two, so of course, I got into trouble again. Husband number three became a gambling addict and wrecked our finances. That was the end of that marriage and the start of divorce number three. After divorce number three came bankruptcy number two. I was in a big mess for a long time before I actually filed for bankruptcy again. I kept hoping I could make enough money to pay back all the creditors, but with the bad state I was in emotionally it was impossible for me to earn that much extra money beyond my living expenses. So I suffered and struggled along.

Finally, with the help of a wise and compassionate spiritual counselor, I was able to make the decision to declare bankruptcy for the second time. She told me that debt is a way of punishing yourself, and asked me if I was ready to stop punishing myself and get on with my life. I was and I did.

Debt is a way of punishing yourself.

Starting from ground zero financially at age 47 like I had to do is not something I'd wish on anyone.

Changing Money Karma

I knew I had to change my rotten money karma and through deep spiritual work, I learned that it was my consciousness and my belief systems that needed to be changed. I read books on prosperity, went to classes and workshops, and asked for individual counseling from my minister. (My favorite books on the subject are listed in the Bibliography).

It took dedicated work to dig out those old beliefs and it took time for the new beliefs to take root, but gradually my financial situation improved. It's like sailing one of those old wooden sea schooners. A small change in the position of the rudder doesn't seem like much as you are doing it, but the result is that you end up at a completely different destination.

Operating under my old beliefs I hated opening the mail because I knew there was not enough money coming in to pay all the bills. I avoided balancing my checkbook because I didn't want to know how much (or how little) money I really had. The thought of writing checks to pay bills gave me a stomachache.

Now it's a whole different story! I'm happy to pay my bills because I always have more than enough. I love looking at my checking accounts, knowing to the penny how much money they contain. Once in a great while I make a mistake, but I don't panic. I look those figures squarely in the eye and calmly figure out what to do. I shift money around, as I need to.

Taking Care of Business

I take care of business and it is no longer a big problem. I am able to deal comfortably with larger and larger sums of money. My willingness to be responsible with money means more and more money is attracted to me. It knows it has a very good home in my hands. I have always dreamed of being a millionaire and I am now on my way.

Being self-employed and a natural-born risk-taker, my cash flow can fluctuate greatly from one month to the next. For example, last year I bought some land and used a large part of my cash cushion for the down payment of $8,000. In just over a year, that land went up in value so much that it is now worth $18,000 more than I paid for it. I more than doubled my investment in less than a year, but I had to take a calculated risk to do so. And I had to live with the consequences of having less cash on hand than I usually work with. I had to keep closer tabs on my cash flow and also make the payments on this investment. I have no complaint about the extra attention that was required of me. I made money on that deal and I stayed solvent doing it. This is a far cry from the old me.

Income Tax? I Love It!

I even changed my attitude about paying taxes. In the past, I resented paying taxes and I believe that attitude was part of the reason I wasn't making much money. The subconscious mind works on automatic pilot and makes no value judgments about our instructions to it. My mind was thinking, "I don't want to pay thousands of dollars in taxes. I hate paying taxes!" So the subconscious created what I wanted. It kept my money magnet set on negative. I attracted very little money, and therefore paid very little in taxes during those years. I got just what I asked for!

Now I'm actually proud of paying taxes because it means I'm really making money. Of course I have a great accountant who makes sure I take every deduction legally allowed so I don't pay more than I need to. But it makes me feel really good when I sign those checks to the IRS for thousands of dollars every quarter. How wonderful (and how usual) that I have enough money to pay my taxes with plenty left for me. How fabulous it is to do what I enjoy (writing, speaking, designing) and make a good profit from my work.

> ***"I very linearly [sic] wish you would exert yourself so as to keep all your matters in order yourself without depending on others as that is the only way to be happy – to have all your business in your own hands."***
>
> ***—Martha Washington***

Every person needs to develop a healthy personal money consciousness and come to the realization that nothing outside of us is the source of our good and abundance. It all flows from God directly to us and it is up to us to be a good steward of our abundance—money and all. Your financial situation is a reflection of your consciousness. Changing it or improving it is an inside job. Martha Washington's advice is right on target for us today: *"Have all your business in your own hands."*

Every person needs to develop a healthy personal money consciousness and come to the realization that nothing outside of us is the source of our good and abundance.

Tithing

No discussion of financial responsibility and success is complete without the principle of tithing. This is the practice of giving away a part of your income to a person or organization where you receive spiritual nourishment or perceive good work is done. Tithing is an ancient principle taught by many religious traditions. The magic of tithing is that it keeps us firmly implanted in the cycle of giving and receiving. It shows us that when we give, we always receive.

A good rule of thumb is to tithe 10 percent of your income. When we believe that all good comes from God it makes perfect sense to take the first 10 percent of what we receive and send it back into circulation to do good. This may seem like a lot to give away if you have been living in the consciousness of lack. You can start with just 2 percent or 3 percent if you need to. The important thing is to start giving and make it a regular practice. The action of tithing sends a message to the universe that you know you always have more than enough. Your willingness to give opens up the channel for you to receive.

The action of tithing sends a message to the universe that you know you always have more than enough.

Since my income can fluctuate I have a different strategy for my tithing. I tithe the same amount of money every week to my church no matter what's in my bank account. I have developed a strong inner knowing that I always have more than enough and my tithing practice proves it to me. At the beginning of every year I give God a raise because I know that means I am getting one too!

The Joy of Being in Control

You will derive great satisfaction and a feeling of real accomplishment when you bring your finances under control and you are no longer ruled by fear. Your ability to see a man's character clearly will not be clouded by his financial assets (or lack thereof). Lack of money is a terrible energy drain that no woman need suffer. Money is a wonderful tool when a woman of power wields it with integrity.

Step 7. Live a Balanced, Healthy Life

It is very easy and tempting for a woman with a strong Star Woman profile to become a workaholic. We are hell-bent on accomplishing our goals and woe to anyone who tries to slow us down. The danger that we risk is becoming so stressed and burned-out that we aren't effective or happy at work or at home. Our loved ones don't get the attention they deserve and we become too emotionally exhausted to care.

Earth Mothers can just as easily slide into the workaholic lifestyle as they focus on doing for everyone else and ignore their own needs. They can be caught in a terrible bind because staying at home to raise the children receives little appreciation in our culture. An artistic Earth Mother friend told me that people make the cruelest remarks to her like, "Gee, you're so talented. Too bad you wasted your life just being a mother." But a mother who goes out to work is then criticized for not being there for her family.

The Way Out

The way out of this bind is to develop your feminine power and use it to equalize the balance of power in your household. If we wait for the men to volunteer, it may never happen! Being a martyr and getting burned out with stress and overwork is a shameful waste of the talents and energy of women.

Develop your feminine power and use it to equalize the balance of power in your household.

A woman thrives when she is mindful to nurture herself, to recharge her batteries so there is always enough energy for all her many interests and responsibilities. This is the time to call on your "Volcano Woman" aspect to stand up for your right to live a balanced life and to help you find ingenious ways to accomplish it.

A woman thrives when she is mindful to nurture herself.

If your life is so harried and stressful that you don't have time for friends and family, only you can choose to make positive changes. Struggling is not necessary. God does not award bonus points for suffering and struggling. But It will respond when you ask for help in reordering your priorities to attain balance. Life is meant to flow in harmony and balance. Look at the world of nature around us. Everything works in an orderly rhythm—the growing cycles, the seasons, the waxing and waning of the moon. Mother Nature never rushes anything and neither should we.

When you align yourself and your purpose to your Higher Power, whatever you need comes to you when you need it.

When you align yourself and your purpose to your Higher Power, whatever you need comes to you when you need it. When you have complete faith that God's plan is always better than your plan, you don't worry and fret when things don't go according to your plan. It just means there's another, better plan in play. When you trust in the Divine, the occasional bout of chaos and disorder in your life is only annoying, not disastrous.

Reclaiming Serenity

Women can be very intense in the pursuit of their goals. We benefit from training ourselves to just stop sometimes and smell the roses. You are not attractive when you are tense and worried. This is when it is so important to have a solid spiritual foundation. The faith and trust you develop over time reduces worry significantly. Your being becomes grounded in peace and serenity. A serene woman has a mysterious air about her that is fascinating to men. They see so many "killer women," aggressive and combative, ready for a fight. A serene woman is a refreshing and welcome rarity.

A serene woman has a mysterious air about her that is fascinating to men.

Our feminine power is not based on accomplishments in the outside world the way masculine power is. It comes from whom we are inside. We are born with it, but in our culture that personal power is easily lost. So we must rediscover and reclaim our unique power center. Living our life in balance helps us do just that.

I believe that living a balanced life begins with choosing and consciously placing your fundamental values in order. My personal priority list looks like this:

1. **God**—My life is built on a solid spiritual foundation. When I take the time to connect with God daily everything else falls into place.
2. **Self**—My physical and mental well-being are essential. Without good physical and mental health I can't accomplish anything else, so I take good care of my body and my mind. I make sure I get enough renewal and relaxation time every week.
3. **Husband**—My partner is the most important person in my life before other family members. Giving him the love and attention he needs keeps our relationship strong and allows him to give me what I need.
4. **Family**—If I had children they would be next on the list, but since I don't I put my immediate family next. Relationships with parents and siblings must be nurtured with regular communication and visits.
5. **Everything Else**—Work is quite important to me because I enjoy it and because it brings income, but rarely do I allow it to come before my higher priorities. When I'm working on a special project and want to push through to the finish I may put it in #2 or #3 position, but only temporarily.

Our lives are so busy and there are so many activities and distractions vying for our time. Without a clear definition of your priorities to guide you it is all too easy to spend your time being pushed and pulled in all directions by other people's demands. Some will look at this list and think it seems selfish to put yourself above your husband and family. The problem is that if you don't take care of your

If you don't take care of your own needs you will soon have nothing left to give others.

own needs you will soon have nothing left to give others. For this reason the airline crew always tells us that if the oxygen masks drop down in an emergency situation you should put on your own mask first, then help your child with his or hers. The same principle applies to your everyday life.

Once you decide what your priorities are it is much easier to make decisions about the best use of your time. Instead of automatically saying yes to everyone's wants, you can stop and consider where they fit in to your list. Make sure that the top priorities and people get the time and attention they need from you first. Learn to say no to things that interfere with your top priorities. You may feel guilty when you begin to do this, especially when you get a disapproving or even angry reaction from someone who has always expected you to be compliant.

There are only 24 hours in a day and once time passes we have no way to get it back or do it over. No one on his or her deathbed ever says, "I wish I had put in more hours at work." We all believe that relationships are precious, yet too often the people we love are relegated to the bottom of our "To Do" list! Balance is a necessary ingredient in a well-lived life. Only you can decide what your exact personal requirements for balance are, but the following guidelines are a good start:

- Take the time to take care of yourself physically, mentally, and spiritually.
- Be clear on what you value and say no to activities, invitations, and commitments that don't align with your values.
- If you value your family spend enough time with them—don't work late every night and most of the weekend.
- If you value your health eat right and get enough exercise to stay fit.

- If your spiritual self is important to you, do what helps you continue growing and learning—activities like classes, yoga, meditation, volunteer work, etc.

Workaholic No More

You're probably not surprised to learn that I once was a world-class workaholic, are you? Oh, yes, I used to believe that the only way to get ahead was to work hard and long. I barely had time for friends and a social life. Sometimes I didn't even leave my all-important business in California to visit my mother in New Jersey for two or three years at a stretch. I actually thought my struggles with my work were more important. It's painful to admit how out of balance I was and how shallow my values were.

It wasn't until I moved to the mountains in Big Bear Lake that I started to live a life that had some balance to it. I was careful to keep my living expenses as low as possible so I wouldn't have to freak out if I had a slow month in my design business. I adopted a dog and started hiking every day. I joined a local theater group, found a church that I liked, started making friends. One day it dawned on me: I was no longer a workaholic. I had a balanced life with lots of people and pleasures in it. Work was just one part of life now, not the large majority, as it once was.

Life In Balance

I'm getting better and better at this thing called "balance."

Now I have people help with my design business so I can concentrate on doing the things I'm best at. Last year I took in more money in design fees than ever before, and worked less hours! I have time to enjoy being with my husband, as well as travel. I dance. I write. I'm very involved with my church, where I'm studying to become a practitioner. I have fun playing keyboard in our church band, "High Spirits." Life Is Good!

No worthwhile man wants a stressed-out worrywart for a girlfriend or a wife.

Don't try to tell me your situation is different and impossible to change. If you keep living a life of too much stress and not enough pleasure, it will be very difficult for you to attract a good man or to keep the one you have. No worthwhile man wants a stressed-out worrywart for a girlfriend or a wife. And what woman wants to be that unhappy?

If this is you, the answer is not to buy a bigger, better day planner or get up an hour earlier. It's in your consciousness. You knew I was going to say that by now, didn't you? It's your beliefs about work and worry that have kept you on that miserable treadmill to nowhere. Choose to take the steps that will ferret out that old mental garbage and grow a beautiful, balanced garden of positive beliefs in your mind, instead.

Pleasure is a Must

Taking time for relaxation and pleasure is not a luxury – it's a must for every woman. The world will not stop turning if you sit down and read a romance novel, get a pedicure or massage, play some music, or engage in whatever your favorite pleasure may be. When we're in struggle mode, that old Protestant work ethic that's etched into our American consciousness makes us feel smug, self-righteous, and justified in our suffering. Stop killing yourself this instant!

Since you haven't yet given yourself permission to live differently, I will do it for you, so pay attention.

> **I hereby give you, gentle, tired reader, complete permission and total approval to live a balanced, healthy life, to make choices that nourish your soul and your body, to establish peace and serenity as the center of your being.**

Now get out there and loaf! Don't DO anything. Just BE.

Being is where we need to live. Being is it. Believe it. Let your life come into balance now. Everything you need is supplied to you. You are becoming the woman you were meant to be. Imagine how good it feels to be powerful, passionate and peaceful – all at the same time. Nothing can stop a woman whose power and passion are expressed from her strong, spirit-filled, calm, confident, peaceful center.

Nothing can stop a woman whose power and passion are expressed from her strong, spirit-filled, calm, confident, peaceful center.

Nothing.

Step 8. Give and Receive Graciously

Some women are fortunate enough to have a large giving nature and a small ego, but I'm not one of them. I was blessed with a big, tough, demanding ego that wanted to go out and conquer the world.

Unlike some wise Native American tribes, our society makes no provisions for identifying, grooming, and educating its future Star Women. As a child I was smart and sassy and naturally assumed a leadership role in almost any group in which I participated.

And too often I delighted in using my powers of persuasion to serve the dark side and inflate my ego. I always had a knack for dreaming up some mischief and getting other kids to carry out my plans. In school other girls labeled me "pushy." I was often exasperated with their relative passiveness and sometimes expressed it forcefully with little regard for their feelings. Had I been more fortunate, I would have been born into a tribe that knew how to shape and focus the energy of their Star Girls in a direction that would benefit both the tribe and the girl.

Learning to Give

It wasn't until reaching my thirties that I began to appreciate the virtues of giving and nurturing. I realized that I was never going to have the kind of love I wanted unless I put down my sword and shield, and let the loving, lovable part of myself shine in the light of day. I had a sincere desire to become softer and more approachable instead of brittle and standoffish.

I launched a mental archeological dig to find those lost parts of myself buried under calcified layers of hurt and disappointment. My ego had done such a brilliant and thorough job of building my defenses that I wouldn't let any man (or even friend) get close to me.

Getting Off the Glass Mountain

Why would any sensible, warm, kind, loving man want to even try to get close to a woman with a chip on her shoulder, a woman who was much more concerned with what she was going to get than what she could give? I was living a fairytale life; only my fairytale was the one about the princess on the glass mountain. One suitor after another tried and failed to scale that cold, slippery mountain of glass. I didn't want to play that game any longer. I had to get off the glass mountain and turn myself into a whole human being whose life would no longer be run by the fears of my ego.

I worked with several therapists, but rehashing the past didn't do much good. When I began exploring the philosophy of Religious Science, I found a practical set of spiritual principles that made sense to me. I learned about the ego and the Higher Self, and decided to put my ego in the back seat and my Higher Self in the driver's seat of my life.

I was in that place where the pain of staying the same was worse than the pain of changing. I wasn't a bad person. I was just dragging around a lot of emotional hurt and pain that had never healed. I didn't even know that what I needed was emotional healing. As I did my spiritual work and study, the healing began to happen for me. How it happened is still a mystery that I don't fully understand, but I am grateful beyond belief for it, because the kind, loving, giving me was able to emerge and blossom.

The Black Hole

In my darker days, I held an image of myself as a person with a gaping black hole just below my solar plexus. I tried to fill that hole with all kinds of things; guys, drugs, alcohol, spending sprees, food, you name it. What I looked for was that feeling of love that I thought was lacking.

As the old emotional pain healed and I grew spiritually, a new understanding came and a new visual image too. As I came to know and believe that I was enough, that everything I need is within me, love started flowing out from inside me – out of that black hole, out to other people, out to the world. It began as a trickle and progressed into a free-flowing spring.

Reverse the Flow

The black hole healed completely when I let go of my fear and just gave without any concern about getting anything back. There was that love and that good feeling I was searching for, within me all the time. All I had to do was reverse the flow. That was a life-changing revelation – a turning point for me. Giving is easy for me now.

Learn how to give – to love – and your life opens up to new depths and real happiness.

I sincerely hope that you are not as tough a case as I was. What a stubborn ego I had (all the better to protect you with, my dear!). Star Women can be real tough cookies. But until we learn how to freely express our loving, kind, giving side, great love with a great man remains elusive. Learn how to give – to love – and your life opens up to new depths and real happiness. To love is a verb. It's not a thing you get or keep; it's a process and an attitude.

Learning to Receive

Women (even us tough cookies) have a much easier time giving than receiving. Learning to receive graciously is a long lost art, except maybe for Southern belles. Those ladies seem to have the knack for it. To be receptive is the very essence of being female. We have so many negative thoughts floating around in our cultural consciousness about receiving. Here are a few of my favorites:

To be receptive is the very essence of being female.

- I mustn't be greedy.
- I mustn't be selfish.
- It's better to give than to receive.
- I shouldn't act ungrateful for this food that I don't like when there are people starving in (pick one): a. Africa, b. India, or c. China.
- Rich people are unhappy, selfish snobs.
- The meek shall inherit the earth.
- Blessed are the poor.

Developing a healthy attitude toward receiving means unlearning all the negative, shaming attitudes and ideas that we grew up with. God doesn't put us here to suffer from lack of anything. There is enough food, air, water, and shelter for every human being on earth. But if we believe we are not deserving of having enough, our subconscious goes right to work on that belief and makes sure that lack is what we experience.

Developing a healthy attitude toward receiving means unlearning all the negative, shaming attitudes and ideas that we grew up with.

> ***"God does not punish us. We punish ourselves with guilt, shame, and fear when we choose not to act in concert with our inherently divine nature."***
>
> ***—Iyanla Vanzant***

What do you say when someone gives you a compliment like, "What a nice sweater that is." Do you say something like, "Oh, this old thing? It's nothing special." Can you instead just say, "Thank you" and simply receive the compliment without diminishing it? If not, you might want to give yourself the assignment to practice saying "Thank you" and nothing else, any time anyone says something nice about you.

Most of our parents were brought up in families in which children were to be seen and not heard. They were afraid that if they praised us too much we would grow up "spoiled" and selfish. They did not know how to give a child a healthy sense of self-esteem and self-respect balanced with humility for self and respect for others. As adults we can choose not to accept old childhood beliefs that we are not good enough or deserving enough.

I grew up with a classic case of what I call "New Jersey Syndrome." When you live in New Jersey, you feel that you'll never measure up to New York. You're always second best. Any New Yorker you meet is happy to reinforce your feelings of inferiority by pointing out the inadequacies of Jersey drivers and the incomparable cultural advantages of the Big Apple. I had to overcome a long history of feeling "not good enough," but I persevered and changed that belief by doing the work necessary to change my consciousness at a deep level.

The Raffle Queen

I knew I was making real progress when I started winning raffles all around town. Big Bear is very big on holding raffles for fundraisers. I never used to win anything when I'd buy raffle tickets, but suddenly I was winning! It was almost like witchcraft. I'd see a gift certificate for ski lift tickets on the raffle table, picture myself up on the slopes and next thing you know, they're calling my name as the winner. I once won four prizes in one night! Sometimes I'd leave the event early and get a phone call the next day, "You won again! Come get your prize!"

People started calling me "The Raffle Queen" and I proudly accepted that moniker! I was no longer second best or not good enough. I was a winner! I believed it and saw the proof in the physical world. This experience might seem silly or superficial to some, but for me it was a milestone in my spiritual growth. Once I truly believed I was good enough and deserved to be successful, my life improved by leaps and bounds. Having good things happen to me and receiving and accepting those things without reservation is now my normal way of life.

Developing New Beliefs

To have a good and happy life, you must first believe that it's okay for you to have it. So if you are harboring any old beliefs that you are undeserving or not good enough, they've got to go! Replace them with the truth. You deserve to be happy and you *are* good enough. You are the beloved creation of the Divine!

You deserve to be happy and you* are *good enough.

Once we have dissolved the old negative stuff, the fun really starts. Then you can begin playing a game with God called "How Much Good Can I Accept"? No matter how much good, joy, pleasure, and happiness you believe you can handle, God never runs out of more to give you. The only limitation is how much love or money or fun you believe you can have. Continually expanding your capacity to receive is a delightful way to spend the rest of your life.

Learning to Receive More

Most of us don't have the consciousness to go from being dead broke one day to being a millionaire the next. Witness the stories of lotto winners who manage to lose all their winnings in a few years (in some cases just a few months!). Their consciousness could not support the idea of accepting and handling the amount of money that they won. They end up right back where they started, bewildered and dismayed, wondering how it happened.

That's why it's better to expand your capacity to receive gradually, one small step at a time. It wasn't that long ago that keeping a four figure balance in my checkbook for one solid month was a thrilling accomplishment. A few years ago I built a small house for myself and was very proud and delighted that I was able to come up with about $17,000 in cash toward the down payment. That was a very big deal for me at the time, especially considering that bankrupt was once my middle name. It was a stretch for me to accept having a checkbook balance that was five figures instead of three or four.

Now here it is, just two-and-a-half years later, and my husband and I are building another house on speculation to sell for a nice profit. I needed a construction loan for a project of this size, so I diligently did all my research on the costs involved and put together my cash requirements spreadsheet. At the high point in the project I will owe about $300,000. I will be paying not one but two mortgages until the "spec" house is sold. This does not scare me. It doesn't seem like a lot of money to me now. I've grown into being perfectly comfortable being responsible for six figure sums. My capacity for accepting money increases and expands step by step. I push myself to go beyond my comfort zone – so with each new adventure, I make sure the project is a stretch, but not too big of a leap. I have no doubt that I will reach my goal of being a millionaire.

Receiving is Fun!

Learning to receive is one of the most fun parts of the process of spiritual growth. Facing your fears and your old limiting belief patterns and changing them takes dedication and work, but it's a prerequisite to reaping the rewards of receiving. To keep your receiver open wide, do as I do at least once a week: Close your eyes, spread your arms out wide, and say out loud: "I'm open, open, open. I'm ready to receive. Thank you, God!"

May all the good of God pour into your life in a never-ending stream every day! May you always be open, open, open to receive it!

> ***"Change does not occur when we try to become someone we are not, but instead when we become more of who we are."***
>
> ***—Jacqueline Small***

Once you have worked your way through the Eight Steps to Power, you should be feeling really good about yourself. Healing old hurts, replacing old beliefs, getting your life in good order, and learning to receive – are all necessary steps to your goal. It's as if you have plowed the field of your life, gotten rid of anything that did not serve you, and prepared rich, fertile soil. Now you can plant the seeds that will grow into a new and happier life for you.

With your newly found (or newly expanded) sense of self-confidence and strength you are ready to tackle the next chapter – *Training Your Man or Why Real Women Don't Do Housework.* Putting the techniques in the next chapter to work requires guts and determination, but that's all in a day's work for a woman of power like you!

Chapter 10

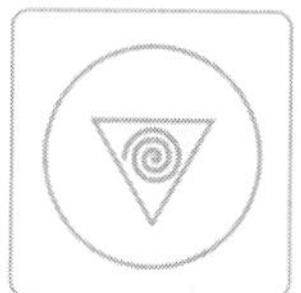

Training Your Man – Or Why Real Women Don't Do Housework

"Don't cook. Don't clean. No man will ever make love to a woman because she waxed the linoleum– "My God, the floor's immaculate. Lie down, you hot bitch."

—Joan Rivers

At last we reach the chapter many of you have been waiting for. This is the chapter that answers the burning question women have been asking for decades: "How can I get my husband to do his share of the housework?" The answer is simple: you train him to do it.

This may be simple, but it is not necessarily easy. It requires your time, effort, and attention. However, the rewards are great. Learn how to train him and you can mold him into a man who knows exactly how to make you happy.

Why Must I Train Him?

Before you start protesting that you don't want to – and shouldn't have to – train the man of your dreams, let me ask you something. Have you ever seen a child running around, out of control – whose mother makes a half-hearted attempt to stop him and then just gives up? Don't you wish she had made some effort to train that child to behave better? You set standards for your child's behavior and then reward him when he behaves the way you want – and punish him when he doesn't. If you don't, you will have a selfish child who doesn't respect you and who only obeys you when he feels like it.

And my experience indicates that if you have been lackadaisical in rearing a child, you will need to change your ways when it comes to training your man.

> ***"A good man doesn't just happen. They have to be created by us women. A guy is a lump like a doughnut."***
> ***—Roseanne Barr***

If you're still having trouble accepting the idea that you must train your man, let's look at it another way. If you have two friends who both have dogs, which home do you enjoy visiting more? The one where the dog jumps up on you the minute you step inside and makes a nuisance of himself begging for food at the dinner table? Or the home where the dog sits down promptly at the owner's command and waits for you to pet him when you come in? In this home the dog stays on his bed while you have dinner. Of course you prefer to be around the well-behaved dog.

"Wait a minute," you're saying, "a man is not a dog!" You're wondering how you can keep your love and respect for your lover if you have to train him like a child or a dog.

Is it easier to love an undisciplined child who runs wild and causes you problems, or a child who is generally well behaved and makes you proud?

Which dog do you love more? The one who messes up the house, constantly pulls on the leash, and won't come when you call him – or the one who comes when you call and heels at your side when you walk him? Come to think of it, which dog is happier?

Good behavior has to be created; it is not inherent in people or animals.

Good behavior has to be created; it is not inherent in people or animals. You will love and respect your man even more when you train him to do things that please you. You will be proud of him and his new skills when you start reaping the benefits, like having a clean house all the time.

> ***"The male is a domestic animal which, if treated with firmness and kindness, can be trained to do most things."***
>
> ***—Jilly Cooper***

If you have chosen your man well, he has the desire and the willingness to make you happy. What he doesn't have is the detailed and specific knowledge of how to do that. He can't read your mind. His approach to life is very different than yours. The male mind works best when given a specific task to accomplish or goal to reach. He is naturally wired to fulfill his mission in the most efficient way possible. He is focused on the end result.

The male mind works best when given a specific task to accomplish or goal to reach.

We must understand how a man's mind works in order to train a man successfully. If you do the training right, he won't even mind being trained, because he will be learning exactly how to please you. Nothing pleases him more than pleasing you!

Training

Training is the process of helping a person learn a skill or a job. You must teach your man how to make you happy. That's his job and doing his job well makes *him* happy.

You must teach your man how to make you happy.

Training is accomplished by using a system of positive and negative reinforcements. The ultimate positive reinforcement for a man is giving him sex and the ultimate negative reinforcement is taking it away. However, we don't have to dangle the possibility of sex in front of him like a carrot. That would be way too blatant and obvious.

His real reward is having a woman who is happy because he did something that made her happy.

What we want him to work for is the possibility that we'll be *in the mood* for sex. If we gave him sex every time he made an attempt to please us, we'd be exhausted. No, his real reward is having a woman who is happy because *he* did something that made her happy. When his woman is happy she is much more likely to want to have sex with him.

Let's give our men some credit here. A good part of the time, your man will do things for you just because he gets a great deal of satisfaction out of it. Most of the time your immediate appreciation of his efforts is enough of a reward. Whatever you appreciate, appreciates. So don't underestimate the power of your gratitude in reinforcing the behavior you desire in your man.

So don't underestimate the power of your gratitude in reinforcing the behavior you desire in your man.

It is imperative that you discard your old ideas about having him "help around the house." He is *not* helping you with *your* work. When you train him to do a task, it becomes *his work, not yours*. Do not be grateful that he is helping you. Do be grateful when he is doing his job well. How many tasks he does is up to you and depends mainly on your leadership and training skills.

Intermittent Positive Reinforcement

Now that you have the basic idea about positive reinforcement, there is an important principle to learn when applying it; it's called *intermittent positive reinforcement*. Training is much more effective when you reward desired behavior only some of the time, not every time. If you reward it every time, the reward system gets repetitive, boring, and ineffective.

Motivation to perform the desired activity remains high if the reward is unpredictable. This has been tested scientifically and proven true. Isn't it ironic that one of the traits thought to be stereotypically female is the very thing that makes us naturally great trainers? So, be as capricious and unpredictable as you like with your rewards.

One of the traits thought to be stereotypically female is the very thing that makes us naturally great trainers.

Negative Reinforcement

Next, we need to understand how and when to use *negative reinforcement* or punishment. First, understand that the opposite of love is not hate, but indifference. For a man, your attention – especially your physical attention – is an important demonstrable sign of your love for him. And when he has committed a serious offense, the worst punishment you can inflict on him is withdrawal of your attention and affection.

The opposite of love is not hate, but indifference.

> ***"Men grow up being disciplined and nurtured by women. Deep inside they still need and desire this."***
>
> ***—Elise Sutton***

You must not overuse this technique because withdrawal that lasts too long can damage your relationship. For normal everyday life, an expression of your disapproval of his behavior can be quite enough. Some women master the technique of "the look". Say absolutely nothing, but give him "the look" and he knows he's in trouble. A short period of the cold shoulder treatment is another good way to motivate him to find a way to scramble back into your good graces.

> ***"Using discipline on your man is like defragging a computer or putting bleach in with the whites. It just works better when you do."***
>
> ***—Litia***

Your man knows full well that when he makes you unhappy his chances for physical affection and sex are close to zero.

Your man knows full well that when he makes you unhappy, his chances for physical affection and sex are close to zero. If you are extremely angry – give yourself a cool down period before you say or do anything. You don't want to say something that is so hurtful that it will seriously harm your relationship.

Not a Good Candidate

We are talking here about dealing with men whose prime directive is pleasing you. If pleasing you is not right at the top of your man's priorities, then he is not a good candidate for training.

You can try these techniques to see if they might wake up a dormant desire to please that still lives somewhere deep in him. But don't expect miracles to happen. On the wrong kind of man, these techniques don't work because he just doesn't care enough about making you happy. (So why in the world are you still with this guy?) On the right kind of man for you – they work wonders.

Show Him

Let's say you want your man to do the laundry. He will make up some lame excuse for why he can't. His real fear is that he doesn't know how to do it the way you want, so he's afraid to try. The last thing he wants is to suffer your disapproval if he does it wrong.

His real fear is that he doesn't know how to do it the way you want, so he's afraid to try.

You have to take him by the hand, show him just what to do, and explain why it's done that way. Men always feel more comfortable if they know how a thing is supposed to work and why. My preferred training method is to allow him to do most or all of the physical motions involved as I supervise. Coach him through it, step-by-step, explaining as you go. Don't do the work yourself while he watches you. He doesn't learn anything that way. We all learn best by doing.

We all learn best by doing.

Sorting laundry right is something that takes some experience, so make it clear to him that, when in doubt, he is to ask you for your opinion. Be sure to praise him for a job well done and let him know how proud you are of him for doing so well his first time.

Some skills are complex enough that they require you to demonstrate correct techniques before allowing him to try. Suppose I'm teaching my husband how to cut up a bell pepper. I will do one as an example, then hand him the knife and let him do it as I coach from the sidelines.

Any household skill can be taught this way and you both can have fun in the learning process. Don't be surprised if his respect for you goes up another few notches once you start training him. You know much more about how to clean, cook, and run a household than you ever realized. Your man will be duly impressed as you impart your knowledge to him, and he will have a whole new level of admiration for how much knowledge and skill it takes to do it well.

The Right Way to Correct

Men (especially the good ones) are sensitive creatures deep inside, and don't like to be criticized in a way that feels like a personal attack. They particularly hate being made to feel incompetent. If you make him feel bad about himself, he'll be resentful and won't be listening as you try to correct him.

Watch Your Tone of Voice

When something isn't the way you want it, don't say, "You put these red socks in with the whites and now my panties are pink instead of white!" The belittling tone of voice that usually accompanies a statement like this is even more hurtful than the words themselves. Instead, say in a nice even tone of voice, "Oops! These red socks must have gotten mixed up with the whites. See what happened to these white panties? The dye in dark colors tends to bleed in hot water. That's why we have to be careful not to put darks in with the whites."

Keep your language objective and throw in a logical explanation for the why. The more scientific the explanation, the better he will feel. Now it's just the two of you calmly discussing how to improve on the result next time. No accusations, no implied blame. Make it like a military debriefing. "Just the facts, ma'am."

Don't overwhelm him with too many tasks at once. Just let him focus on learning to do one task well at a time. When he sees how happy it makes you and hears how much you appreciate what he has done—he will be motivated to do more.

The Art and Science of Folding

When he first takes over the laundry, don't get too picky about how he folds things. He will no doubt give everything the ugly universal male fold – fold it in half, then fold it in half again and he thinks he's done. You may have to grit your teeth at the state of your linen closet when he does this to the towels, but do not criticize. Be happy that he's folding anything, no matter how pathetic it looks when he's done. When he's doing well with the sorting, washing, and drying, then you tackle the folding.

Be happy that he's folding anything, no matter how pathetic it looks when he's done.

When I first tried to teach my husband the more elegant and stylish female folding method (fold in thirds) he could not understand it. His efficiency-minded male brain could not comprehend why you would fold something in thirds when folding it in half was less work and took less time. I had to reframe the goal for him. I showed him how folding in thirds makes everything look nice and neat because no crinkled, raw edges are showing.

"I love how organized and beautiful the linen closet looks when the towels are all folded this way," I said, "It makes me so happy when I see it like that." Then to satisfy his need for logic, I showed him how easy and efficient it was to partially unfold a properly folded towel and hang it on a towel holder, still folded in thirds with no edges showing.

> ***"There is something deeply satisfying about a nice, clean, folded towel."***
>
> ***—Margaret Atwood***

Now he understood. The desired end result was not to get the towels folded as fast as possible. It was to make our linen closet orderly and aesthetically pleasing to me, and to extend that beauty and order to the way the towels are hung on the towel bars. He got it. I now have the best looking linen closet in town and towels arranged as beautifully on the bars as in any model home.

I am fortunate that my husband has higher standards of cleanliness than the typical male and is an outstanding organizer to boot. When he and I first started living together he got double bonus points from me when he volunteered to clean and reorganize the shed in our backyard. He did a masterful job of it, and I am thankful for it to this day.

If your husband's motivation for doing housework is not yet up to the level that you would like, just show him the following quote from the book *The Seven Principles for Making Marriage Work* by John M. Gottman, Ph.D. I did not make this up. Dr. Gottman spent years studying couples to discover the principles that make for a happy marriage and this is one of them:

> ***"Maybe this little fact will spark a husband's enthusiasm for domestic chores: Women find a man's willingness to do housework extremely erotic. When the husband does his share to maintain the home, both he and his wife report a more satisfying sex life than in marriages where the wife believes her husband is not doing his share...The key is not the actual amount he does but his wife's subjective view of whether it's enough."***
>
> ***—John M. Gottman, Ph.D***

Affectionate Reinforcement

It's good to give your man positive reinforcement now and then as he is doing his chores. Combine the physical with your verbal appreciation to show him how much his efforts mean to you.

Praising him for doing a good job is nice, but giving him a little smack on the butt and telling him how cute and sexy he looks when he's doing his chores, is even more effective.

Get him to wear a special outfit that shows off his physique when he works around the house, like clingy knit shorts if he's got good legs or a tank top if he's got a great chest or arms.

Men love to receive compliments on their physical attractiveness. Don't be above grabbing him and giving his private parts an affectionate squeeze or two as he goes about his duties. This helps to connect doing housework with sexual arousal in his mind. That connection keeps him going in the direction you want him to go.

Men love to receive compliments on their physical attractiveness.

As you progress in your training program, continue adding chores one at a time. Every time you talk to him about taking over another chore, make sure you emphasize how much pleasure you'll derive from being relieved of this task. If there's any domestic chore that I truly despise, it is mopping the kitchen floor. The day my husband took over that job was one of the happiest days of my life. Now, of course, I have to suffer his displeasure if the dog or I track muddy footprints onto his nice clean floor. We try very hard not to mess it up for him – it's such a small price to pay for domestic tranquility!

Talk to Him at the Right Time

Timing is critical in choosing when to talk about housework issues with your husband. Choose a time when things are good between you. Don't try to talk things out when you are feeling angry or resentful because he hasn't done "his share." Chances are he has no clue what "his share" is supposed to be. You are the one who determines how much he does. He needs to do enough so that you feel good about it.

Some women are pleased if their men just take care of the things disliked the most – like the bathrooms and the floors. This will secure her satisfaction and happiness.

"Nature abhors a vacuum. And so do I."

—Anne Gibbons

Real Women Don't Do Housework

When I ran across the phrase *Real Women Don't Do Housework* on the Internet I adopted it as my personal motto. I have always hated housework of any kind. If you hate housework as much as I do, you may decide to go for the gold, the ultimate achievement in domestic management for women. That's when "his share" means he's doing it *all.* This is entirely possible, especially if you've got a Comet Man who takes to training like a duck to water. Don't be afraid to train your man to do as much of the housework as you like.

Even if you hire domestic help, a professional won't always do everything just as you like it. Whether your man is a heavy hitting lawyer, deputy sheriff, factory worker, or computer geek, it doesn't matter. Pick out the tasks that make you feel really good when they are done perfectly and train the love of your life to do those for you.

The truth is that a man who has submissive tendencies **wants** ***to do domestic tasks for his woman, even if he can afford to pay someone else to do them!***

The truth is that a man who has submissive tendencies *wants* to do domestic tasks for his woman, even if he can afford to pay someone else to do them! He enjoys perhaps even more doing the tasks that a personal maid might do, like preparing her bubble bath, giving her a foot massage, etc. The point of the man doing things like this is for him to personally perform some task that brings her pleasure. It doesn't matter if he's a CEO or a security guard. The kind of man we're talking about derives pleasure from and finds it a sexual turn on to do things like this for his woman.

As long as you are willing to put in the time and effort, there is no end to the things you can train your man to do for you. Train him to do whatever you can think of to make your life more pleasant, easier, and smoother. You will both be happy that you did!

The Magic Formula

Getting your man to do his part of the housework can be a fun and rewarding process for both of you. It is easy as long as you remember the magic formula:

Clean House = Hot Sex

Messy House = No Sex

Nagging, whining, and criticizing don't work, but the promise of sex always does. Make sure that when your man completes a task successfully, you always notice it and praise him. Combine your praise with some physical affection and he will beam with pride. Give him an occasional reward of great sex – but only when the house is up to your standard of cleanliness.

Never have sex with him when you are dissatisfied with the state of your home.

Never have sex with him when you are dissatisfied with the state of your home. Say something like, "Sweetheart, it's just impossible for me to feel sexy when the bathroom isn't clean and the house needs vacuuming. I feel much more relaxed and in the mood when the house is clean." Then be true to your word.

I never fail to appreciate the way my husband takes care of our home, inside and out. It makes me feel so loved that he willingly does all those domestic tasks that I dislike, and moreover, I don't have to nag him to do it. When the house is freshly cleaned and in order, my heart goes pitter-pat and my desire to make love to him just naturally starts to grow! My husband knows that giving me flowers, sweet words, or a kiss is nice but nothing turns me on like a clean house.

Nothing turns me on like a clean house!

Lead him to connect the clean house with the high probability of sex. Keep that connection solid by holding fast to the magic formula and watch how easy and pleasant your life becomes.

Bedroom Training

All the principles and techniques of training that we have outlined above, apply in your sexual relationship just as much – if not more. Most women will want to get their feet wet by first training their man in the domestic arts. When you see you are getting the results you want in that area, it will be much easier for you to apply your training techniques to sex.

It's possible that your man is in agreement with Platinum Rule #1 *(sex is primarily for the woman's pleasure, his is secondary)*, but he hasn't yet seen the wisdom of Platinum Rule #2 *(the woman decides if, when, where, and how)*.

You must show him that it is in his best interest to agree to Rule #2. You do that by using positive and negative reinforcement. When your man tries to initiate sex with you, act disinterested and bored. You might decide to be magnanimous and allow him to have intercourse with you, but he won't enjoy it all that much without any enthusiasm on your part.

A Talk and a Treat

At another time, *you* initiate sex and take control of him and everything that happens. Enjoy yourself and have as many orgasms as possible. When you are thoroughly satisfied, rest for as long as you'd like, but stroke his erect member with your hand to keep his interest level up. He is now highly aroused – and this is the time when he is most suggestible and receptive to your desires.

Keep stimulating him just enough to keep him on a medium boil. Point out to him how much better it is for him when you are in charge – how much more you enjoy yourself when you pick the time and place. Get him to agree with you. He'll agree to just about anything at this point. Once you have gotten his agreement, tell him he has made you very happy so you are going to give him a treat. Then give him a tremendous orgasm. You know him well enough to know what turns him on and what particular position or technique is a sure-fire mind-blower for him. This is the Granddaddy of positive reinforcement – so only use this special reward sporadically, and for really important issues.

> ***"If you've got them by the balls, their hearts and minds will follow."***
>
> ***—John Wayne***

This *Talk and Treat* procedure can be used any time you want to ramp up your influence on your man. If your man has trouble really opening up and talking to you in the intimate way you would like, this procedure has the potential to change all that. It's especially good for extracting promises about future behavior. Don't forget the always-important principle of intermittent positive reinforcement. He doesn't always need to get the treat at the end. It's your choice.

You can use a variation of this procedure when you are just snuggling in bed, sharing pillow talk before you go to sleep or when you wake up in the morning.

Your pillow talk will be remembered and acted upon if you combine it with physical pleasure for him.

Get him all nice and relaxed and receptive with some lazy stroking. Your pillow talk will be remembered and acted upon if you combine it with physical pleasure for him. Don't take it above a low boil unless you have finished talking and decide you want to give yourself a treat (and maybe him, too).

If you want your man to feel really loved, then once in a while just stroke him like this and tell him how happy he makes you. Tell him in detail just what he did and how it made you feel. Don't make him do anything for you. Let him just drink in your words of appreciation and love, while you pleasure him at the same time.

Vary the sensations he's receiving in whatever creative ways you like. Teasing him with light strokes that barely touch the skin is exquisitely effective. Then stop talking and just torture him with pleasure. Keep it up long enough and he could have one of the most incredible orgasms he's ever experienced. You will enjoy the feeling of power you get from giving him such an experience. He will start thinking of you as his Goddess if he doesn't already. It's good to be the Goddess!

"The art of love... is largely the art of persistence."
—Albert Ellis

Intimate Talk

Training a man to please you in bed is, in theory, no different than training him to do the laundry, but it is likely to be a more emotionally charged issue for you. You will have to overcome any personal reluctance to talk about your most intimate sexual likes and dislikes.

If you are just dating or living with your man, you both need to build enough trust in each other to be able to talk about sex in a way that deepens your relationship. When you are in a long–term, committed relationship like marriage, it should be easier. I say, "should" because we Americans haven't yet shed all the shame, guilt, and puritanical attitudes that our forefathers placed in our cultural consciousness about sex.

Men usually have less of a problem than women in expressing their sexual preferences. Haven't you noticed that, if you let him, he will happily slip into the role of director when you are making love? "Move here, turn over, do it this way." Men have little inhibition when it comes to directing the action in bed. We need to drop our hesitancy and learn to do the same.

Men have little inhibition when it comes to directing the action in bed. We need to drop our hesitancy and learn to do the same.

What really helps us in this area is to first talk about it with him and get his agreement that it is good for you to do some or all of the directing. As explained earlier, most men will welcome the opportunity because, unless he is told or shown what you like, all he can do is guess. If you are a little shy about showing him, his reassurance that he really wants you to show him can help you take your first steps in this direction.

Tigress in the Bedroom

Bedroom training requires boldness. This is no place for the compliant, eager-to-please, sweet side of femininity. We can also be fierce, free, and uninhibited when making love. Whether you are an Earth Mother or Star Woman, there is a sexy, wild tigress within you, and if you let her out to play, your man will love it. When he is making love to you and he starts doing something that really rings your chimes, you must tell him in no uncertain terms how much you love it. Men are not stupid. If whatever he just did really pleased you, he will remember it and give you even more of it next time.

The hardest part of this process for a woman is learning how to simply open her mouth and ask for what she wants.

The hardest part of this process for a woman is learning how to simply open her mouth and ask for what she wants. Even Star Women, as mouthy and brash as we can be in the outside world, often get tongue-tied and reluctant to tell our men what we really want in bed. This is why the Three Platinum Rules of sex are so important in a relationship. It establishes in your mind – and his – that your pleasure is the primary goal. When your man openly agrees to this, there is no reason for you to hang back. He gallantly opens the door to the Pleasure Palace for you, but you are the one who has to step through it.

No one would ever accuse me of a lack of boldness, courage, or feistiness, yet I was taken aback the first time my husband (then boyfriend) told me he wanted my pleasure to come first. It took some time for it to really sink into my awareness that this was not just okay with him – it was what he really wanted. No other man had ever given me this outspoken, total freedom to just enjoy myself and not worry about his pleasure. If I wasn't already in love with him by then, that did it. I decided that this man was a keeper.

It didn't take long for me to get over my amazement and shock, and start having some real fun. It was like being released from an invisible cage. I didn't even know I was in that cage until my man pulled me out of there! We have been so conditioned to be more concerned about a man's pleasure than ours, that when we are offered a different approach, it is a shock to us.

Let us learn to receive and accept pleasure with as much ease and delight as we receive money.

Accepting Pleasure

Let us learn to receive and accept pleasure with as much ease and delight as we receive money. Few people feel ashamed or guilty when good fortune flows into their life and they earn or receive money. If the receiving station in your consciousness is set to *open,* and no harm has been caused in getting the money, there is no guilt involved in receiving it. Why can't we have the same attitude about pleasure?

We also need to train ourselves to feel deserving of pleasure.

Practicing Pleasure

Not only do we need to train our men in how to pleasure us, we also need to train ourselves to feel deserving of pleasure. To get you started, here is a nice, non-threatening exercise you can practice with your man to increase your ability to receive pleasure.

Choose something sensuous for him to do for you that you particularly enjoy. Some possibilities are a bubble bath, body massage, or foot massage. It must involve him touching part or all of your body, but it should not involve sexual activity.

Having your man give you a bath is a particularly good choice. You must, of course, direct him in what to do and how to do it. You can even have him shave your legs (slowly and carefully!). He will have a whole new appreciation for all that you do to make yourself beautiful for him.

As he attends to each part of your body, you may feel uncomfortable when his attention is on a part that you don't like. Your assignment is to relax and send some love to the part of you that you treat like an orphan. He loves that part of you more than you do at the moment. Just breathe and imagine how it would feel to accept and care about that part of you. Let him pamper you as if you were the Queen of Sheba and he, your lowly bath slave. Allow your belief in how much pleasure you deserve, to expand and grow.

Just as training your man in the art of pleasuring you will take time, so will increasing your ability to receive that pleasure and accept it as your birthright. The two of you will grow in this process together.

You may find that when you make love, sometimes one of you will be in the mood to be the more active one – let the other just receive and enjoy their climax. Being held close after he pleasures you in this way – knowing that he wants nothing in return – makes a woman feel so loved and treasured. This is a wonderful gift to give your partner now and then, and a wonderful gift to receive as well.

In a woman-led marriage, you never get bored with sex. The romance is kept alive because your man is always courting you by doing things for you and making your happiness his priority. The little things can mean more than the big ones.

Little Things Mean a Lot

My husband prepares the coffeemaker every evening and sets the timer so there will be fresh coffee ready for me when I get up. I'm usually awake at the crack of dawn, eager to get to work on my latest project. He's a night-owl musician who's up late most nights and whose natural wake-up time is more like the crack of noon. When I come out into the kitchen and find my coffee ready and waiting, it feels like a little caress to me. He thinks of my needs and shows me with his deeds. That's real love.

Most men don't understand how much little things like that mean to their women. That's why you have to educate your man in very specific ways, on what you like both inside and outside the bedroom.

A man who attends to those little things to make her life easier, makes his woman feel loved on a daily basis. That keeps your heart open to him. And a woman who feels loved, naturally wants to make love to her man.

A man who attends to those little things that make her life easier, makes his woman feel loved on a daily basis.

Are you starting to see how brilliant those Three Platinum Rules really are? I can't take credit for inventing them. Some women have known about them and used them ever since the prehistoric days of Goddess worship.

Men have always had an inborn desire to pursue goals. They really enjoy focusing their energy on accomplishing a goal. The pursuit and the striving for the goal are what they love. If you don't believe it, just think about the last time you saw a group of guys watching football. When that ball is in play, they are totally focused on it and are in their full glory.

Keep Him on His Toes!

The Platinum Rules set up your relationship so your man is always striving to please you. When he does something that makes you happy – he knows he's moving toward the goal line. When he does something that invokes your displeasure, he knows he's moving in the wrong direction away from the goal. The fact that you are in control of when he scores, serves to make the game that much more interesting. He is never sure of when you will be *in the mood*, so it keeps him on his toes!

As you become more confident and less inhibited, you will feel free to explore new avenues of sexual pleasure that interest you. The possibilities are endless. You don't waste your energy on power struggles, as so many couples do. Instead it's a team effort to see just how happy the two of you can be.

Happy training!

You now know the secrets of how to create a happy life of domestic bliss with a man who knows how to please you both in the bedroom and out. It's easy once you know how. And isn't it wonderful to realize that you can be your own serene, gracious, sexy self as you accomplish your goal. Your man is happy living in a home where the rules are clear and he knows what works and what doesn't.

Our journey is nearing the end. In the final section of this book we take a look at the all-important subject of how to maintain love and respect in your relationship. And last but not least I'll give you this Star Woman's vision of how the rise of feminine power impacts the future of the world.

Venus
ON TOP

SECTION FOUR:

Forging Ahead

Chapter 11

Maintaining Love and Respect For Your Man

"To love someone deeply gives you strength. Being loved by someone deeply gives you courage."

—Lao Tzu

For any kind of marriage, maintaining respect and love for your partner is an absolute essential. For the woman-led marriage, it is essential – but even more challenging – because our lifestyle is outside today's norm. If your sense of self-worth depends on other people's opinions, your attempt at this kind of relationship is likely to fail. Both partners need to be strong enough and mature enough to forego mainstream society's approval. The only thing that counts is what you think of each other.

Accepting Your Role As Leader

The biggest problem most women have in accepting their role as leader in their marriage is the fear that they can't respect a man who allows them to lead. The woman-led marriage has a different balance of power than we are conditioned to believe we should want. It's much like ballroom dancing. On the dance floor the man is the leader. However, he cannot lead unless the woman agrees to follow.

The woman-led marriage has a different balance of power than we are conditioned to believe we should want.

If both people are trying to lead, the result is a disaster and neither partner enjoys the dance. But if the woman graciously takes the role of follower and allows the man to lead, she has a wonderful time. Of course, she must first choose a partner who is a good leader – a partner she deems worthy of being given the power to lead her.

If she chooses well and then willingly allows a good leader to lead, dancing together is a joy and a pleasure to experience. All she needs to do is respond to his lead. In fact, on the dance floor, a woman who is a great follower can make a man who is just an average dancer look good. The follower has a lot of power to affect the end result. The leader cannot lead without the follower's conscious consent.

The leader cannot lead without the follower's conscious consent.

What does this principle have to do with the woman-led marriage? Everything! The reason I respect my husband is because he gives his conscious consent to my leadership. Without his willingness to follow, I cannot lead. He recognizes that I am very competent at directing most aspects of our partnership. With the gift of his consent and cooperation, our life is mostly smooth and harmonious.

Handling Conflict

Does this mean that everything is always perfectly peaceful in our household? Of course not! We are both only human and we still have a lot to learn. We still experience occasional little quarrels, disagreements, and emotional upsets. The difference is that one or the other of us cools down the emotional fire with a humorous comment, a cooling off period, or an expression of understanding for the other's feelings, before it explodes into a destructive raging inferno.

Making Repairs

We have learned to own up and apologize to each other for our part in the upset, as we regain control of our emotions and start thinking calmly again. This willingness of both partners to "make repairs," as Dr. John Gottman describes it, is another of the keys to a successful long-term relationship. Discovering how to confront difficulties head-on and get back on a good footing with one another is a skill that most happy couples develop. Having that skill means you repair the hurts before they have a chance to grow into deep resentments that threaten the survival of the relationship. You learn to do what it takes to maintain respect on both sides. And there are always plenty of opportunities for learning!

Minimizing the Mayhem

We have an agreement in our household that sounds silly but is really very effective in keeping anger and emotional upsets to a minimum:

Only one partner is allowed to go crazy at a time.

No one can be calm and even-tempered 24 hours a day, except perhaps the Dalai Llama. I bet even he would admit that he has his moments of anger now and then. So it is unrealistic to think you can completely eliminate those moments in life.

Better to accept that your partner will be cranky, upset, or in a bad mood now and then. If you both have a sufficient level of maturity and some self-control, you can make an agreement with your partner that allows you to express and release those emotions without creating major hurt for either of you.

To apply this technique successfully you both must have some experience in stepping out of the situation and becoming the observer of your emotions. When you have learned how to detach from your own out-of-control emotions and are in the habit of being the observer, you will have a much easier time doing so when there are two sets of emotions in the mix.

When only one partner is allowed to go crazy at a time, it's up to the other one to stay sane and centered. Whoever notices the craziness of emotions going out of control first has a sacred obligation to exercise self-control and stop reacting to it. Suppose I'm having a bad day and I make a snippy remark to my husband. If he's having a bad day too he might fire a verbal volley back.

Whoever notices the craziness of emotions going out of control first has a sacred obligation to exercise self-control and stop reacting to it.

Within the space of the next few minutes one of us realizes that some craziness is going on. The one who sees it first must do something to interrupt the process that has gotten started in the other. We do that by simply going silent and not responding to the remarks, or calmly withdrawing from the room. Sometimes all it takes is a humorous remark like, "Dammit, now you get to have all the fun because I just realized what's happening so I have to stay sane, but you don't!"

Obviously if one partner is continually going out of control and the other is constantly trying to stay cool, the relationship has serious problems and may require some professional help. However, for the average couple this little technique can be very effective for keeping little upsets from turning into big hurtful ones.

Money Matters

Disagreements about money are the number one cause of most marital strife. We don't fight about money. I manage all our money, pay the bills, and decide on investments. My husband, Stephen, knows I am responsible and fair. He trusts my judgment.

> ***Why would you* not *respect a man whose attitude contributes so greatly to the harmony and peace of your household?***

I don't make major decisions without telling my partner. I talk it over with him and explain why I want to take each financial step. If he has questions, I answer them. I take his opinions and feelings into consideration and then make a final decision that will work best for both of us. There is nothing to fight about. I am grateful and appreciative that my husband respects my ability to handle money. Stephen's willingness to do that makes him worthy of my respect. Why would you *not* respect a man whose attitude contributes so greatly to the harmony and peace of your household?

This is a refreshing and welcome change from the money troubles that plagued my three previous marriages. After experiencing the trauma of having to rebuild my finances and my life – not just once, but three times – you can imagine how reluctant I was to put myself in a vulnerable financial position again. My husband understood and respected my feelings about money. He had no problem signing a prenuptial agreement that effectively allows me to decide which assets will become community property and which will be my separate property.

My husband is not irresponsible with money. He doesn't spend money on foolish male toys and is quite frugal in his ways. He's a low maintenance kind of guy. In his previous marriage, he was the sole support of his wife and two children for a large majority of the 21 years of the marriage. He was a professional musician for some years before he married, but in his late twenties he was burned out by the loneliness of being on the road. He decided that he wanted to have a family and be able to spend enough time at home in order to enjoy them. So he married and became a plumbing contractor so he could support his family and be a good father. I call that being very responsible.

He never gave up his music completely. He continued to play drums and do one-night and occasional weekend gigs to keep his hand in it. When his children were grown, he wanted to go back into music full-time, but his wife would not support him in pursuing what he loved. They divorced and I met him a couple of years later.

I am blessed that my husband is an emotionally stable, secure person who has no preconceived notions about the man being in control of the money. For the last ten years of his marriage Stephen ran his own plumbing business, supervised six employees, and managed both his business and home finances. He was the main breadwinner for all 21 years of his first marriage.

When I met him he had shed the financial pressures of maintaining his previous lifestyle. Gone was the big house on five acres, the boats, the motorcycles, and the trucks. After the divorce he closed the business and lived a simple, financially uncomplicated life in a small apartment, glad to be out from under the burden of making enough money to support all the "things." He found a dream job for himself that involved one of his other loves: propeller-driven aircraft. He worked for a company building full-size working reproductions of 1930's era racing aircraft for national air shows.

There is no question about Stephen's competence at making and managing money. He chose to live a simpler life without the pressure. He was perfectly happy to turn the money management over to me when we married because he saw that I am not only very capable of doing it, but also enjoy doing it and feel more comfortable being in control of our money.

Money and Emotions

My husband's calm acceptance of our financial structure doesn't mean that emotional issues don't sometimes arise regarding finances. For example, I bought my car some years ago with cash, so I would have no car payment. My husband came into our marriage with a nice SUV that required a monthly car payment. I began using his car for business instead of mine, so I suggested putting the SUV in my name so my corporation would make the payment and I would get the benefit of depreciating it. This seemed like a simple, rational business decision, right? But after he signed his car over, he had an emotional reaction that surprised both of us.

Being a kind and generous person, he gave his wife nearly everything when they divorced. He was left with just enough cash to lease an apartment and buy a car – and start over. He also was paying alimony and child support until his youngest child turned 18. He did not shirk his responsibilities or resent them. This is how a good man behaves and I was impressed that he navigated his divorce with a minimum of strife – and without the typical childish fights over incidentals such as furniture.

Because he had closed his plumbing business due to a back injury that made it very painful for him to continue with the hard physical labor – signing that car over to me meant that he now literally owned nothing but his clothing and his drums.

Stephen was starting back into the music business from ground zero – having to make all new contacts like an unknown twenty year old – except for the reality that he was 50. It was not easy. He had some promising opportunities on the horizon, but no money coming in. His career start-up struggles plus giving up ownership of his car was a big deal for him – but he did it because he loved me. Men in our culture are judged by the size of their wallets, and it takes a strong man to go against that standard. My love's pride may have been wounded, but he did not react to those feelings by drinking, drugging, or picking fights the way a man of lesser character might have done. He kept his cool and stayed the course.

Men in our culture are judged by the size of their wallets, and it takes a strong man to go against that standard.

A Tough Financial Test

This long-term financial situation became an equally tough test for me. I was bringing in all the money and supporting us both. I wanted control of the finances, but the old tapes were still playing in my head:

- The man should be making the money.
- A man who doesn't make money is a bum who is taking advantage of the woman.
- A woman should not have to worry her pretty little head about money.

Without our faith in God and knowledge of spiritual principles, this situation could have wrecked our relationship. If I had let my old beliefs about money take over, I would have lost respect for my man. It's very difficult, if not impossible, to love a man if you don't respect him.

Our belief that God is our source of supply and that It supplies all our needs including money was vitally important during this phase of our relationship.

When you believe that your job, your business, your spouse, or your parents are the source of your money, you are setting yourself up for disappointment. So this was my test of faith. Am I going to judge my mate, find him lacking, and thereby lose my respect for him? Is his true worth to me dependent on how much money he makes? Is my love that shallow?

Is his true worth to me dependent on how much money he makes? Is my love that shallow?

I thought about what would happen if the situation were reversed. What if I was making no money and he was making a lot? Would he be having the same tough struggle? No, he would easily and generously give me every dime he made with no judgment and no strings attached. He knew how to be a real partner better than I did.

I was still stuck in thinking, "I worked for it, so the money is *mine*." That kind of selfish, immature thinking threatened to destroy the best relationship I ever had.

I had to meditate and ask for guidance on this one. I needed to see that money flowed into the partnership – not just to me. My role was to be a good steward of that money for both of us.

Our income was coming to us through my business, but he was definitely making an important contribution by taking care of all the domestic chores which I hated doing. For the first time in my life I had the kind of support I needed from a partner. Never had any other man supported me this way. My mind was free to focus on my work. This is how traditional, successful men have always succeeded at their careers.

The vast majority of CEOs and top executives are married men. Their success is a result of the work of both partners, not just his work. Without his wife to run the home and family, entertain business associates, and take care of living arrangements while he's away on business, he would not be as successful as he is.

No longer did I have to worry about those dreaded household chores. I had time to go to dance classes, work out at the gym, play keyboard for my church band, study to be a Religious Science practitioner, and go on weekend getaways. The only ways I balanced the work and joy in my life before living with my partner was to hire a housekeeper. I no longer needed to pay a housekeeper – and our life together was so much richer than single life.

And as I meditated on all the benefits brought into my life by my husband, the list grew quite long. Going on any kind of trip had always been traumatic for me. I hated packing and would always leave it to the last minute. Then I would become frantic because I knew I'd forget something. Rarely did I depart for the airport on time, so I was stressed before I got on the plane. Now all I have to do is lay out my clothes. My master organizer, Stephen, packs the suitcases, attends to all the details, and makes sure we leave for the airport in plenty of time. What a difference! I have a balanced life that runs easily and smoothly because I have a great partner.

The only thing that could stop me from enjoying and appreciating my new life was my old belief system about marriage and money.

I sat myself down and worked through another "Old Belief Into New Belief" exercise about the situation. From time to time, I'd review what I'd written and add to it. With time and repetition, the old tapes faded and were replaced with ideas that serve me better.

For years I prayed for God to send me the right partner who would help me to grow spiritually. When he showed up, he was quite different than what I had expected.

I hadn't a clue there was such a thing as a woman-led marriage, nor did I know that it was the kind of marriage I needed – God's plan for us is always better than our own. Being with my husband has made me grow in ways I couldn't have imagined.

God's plan for us is always better than our own.

Attitude Adjustments

Now his music career has begun to take off. Stephen will be on tour and I will have to learn to live without him for several months at a time! When I attend his performances no one knows or cares that I'm a semi-famous author. I'm just the rock and roll wife or groupie girlfriend to people in the rock music scene. As he makes more and more money, I will need to make some more attitude adjustments. Do I detect the seeds of some resentment and jealousy deep in my psyche when I consider that he might make more than I do or become more famous? How about my own sense of self-worth? If it is built on how much money I make or how many people think I'm great, I will need to start looking at whether that's just my ego trying to run the show.

When thoughts like this come up I am so grateful that I now have enough awareness and maturity to observe what is going on within myself instead of blaming my partner. I contemplate, meditate, and write in my journal to clarify the situation for myself. I also use the "Old Belief into New Belief" procedure when needed.

Never a Boring Moment

Being confronted with soul-searching questions like these makes living on the edge of the relationship frontier an exciting adventure. I got bored in my previous relationships. In this partnership, I know I will never be bored. There is always more to discover, more to look at, and more ways to grow.

There is always more to discover, more to look at, and more ways to grow.

When I tell friends that this book went from creation and idea stage to completed rough draft in less than four months—they are astounded. I kept my design business going during those months as well. Without my husband's help, I could not have done it. Some days I was writing for twelve or fourteen hours with just a few eating and dog-walking breaks. On days like that he brought me lunch and dinner without my even asking. He wasn't getting as much emotional or physical attention from me as he would have liked while I was wrapped up in the writing, but he didn't complain. He really was "the wind beneath my wings" on this project, and for that I am eternally grateful to him.

What kind of creative and wonderful things could you accomplish with a partner like that?

Blazing New Trails

A smart woman does not judge her man by society's standards. The only standard that matters is if he makes you happy. If you have suffered through a string of bad relationships as I have, it shouldn't be that difficult for you to ignore what other people might think or say. Their rigid, old-fashioned ideas will never work for women like us. We were born to be trailblazers and this new form of relationship is one heck of a fascinating trail to blaze!

A smart woman does not judge her man by society's standards. The only standard that matters is if he makes you happy.

The key to your happiness as either a Star Woman or an Earth Mother is to choose the right kind of man for you as your partner. This is something that neither your mother nor your shrink could prepare you for. This is a matter of directing your own destiny!

The tips in this book come from a woman who's been through it all, found some answers, and succeeded in climbing a little further up the trail. I hope I have been able to open your mind to new possibilities that will make your life a positive adventure, and get you thinking in new directions about yourself, men, and marriage.

The key to your happiness as either a Star Woman or an Earth Mother is to choose the right kind of man for you as your partner.

"Do not follow where the path may lead. Go instead where there is no path and leave a trail."
— Ralph Waldo Emerson

You *can* be a strong, powerful woman and have a great relationship with a man you love and respect. If I can do it, you can do it!

I believe that by sharing my experiences and the hard-won wisdom that I earned through them I have opened up a path to happiness for you. Use the tools, tips, and techniques in these pages to create and maintain a beautiful relationship for you and your partner.

So, my sisters, we come to the next and final chapter. I am wrapping up our journey with a vision of the future, a future that you can help to create. This Star Woman calls to the Star Woman in you. Let's release ourselves from the old thinking and the old ways that no longer work for us, and go forward as the Modern Goddesses that we are.

Now, get ready! I'm stepping up onto my soapbox and I'm holding nothing back!

Chapter 12

Feminine Power and The Future of the World

"If you don't like the way the world is, you change it. You have an obligation to change it. You just do it one step at a time."

—Marian Wright Edelman

After taking this journey to become a true woman of power, you can understand that the problems you've had relating to men are deeply rooted in thousands of years of cultural conditioning. If you are not in a sufficiently loving and supportive relationship, it does not mean you are neurotic, inadequate, or unlovable. You are enough and now you know what you need to do. If you are truly willing the path opens before you and you are led to the right people, places, and activities to help you free your feminine power. You radiate strength and confidence from a calm, solid center. You are a magnet that attracts the right partner, friends, and associates. You align yourself with the power of Spirit and you proceed toward your heart's desire.

I firmly believe that the hope of the world lies within the hearts and souls of women. There is a great imbalance in our world and we are the only ones who can fix it.

> ***The hope of the world lies within the hearts and souls of women.***

We can no longer let the world be dominated by the masculine. Every woman needs to develop her own feminine power, and learn how to use it to first better her individual life, then that of her family, her community, and ultimately, the world.

> ***Every woman needs to develop her own feminine power, and learn how to use it to first better her individual life, then that of her family, her community, and ultimately, the world.***

A New Social Order

We can forge a whole new social order based on the acceptance and celebration of differences, not on one group dominating another. The rise of the *feminine* does not mean the demise of the *masculine*. It means creating a way of life that includes and honors both principles. It means creating a society where individuals are free to express their gifts and talents without being limited by gender, age, or race.

> ***The rise of the* feminine *does not mean the demise of the* masculine.**

On the surface, women in America appear to have a lot of freedom and few limitations, compared to most other countries and cultures. We are still far from living in true equality, but we have definitely started a cultural transformation that cannot be stopped. Many of the difficulties we face in our relationships are a reflection of the underlying patterns of a patriarchal, male-dominated society in the process of change. If we can make the transition to a new society that accepts and blends the best qualities of the masculine and the feminine, we will usher in a new Golden Age for the human race. If we don't make this transition in time, we may very well damage our planet and our civilization to the point where we slide backwards and cause the demise of the human race.

> ***"When you are trying to change the old culture, you must not accept the solutions supplied by that culture. You have to discover or invent your own."***
> ***— Sherry Ruth Anderson, Ph.D. and Paul H. Ray, Ph.D.***

To create momentum for this transition, women need to push their feminine power to the forefront. Overcoming thousands of years of conditioning calls for those of us at the spearhead of the movement to exert our power most fully right now at the *beginning*. That's why this book is titled *Venus on Top* and not *Venus on the Same Level*. Getting to a point of balance and equilibrium is a pendulum-like process. The pendulum has swung too far to the masculine side. The only way we will get to the goal of being equal is if we swing it hard to the feminine side first. If you want to be equal, first you've got to get on top! Why continue at a slow crawl toward the middle when you can get there faster by getting on top!

If you want to be equal, first you've got to get on top!

This does not require marching in the streets, strident rabble-rousing speeches, or bra burning. It simply requires you to do your part within your own personal sphere of influence – whether that includes just one man, or one child, or a large family.

The New Sexual Revolution

The Three Platinum Rules herald the start of a new sexual and Cultural Revolution. The so-called sexual revolution of the sixties was nothing compared to this. All that revolution gave us was the freedom to be used by men because it freed women to have casual sex. It gave us the freedom to have sex the way males have always enjoyed sex — lots of partners with little commitment. If we were lucky, a guy would be decent enough to have some concern for whether we were satisfied, but that revolution didn't go far enough.

The Three Platinum Rules have started another sexual revolution – one that will truly benefit women. Imagine what will happen when we only date and mate with men who believe in and practice the Three Platinum Rules!

Imagine if we teach our sons to respect and revere all females and the values we hold dear.

Imagine if we teach our daughters to respect themselves and to spurn any male who does not treat them with the highest respect.

In just a few generations the Bad Guys will have died out because no women will have their babies. The pleasuring gene will become dominant in the majority of the male population. Relationships between men and women will be partnerships in the purest and best sense of the word. These couples will teach their children to respect and care for all people and for our Mother Earth. Next thing you know, peace will have broken out all over the world!

Suppose we all choose to vote with our considerable spending power and only support those businesses that use our natural resources responsibly. More women reaching top positions in the halls of government and the towers of corporate America will certainly help. But the average individual woman can make a tremendous difference by making sure that there is a new balance of power within her own household, and that she exercises her power in service of her highest values.

"All bonafide revolutions are of necessity revolutions of the spirit."

—Sonia Johnson

The new revolution is rooted in love, not anger.

The women's movement began as a reaction of righteous outrage to injustice, but now we are moving into a more visionary and spiritual time where women are redefining the *feminine* and rediscovering their power. The new revolution is rooted in love, not anger. The attempts of those in power to rule through fear cannot withstand a growing cadre of women and men who believe that gender does not determine our fate.

We exercise our power in the service of values that are natural for women: caring for the well-being of our families, our fellow human beings, and our planet.

"Women really do rule the world. They just haven't figured it out yet. When they do, and they will, we're all in big, big trouble."

—"Doctor" Leon

Men are not the enemy. They just need our love, guidance, and direction.

Men are not the enemy. They just need our love, guidance, and direction. As we direct more male energy and talent toward humane goals, the tide must turn.

You now have the blueprint and the tools, my sisters. First take care of your own life. Create a great partnership for yourself and train that man to make you happy. Then turn your attention to the outside world. It's so much easier to save the world when you don't have to worry about who is going to do the dishes or pick up the kids.

One of the best things women can do for the future of the planet is to raise children who respect each other and the earth. As we use our influence to bring the *feminine* and *masculine* into balance, we will reverse the shameful devaluation of child-rearing in our society. A woman who makes caring for children her main focus will command respect equal to any other career choice.

One of the best things women can do for the future of the planet is to raise children who respect each other and the earth.

The process of this great change has already begun in the most highly developed nations like the United States, Canada, and much of Europe. It is up to us women to accelerate the pace of change by taking charge of our individual lives. Every woman who educates herself to become economically self-sufficient hammers one more nail into the coffin of the old patriarchal order. Every woman who refuses to allow anyone to mistreat her or her children plants another healthy seed that grows our new society. Every woman who appreciates and respects men for their character, instead of their bank accounts, breaks the chains of bondage to the rigid cookie-cutter hand-me-down roles that limit the potential of men and women alike.

The only way that a happy future for our species is assured is if we create it—one woman and one mind at a time. The future is in your capable hands.

> ***"We are volcanoes. When we women offer our experience as our truth, as human truth, all the maps change. There are new mountains."***
>
> ***—Ursula K. Le Guin***

Send in Your Success Story

How has this book changed your life? How has it helped you to find your soul mate or improve your relationship or marriage? Send me your success story (no more than three typewritten pages) and your story could be included in my next book. Be sure to include all your contact information (name, address, phone, e.mail). Your real name will not be used without your permission.

Preferred submission format is within an e.mail message – no attachments, please.

Send your e.mail to: *goddess@venusontop.com*

Barbara Wright Abernathy
1521 N. Jantzen Ave., Suite 379
Portland, OR 97217

Toll-free **(888) 22 VENUS** (888-228-3687)
Fax **(503) 289-7598**

e.mail: *goddess@venusontop.com*
Website: *www.VenusOnTop.com*

Engage the Author

Let Barbara Wright Abernathy entertain, educate and inspire your group with her witty and provocative insights about men, women and relationships and perhaps a bit of belly dancing, too! Inquire about how Barbara can custom tailor a presentation for your group.

For information on speaking, seminars and workshops, contact Barbara at:

Barbara Wright Abernathy
1521 N. Jantzen Ave., Suite 379
Portland, OR 97217

Toll-free: **(888) 22-VENUS** (888-228-3687)
Website: *www.BarbaraWrightAbernathy.com*
e.mail: *info@BarbaraWrightAbernathy.com*

Bibliography and Suggested Reading

Belly Dance

Al-Rawi, Rosin-Fawzia B. *Grandmother's Secrets: the Ancient Rituals and Healing Power of Belly Dancing.* Brooklyn, NY: Interlink Books, 1999

Djoumahna, Kajira. *The Tribal Bible.* Santa Rosa, CA, Black Sheep Belly Dance, 2003

Culture and Transformation

DeMott, Benjamin. *Killer Woman Blues: Why Americans Can't Think Straight About Gender and Power.* New York: Houghton Mifflin Co., 2000

Douglas, Susan J. *Where the Girls Are: Growing Up Female With the Mass Media.* New York: Three Rivers Press, 1994

Eisler, Riane. *The Chalice and the Blade.* New York: Harper Collins, 1987

Gladwell, Malcolm. *The Tipping Point: How Little Things Can Make a Big Difference.* New York: Little, Brown & Co., 2000

Ray, Paul H and Sherry Ruth Anderson. *The Cultural Creatives: How 50 Million People Are Changing The World.* New York: Harmony Books, 2000

Small, Jacqueline. *Transformers: The Artists of Self-Creation.* Marina Del Rey, CA: DeVorss & Co. 1997

Sykes, Brian. *The Seven Daughters of Eve.* New York: W.W. Norton & Co., Inc., 2001

Feminine Power

Argov, Sherry. *Why Men Love Bitches.* Avon, MA: Adams Media Corp., 2000

Bolen, Jean Shinoda. *Goddesses In Every Woman: A New Psychology of Women.* New York: Harper & Row, 1984

Borysenko, Joan. *A Woman's Journey to God: Finding the Feminine Path.* New York: Penguin Putnam Inc., 1999

Herron, Elizabeth. *The Fierce Beauty Club: Girlfriends Discovering Power and Celebrating Body and Soul.* Boston: Element Books, Inc., 2000

Thomashauer, Regena. *Mama Gena's School of Womanly Arts: Using the Power of Pleasure to Have Your Way With the World.* New York: Simon & Schuster, 2002

Goddess History

Campbell, Joseph and Charles Muses. *In All Her Names: Explorations of the Feminine in Divinity.* New York: Harper Collins, 1991

Gimbutas, Marija. *The Language Of The Goddess: Unearthing The Hidden Symbols Of Western Civilization.* New York: Harper Collins, 1995

Gordon, Elinor W. *The Once and Future Goddess.* New York: Harper & Row, 1989

Starhawk. *The Spiral Dance: A Rebirth of the Ancient Religion of the Great Goddess, 20th Anniversary Edition.* San Francisco: Harper, 1999

Stone, Merlin. *When God Was a Woman.* Orlando, FL: Harcourt Brace, 1976

Money

Dominguez, Joe and Vickie Robin. *Your Money or Your Life: Transforming Your Relationship with Money and Achieving Financial Independence.* New York: Penguin, 1992

Hansen, Mark Victor and Robert G. Allen. *The One Minute Millionaire: The Enlightened Way to Wealth.* New York: Harmony Books, 2002

Nemeth, Maria. *The Energy of Money: A Spiritual Guide to Financial and Personal Fulfillment.* New York: Ballantine, 1997

Wilde, Stuart. *The Trick to Money is Having Some!* Carlsbad, CA: Hay House, 1995

Relationships

Gottman, John and Nan Silver. *The Seven Principles for Making Marriage Work.* New York: Three Rivers Press, 1999

Gray, John. *Men Are From Mars, Women Are From Venus.* New York: Harper Collins, 1992

Vanzant, Iyanla. *In the Meantime: Finding Yourself and the Love You Want.* New York: Simon & Schuster, Inc., 1998

Vedral, Joyce L. *Get Rid of Him.* Warner Books, 1993

Sexuality

Bodansky, Steve and Vera Bodansky. *Extended Massive Orgasm: How You Can Give and Receive Intense Sexual Pleasure.* Alameda, CA: Hunter House, 2000

Easton, Dossie and Catherine A. Liszt. *When Someone You Love Is Kinky.* Greenery Press, 2000

Eisler, Riane. *Sacred Pleasure: Sex, Myth, and the Politics of the Body.* New York: Harper Collins, 1995

Mistress Lorelei. *The Mistress Manual: The Good Girl's Guide to Female Dominance.* Emeryville, CA: Greenery Press, 2000

Spirituality

Anderson, Sherry Ruth and Patricia Hopkins. *The Feminine Face of God.* New York: Bantam Books, 1992

Dyer, Wayne. *Manifest Your Destiny: The Nine Spiritual Principles for Getting Everything You Want.* New York: Harper Collins, 1997

Ford, Debbie. *The Dark Side of the Light Chasers.* New York: Penguin Putnam, 1998

Holmes, Ernest. *This Thing Called You.* New York: Jeremy P. Tarcher/Putnam, 1997

Myss, Caroline. *Spiritual Madness. (Audio, Unabridged Edition)* Sounds True, 2002

Walsch, Neale Donald. *Conversations with God (Series).* Charlottesville, VA: Hampton Roads, 1995

Appendix A

Interviews for Chapter 7: The Man's Perspective—Why She Leads

Chapter 7 summarizes the insights I gained from interviewing three men who are proud partners in a woman-led marriage. These are the interviews in full. This is not a large or scientifically selected group, but I believe you will find it enlightening to hear how these men feel about their marriages and their partners in their own words. Their names have been changed to protect their privacy.

First is Robert, a graphic design consultant whose wife is an editor and writer. Second is Alex, a retired electrician whose wife is a minister. And third is my own husband, Stephen, a musician.

Interview 1: Robert

B: Do you consider yourself a Comet Man or a Meteor Man and why?

Robert: After reading some of your book I guess I'm going to say that I'm a Comet Man. And it's not that it really described what a Comet Man is, but more that it said that a Comet Man is an ideal partner for a Star Woman...that her energy and zeal lights my fire.

B: And you identify with that?

Robert: Yeah, I really do. I'd have to describe myself as one of those people who doesn't get up and go and do things unless somebody's making it happen for me. I have dreams of going places and doing things, but somebody else has to plan it out and make it happen. My wife, Karen, is that perfect person.

B: So it sounds like you are the perfect support person?

Robert: Yes, I think so.

B: So would you characterize Karen as a Star Woman?

Robert: I would definitely put Karen in the Star Woman category, but I know she's got the other Earth Mother influences in her too.

B: All women do have both, but some of us are more heavily weighted toward being a Star Woman – the majority of women are mainly Earth Mothers, with some Star Woman characteristics too. That would be my guess about Karen as well – so you're the perfect match for her being a Comet Man.

Robert: It's a good match. It really is a great match.

B: What I've been doing in writing this book is studying what makes a great match for a strong woman and why. Now before you met Karen, what were you looking for in a woman?

Robert: The list is incredible, but basically someone who was just down to earth, normal, no weirdnesses and I don't know if that comes from upbringing or good parenting or what, but someone who didn't have any strangenesses about them, who was fun, childlike, who loved to get out and play. Those were some of the most important qualities.

B: Both of you had grown children from previous marriages before you met?

Robert: Yes, they were all finishing high school or older.

B: Was this always the kind of qualities you looked for in a woman or has that changed from your younger days?

Robert: No, I think that's what I always wanted. And it's a tough find. I really found that out. I was married 22 years and being single again had its issues or unhappiness. I met a lot of women and dated quite a bit. And I just couldn't find a woman that had those qualities. I wanted a woman who was exciting and not strange and very easy to get along with. It took a while for Karen to finally look in my direction. It was hard to find a match.

B: What were the qualities in the women that you did meet that turned you off?

Robert: Jealousy was one. Then there were the little weirdnesses, like on the Seinfeld episode where Evelyn dances really funny and stomps her feet. I found myself having an issue like that. There was one girl I dated who always wore boots and when she danced she'd just stomp the bejeebies out of the floor. And it was one of those things where you say, 'I don't know if I can live with this the rest of my life.' It was kind of bizarre and weird.

B: So they had quirks that you just couldn't live with?

Robert: Yeah, things that I just wasn't happy with. Whether it was clinging on, hanging on tight, or just strange weirdnesses about their personalities, or jealousy.

B: Sounds like some of it was emotional insecurities and immaturity.

Robert: Yeah, that's how I'd describe it. And that's why I go back to that normal thing – wanting someone who is confident in herself, who's fun, who's excited, who doesn't have to worry about getting jealous, who knows that I'm there and I'm not going to go out and play around. I guess it's all about confidence and having a good strong feeling about themselves.

B: Do I understand correctly it took a little while for you to get Karen's attention, but you were very persistent?

Robert: Yes I was!

B: Because...?

Robert: Because something sparked me about her, there was this inner feeling. This woman walked with confidence, she was always smiling and happy and I guess I looked for that, too. I want somebody who is happy all the time. She definitely had a spark that just had my attention. It's funny because I didn't really know her personality that well; just from what I saw of her through the freelance work I was doing for her company. There was just something about her.

B: Once you did get together and dated and started thinking about marriage, what were your objectives and strategies for the long-term success of your relationship?

Robert: Wow, you know I never even thought about that one. Strategies? Long-term? I guess it just boils down to – hate the word fate, but – knowing this is the right person. You know when you date somebody for a year or two; you pretty much know that there are no problems, no issues, no strangenesses. Everything just flowed so smoothly. You're happy all the time.

You know people always say that marriage takes work. My whole life I always thought, *why would marriage take work?* It's almost like being with your best friend, where you just get along so well and everything rolls along nice and smooth and easy. That doesn't take work. That just kind of happens. If you think back on all your friends and relationships that you really got along with well – once in a while maybe you bumped heads in your younger years, but as adults I think it just flowed along so smoothly. And I guess that's what I always pictured a good marriage to be – that you just got along so wonderfully that there was never any work or never any thought of, "Oh, I better do this to improve or I better do this to make the other person happy."

B: So it sounds like you didn't have to have any particular objectives; you just saw that there was this great compatibility.

Robert: That's something I've always looked for, thinking that's what a great relationship is all about. It's beautiful companionship and compatibility, and I just assumed in my first marriage that's what was going to happen. You think that's always forever. Maybe that's what I was looking for, that was the missing link in all my other relationships – that it didn't flow so perfectly all the time. There were little flaws, there were just things that weren't right.

B: Did that seem like too much work?

Robert: Not even too much work. I just don't want to do *any* work! It's like life; you just want it to go so beautifully and wonderfully. That's what I expected, that's what I wanted and fortunately that's what I found with Karen. It just works beautifully.

B: Would you say that Karen is the leader in your marriage?

Robert: I would say yes, absolutely. She's got a good strong personality, she's articulate, she knows what she wants, and she's a great planner. She's thinking way ahead. And I'm your basic kind of guy – I eat, drink, and maybe think about what am I going to do tomorrow. I don't plan a lot of things out ahead of time. So I think that's what works very well for us. She's a planner and I'm not. I love to be the doer, to go out and play, and have fun, and do trips and travel. Karen makes that all happen. She plans it, puts the budget aside for it, and we do it.

B: Do you think being in different phases of life would make it more or less likely that a woman would lead in a marriage, or do you think it's more personality?

Robert: My life experience has shown me that as people get older they get more set in their ways. Men tend to be grumpier and they want to have their specific things their way. And I've seen so many women all my life just go with that flow, because that's the guy they married. In our day and age right now seems like women are saying, "No, I want to make me happy. I don't want to be the tagalong in this relationship, the maid, the servant, the sex partner, the wife in the relationship. I want equal status. I know where I'm going. I have a direction and I want to go that way."

So it could be just that women have a lot more of that power these days. It's a wonderful time to be a woman. But I think that's what life is all about. Why should anybody be the slave? You've got to be able to go after what you want, and you've got to have a supportive spouse to go along with it.

B: How does the decision making process work in your marriage, like making major financial decisions?

Robert: I think that's pretty much a 50/50. We pretty much talk about what we're going to do, where we're going to go with it, and what the goal and the objectives are with the money. Like purchasing a car, when the best time is and getting the money lined up for our next car.

B: Is one of you the financial manager or do you share that?

Robert: Karen absolutely loves doing bills. She pays the bills, she looks at them and says," Oh, boy, look what I've got left!" When I pay bills, I'm going, "Darn, I hate them taking all my money!" So we look at it completely different – it's the glass half full, glass half empty thing. Therefore, Karen is thrilled to do the financial paperwork because all it does is depress me. She is thrilled to handle the bills and the money and I'm perfectly okay with that. I have no problem with that because it saves me a lot of grief, a lot of headaches, and a lot of disappointment that my money is going other places instead of in my own pocket. It works out really good. So, yes, she is the money woman.

B: Do you feel your viewpoint is heard when there are decisions to be made?

Robert: Oh, absolutely. I think Karen considers very carefully everything that goes in. I think she has a much better thinking process than I do in those categories.

B: What did you envision in this marriage as far as affection and sex go?

Robert: Great sex. That is important. It was lacking in the past. And again that's part of that good partnership you're looking for when you're dating. I didn't want any weirdness. I wanted somebody who was free and hands on and willing to try all kinds of things. Just a wonderful good warm healthy relationship and that's hard to find, too, sometimes.

B: Do you think Karen has trained you so that you know what pleases her and what doesn't, or have you kind of trained each other?

Robert: For us I don't think there was any training involved. For me, I'm pretty open and happy with who I am and what I'm capable of doing. I just wanted equal time for myself. Maybe that's a little selfish on my part, saying I know what I want and I know what I need. As far as Karen goes, I don't think it was any real training. I think for her it was having a great partner who doesn't laugh or mock when you bring up a new subject or want to try something new. I'm right there to back her up and say, sure, let's give it a try. So I think she's able now to experience and just totally be free without anybody saying, "What's wrong with you?" It's just, let's play and have fun. I think that's pretty healthy. I think I'm pretty aware of what she likes and she's aware of what I like and it all fell into place.

B: How about when it comes to sharing the household chores?

Robert: That one is interesting. That one just kind of happens. If I know the floor needs to be vacuumed, I'll just get up and do it. If Karen cooks the meal, I'll do the dishes. If I'm cooking, she'll say, "Hey, I'll do the dishes." I think there's a real easy balance there. There's no saying, "Okay, here's the man's list, here's the woman's list." No "my chores, her chores." We just kind of jump on whatever needs to be done. Some things I'm definitely better at; some things Karen is definitely better at. Again, it just fell into place wonderfully.

B: It sounds like when you see something needs doing and you know how to do it, you just go ahead and take responsibility for doing it. She doesn't have to nag you.

Robert: No, not at all. Well, maybe on a few things. But for the most part, no – for example, if I get up in the morning and she's already at work in the office, I make the bed. And for dishes, if something's lying there, one of us will just take care of it. There's no real nagging. She might have to remind me once in a while, like "This computer's been sitting out here on the table for a few weeks; it's probably time to move it soon." Those are nice little hints, but certainly not nagging.

B: Would you say that one of your major goals in life is to see that she is pleased?

Robert: Absolutely. But I think that's the same with anybody you love, like your family. You never want to hurt them; you want to make sure that they've got a good, happy life. With your children, there's a difference between spoiling and pleasing. You don't want to spoil them too much, which I have a tendency to do with my children. But yes, you want your partner to be happy, so pleasing is definitely in the best interest. I mentioned before about expecting a wife to be a slave and cook the meals, do the dishes, make sure the bed is made, and I've got clean socks in my drawer. That's not what a relationship is about. You want to have a good time. You want a lot of love, a lot of laughter; you want to enjoy your time together. For me, that's the bottom line with anybody. So, yeah, I want to make sure she's happy and pleased.

B: When there is conflict, how is it handled?

Robert: I don't think we ever have conflict. I don't think we've bumped into anything like that.

B: How long have you been together?

Robert: Oh, about 3 or 4 years now.

B: And you never disagree about anything?

Robert: Only minor little things really. Once in a while one of us might do something that bugs the other one, but we just say, "Please don't do that again." So they don't do it again and that's it. We've been very fortunate.

B: So do you think it's a function of the fact that you were so compatible at the outset that you don't have areas where there are any major disagreements?

Robert: That's probably it and I think that's a rarity. But that's what I've always looked for. I always thought this is the way it's supposed to be. I think I've finally got what I think a marriage is supposed to be all about. I feel very fortunate there.

B: Since you readily recognize that Karen is a leader-type and she's more the leader in your marriage, did it take you some time to realize that this was the right kind of woman for you? Did you maybe not understand that about yourself in your younger days?

Robert: I think what I've always understood is that I want to go places, I want to do things, I want to explore life, different places in the world, hiking, camping, traveling, seeing, experiencing. All that is very strong inside of me but I didn't have the planning ability to go out and get it done. Quite a few things happened for me, but not to the degree that I thought I should be experiencing life. So, if I stop and think about it, I'd say, yeah, I realized that about myself, that I probably needed more that leader kind of partner. But I never even thought about it like that's what I should be looking for. I never even looked at it until just now when you were asking me this. That should have been an issue. That should have been on the list of things I was looking for.

B: You see, this is the reason why I'm writing this book, because the kind of relationship you have and the types of personalities that you and Karen are, and Stephen and I are – we have no models for this. It's not up there on the radar screen for relationships. And people that are our personality types don't realize that we need a different kind of partner than Cinderella or Prince Charming.

Robert: You have to study, take a test and pass it to get a driver's license and drive a car. You can't drive a car without a driver's license. You have to go to school and get a degree to be a professor or doctor. You have to do all these things to get somewhere, but any person can make children and have a relationship, probably the two most important things in the world.

B: But nowhere do we have to demonstrate any competency, is that it?

Robert: Yeah, you can go out and look for classes on childrearing and relationships or read books, but it's not a mandatory requirement and it should be. There should be books and information that are mandatory in school that show here's how to have a good relationship, here's how to treat people properly, here's how to raise children properly and so on. But nowhere do we have to learn anything before we marry, make babies, and raise them. I'm amazed at this. It's incredible.

B: What would you say to other men who might think that being in this kind of relationship would detract from their manhood?

Robert: It doesn't at all for me, but maybe that's because I'm comfortable with who I am and who Karen is. Other men might not be. There are men who want to be in charge, who want to be the boss, who want to handle the finances. Now whether they're good at it or not in any of those areas is a different story. I think Karen is very easygoing, but I know that she's bumped heads in past relationships and maybe it is because of her personality – that scares them. They think, *well, I've got to be the man; I've got to be the tough guy.* That's all bull. Those are just ego problems that a lot of men have.

B: So when you don't have that ego problem, it frees you to do what's right for you and to have the kind of relationship that's right for you?

Robert: Yes, which is the relationship I wish everybody had. Just have a great time with it. Be comfortable with who you are. And as long as you get to be you and your partner does too, then life is wonderful. There's no holdback for anybody.

B: What would you say are the advantages and the disadvantages of having a powerful woman as your wife?

Robert: Disadvantages? Absolutely none. Well, I guess if I go to a party, I can't say I'm the man of the house – big deal! Who cares? The advantages are that I have done more in my life since knowing Karen than I ever did in the 22 years I was married before. I have gone more places, seen more things, and experienced so much more of the world than I ever have before just in the short time we've been together. Because she plans things and gets things done and off we go. For me that's incredible. She has just opened the doors to a lot of avenues that I never would have done myself.

B: Do you like the fact that she stands on her own two feet and is not dependent on you?

> ***I catch myself constantly looking at her, just thinking, "I'm so proud of this woman!"***

Robert: I'm proud of that fact. I think it's exciting. When she's talking or telling stories or hanging out with friends or going wherever she's going, I catch myself constantly looking at her, just thinking, "I'm so proud of this woman!" It's unbelievable the way she smiles, the way she talks, the way she articulates, the way she stands on her own two feet. I'm impressed!

B: So her accomplishments don't make you feel less than?

Robert: No, it doesn't affect me at all. I'm thrilled for her.

B: In closing, is there anything you'd like to say to the rest of the male population out there?

Robert: To the average man out there I think the bottom line is, just get off the ego trip, get off the male I'm in charge thing and just go have fun. My gosh, once you get rid of all of that "I want to be the boss, I have to be in charge, I'm going to go buy this sports car without any permission from my partner" stuff you'll see you've lost so much. Just have a great time in life sharing it with your partner and treating them special. You're going to get it back very easily when you stop being a dominating son of a gun, which I think most guys are. They want to be the boss, be in charge, and have control. Get off the ego trip. Take off your pants and shut up, and you're going to have a blast!

Interview 2: Alex

B: How long have you and Rev. Joanne known each other?

Alex: We've known each other for 18 years and we've been married for 10 years.

B: How did you meet?

Alex: We both worked for the local school district. I was an electrician and she was a landscape maintenance supervisor. I actually met her coming out of a bush! Back in those days she dressed down in bib overalls and a flannel shirt, hair in two little short pigtails, one went one way and one went the other. I thought that was a little weird but after I talked to her for a while, she said she did that on purpose because nobody paid any attention to her when she dressed down. She sometimes had to be in a kind of rough part of town so I understood why she did it.

We got to know each other through the staff parties they used to have on Fridays, a TGIF kind of thing. That's how we actually got together to talk and it just went from there.

B: What were you looking for in a woman?

Alex: I wasn't actually looking for a woman at all. I had just come out of a difficult marriage. I thank Joanne for coming into my life because if she hadn't, I probably would have drunk myself to death. I was in a bad situation, having a hard time just coping with the whole idea of being divorced from my first wife who I'd been married to for a long time. Joanne really helped me out a lot and it just kind of worked from there. We became very good friends and buddies actually. She'd show up on my doorstep at some of the weirdest times, but it was kind of a godsend because it was like, she knew I was in trouble and she just showed up. It worked that way.

B: What attracted you to her?

Alex: Joanne is a very smart person. She's got a really outstanding memory. I think it was the fact that she was very soft with me and helped me work out of my problems. That's what really attracted me to her. Just the friendship part of it was the start of the whole thing and it just went on from there. We really enjoyed each other's company and it progressed from there.

B: So you were friends and then dated for some 7 or 8 years?

Alex: Well, I got into a financial bind. I was making a lot of money, making more overtime money than regular money, but I was spending it because I was by myself. She said, "You've got to stop doing this. You've got to put some money away." So she got me into a 401K, got me to put money in a savings account, got me a checking account, and even taught me how to buy groceries. I'd just go through the grocery store – I didn't know how to buy groceries. I was living by myself at the time. Like buying bananas – you don't buy six ripe bananas, you buy five unripe bananas and one ripe banana. And things like that. She really helped me out financially. I don't mean she helped me financially—she helped me get myself financially straight.

B: How did marriage come into the picture?

Alex: Well, we started dating, I mean seriously dating. We decided to live together. I'm 20 years older than Joanne and I didn't know if that was going to work, so we lived together for a while to see how it was going to work. And it worked out pretty good, so we decided to get married. I started going to Joanne's church. Before we even started going together, Joanne said she wanted to be a minister and I kind of laughed, because Joanne worked with a crew of at least 21 guys and they were tough. And she was tough on them. In fact, I used to tell her that if she were the only person in the world to work for, I wouldn't have a job. But we decided to get married and it has worked for 10 years now. Nothing's perfect; it's not a perfect world but we're striving to get it there.

B: Did you both make a conscious choice that Joanne would be more of the leader in the marriage?

Alex: I would say yes to that. Joanne helped me get myself out of debt and get me financially straight. Joanne's very good with money – saving it and putting it out. She makes it possible for us to go off for a couple days vacation pretty often. She makes it possible for us to stay at some really nice hotels. We've been to Europe, we've been to Alaska and it's all because Joanne knows how to handle the money to pay for different things. We don't have any outstanding debts. We pay our credit cards off every month. She's a good, good money manager.

She's a good, good money manager.

B: So you're happy to let her handle the finances?

Alex: I am. And she shows me what's going on so I know. In my first marriage, I just handed my paycheck to my wife and she handled it. Well, that's one reason why we're not married anymore, because she wound up giving all the money away to our grown children, which I didn't think was right. But Joanne and I work together with the money and if I overstep she lets me know about it. Some things I buy that I shouldn't, and she says, "Don't do that anymore. Let's talk about it first."

B: How does the decision making process work in your marriage?

Alex: The decision process is between the two of us. If we decide we want to do something or go someplace, we talk about it.

B: What do you think your compatibility is based on?

Alex: We just get along. We love each other. We laugh a lot together. We have a good time together. So I think that's half of living together.

B: Do you feel that your viewpoint is heard on decisions?

Alex: Yes, I really do.

B: Do you think that Joanne has had to train you in some areas, or do you think you've trained each other?

Alex: I was pretty much set in my ways because of my age and Joanne kind of taught me that what I believe isn't always right. I'd sit back and look at that and go, "You know, she's right." This is a different life than I had before so things have to change. We talked about that. It's a mutual thing with us. Yeah, if you want to say she's trained me, I'd go along with that. She has shown me the way.

B: Was there a least favorite training process?

Alex: I did have a little problem with her telling me what to do with my money, but when I sat back and looked at the big picture...well, I'm 20 years older and I was getting ready to retire. I have a good retirement package, but yet I was spending money so fast, I needed to put something away just so we could have fun on top of my retirement. Again, Joanne taught me how to do that and it worked in to the picture quite well.

B: When there is conflict between you, how is that handled?

Alex: We've had a few words; I think everybody does. I don't hear well and sometimes I don't hear what she's said. Or I hear it wrong. I wear hearing aids and I don't like wearing them, but I have to because otherwise I can't hear right. So we get into arguments about things that she's said that I don't hear right. We might yell a bit, but I realize that 90 percent of it is me and not her, because she's trying to direct me in the right direction. I know that's what she's doing. She doesn't play games with me. When we have talks it's serious stuff, and when we play, it's play stuff. So the problem comes when I don't hear her; maybe I should learn to read lips!

B: What about the path that led you to be in this kind of marriage? Did you realize that this is what you wanted or did it just happen?

Alex: I didn't really want to get married. I didn't want to settle down with anybody after my divorce. I just figured I'd live alone forever. I asked Joanne out a couple times just to have a drink because I liked the way she talked. It was the seriousness about her in the things that I was doing. I liked that. I liked what she was saying to me. After the talks we had and what she had done for me, I decided that she was probably the more dominant of the two of us. I didn't have a problem with it because we both talk over everything that we do when we do something serious. So it's still a mutual thing with us.

B: Now that's very different from most men in your generation.

Alex: Yes it is. Most men my age want to be the dominant one. I know most of my friends do. But I'm willing to let Joanne lead because she's such a good leader. I decided that I could live with that. I could be with this woman and live with her being a good leader, and leading me, which she has done a lot of. I think it's kind of an 80/20 situation with Joanne and I – and I have no problem with that. She supports me in doing a lot of things. Like if I want to go and see my friends, she has no problem with that. She doesn't say, well, you can do this but you can't do that. It's always worked well.

B: What would you say to other men who might feel that this kind of relationship would detract from their manhood?

Alex: Well, you've got to look at the big picture. If you don't want to give in to any of that stuff, then you won't. But if you want to have a good relationship with a partner in this day and age, you should do that. I will admit that Joanne was very macho when I met her, probably more macho than any woman I've ever been with. I would say to the guys, that if you have gotten into a relationship where you think the woman is more dominant than you, then you should talk about it. See how it works out. I'm much older than Joanne; in fact, she could be one of my children, but I have no problem with her being dominant because look what we have! We have a lot of things that I would have never had if I hadn't gotten with this lady. I have a nice house, a new car, and new furniture that are all paid for! I would have never gotten here if it hadn't been for Joanne.

If you're looking at the opposite sex and thinking, hey, this isn't going to work because I'm the dominant male, you had better look at both sides of the picture. Because the side I'm looking at, I really like!

B: What are the advantages and the disadvantages of having a powerful woman as your wife?

Alex: Well, the disadvantage could be I'm a male and a woman shouldn't be telling me what to do. But that's old school thinking – I don't have a problem with it. The plus part about it with my lady is the things we get to do and the places we get to go and the compatibility that we have. I don't see any disadvantage at all, really.

B: So you prefer having a woman who can stand on her own two feet?

Alex: Oh, you betcha! I don't have to push her along. I don't have to follow her around or pick up after her at all!

B: Tell me a little about how you support Joanne in her career as a minister. I know that you support her by doing much of the background work that's needed for church service to run smoothly.

Alex: I'm retired. If I had a job, it might be a different situation because I'd be tied up doing other things. When Joanne told me she wanted to be a minister I had some doubts about it at first. But she put herself through ministerial school while she was still working. Then she was offered the job at this church and I was happy to move to this beautiful place. I rather enjoy supporting her in her career. I have the time to do it and so it's fun for me.

B: When you got married were you aware that she wanted this for her career?

Alex: I was because she was already going to school for it. In fact there was a time that we thought she might have to go to school over 80 miles away, so we were going to buy a motor home so that when she got off work I could drive her to the school that was a couple hours away. Then when class was over she could sleep all the way home and we'd park at her jobsite so she'd be right there for work in the morning. That's how I was going to support her with that, but it ended up that she was able to do her training near our home after all.

B: Is there anything that you'd like to tell the rest of the male population?

Alex: If you ever get a chance to marry a young minister, it's a fun thing. I get to go to all the weddings and all the rest. Marrying a younger woman doesn't hurt. She sure has kept me going. I get up every morning with a smile on my face. It's great being married to a powerful woman.

I get up every morning with a smile on my face. It's great being married to a powerful woman.

Interview 3: Stephen Abernathy

I asked Stephen to pretend I was a reporter who was trying to understand why and how a man could feel comfortable living with a strong and powerful woman at the helm. So in his answers he speaks of me in the third person.

B: What were you looking for in a woman?

Stephen: I wanted to find an intelligent, mature, responsible woman that I could relate with, that was from my generation. I wasn't looking for youth. I had 21 years of a good marriage with some ups and downs like any marriage.

I wanted to find a woman who was mature in her ideas. Spirituality played a big part in it, but not any kind of organized religion. I wanted a woman who was adventurous, someone I could go camping with, hiking, flying, any kind of activity like that. I also wanted someone who would be interested in my music and my career because my ex would never come to any of my gigs.

B: What characteristics had to grow in you in order to appreciate such a woman?

Stephen: I think they were always there but they were repressed in my last marriage. When I came out to California in the early 70's I found more enlightenment in the women in general. After my marriage, I just had to learn to look for things in a person that I didn't want to continue the second time around. I didn't really plan on getting married again. After the divorce I just wanted to date other women, have fun, and see what was out there.

Barbi, to me, is the epitome of a woman unleashed, the new woman – idealistic in one sense but so ethereal and mysterious at the same time. I wanted to get to know her better when I first met her. The first time I met her I gave her a hug. There was an aura about her.

When we sat next to each other at the coffee shop on our first date...she had these leggings on with little mountain boots, a cute little blonde. I felt very comfortable with Barbi. Then when I found out she was from New Jersey, I said, "Uh, oh!" I thought she was going to be one these typical East Coasters like I used to date back in the 70's when I lived there, but lo and behold, she came out to California and got enlightened.

JEEZ! She was from Jersey, Italian, lots of family back there. Me, from Brooklyn, Italian, lots of family back there! Imagine, meeting in California! Then we discovered that our families back there lived thirty minutes away from each other. And on and on it went.

My god, we talked for hours and then the night was over. Long story short…our next date was 13 hours, an all day affair, and then we started seeing each other seriously.

B. Once you did start thinking about marriage, what were your objectives and strategies for long-term success?

Stephen: When we were dating I wasn't thinking about marriage and I don't remember when the issue came up. When I moved in with her – then the goal was marriage. Let's see if we can live together first. There was no real strategy involved.

B. Do you think the different phases of life make it more or less likely that a woman would lead in the marriage?

Stephen: I think a woman-led marriage could happen in any phase of life. It depends on who is the more qualified of the two. Since I was more qualified to handle the finances in my household for 21 years, I did it. I would say that the most qualified person of the two should be the one to handle the finances. And whoever handles the finances doesn't make it a woman or man-led marriage; it just means that the financial head is the person more capable.

But as far as making decisions and things, I think that a man should be more open-minded in the way he perceives a woman and her abilities, because of the way women have been pushed down for so long. Although I'm not a proponent of the women's lib movement per se, they did start out good. They just ended up putting women in men's suits with padded shoulders, you know, and tried to make men out of them when that really wasn't the goal.

The goal was for a woman to have her freethinking spirit open up and blossom like a flower. And it was to have men understand that all a woman wants is to be listened to. And if he gives her that right, that respect, that he can sit and listen to her and understand where she's coming from, whether he leads the marriage financially or not, that's the key. The understanding is that men and women are not that different, but in some ways we are that different. Women don't necessarily want us to solve their problems; they just want to be listened to. Then they'll do the solving themselves.

B: How does the decision making process work in your marriage?

Stephen: Barbi comes up with an idea, and then she discusses it with me, or vice versa.

B: Do you feel that your viewpoint is heard?

Stephen: Well, certainly. If I didn't, I wouldn't be here.

B: What do you want in your marriage as far as affection and sex goes?

Stephen: Umm.... As much as possible. Especially from her. She's the mistress of the bedroom, takes very good care of me.

B: Do you feel that Barbi has mainly trained you, or do you feel that you have in a way trained each other?

Stephen: Probably, trained each other. When we came into this relationship it was a new concept. That's maybe why we were a little jittery. I knew it was an open-ended thing. I was going to come up to the mountain and we were going to see if it would work. It was a new revelation to me that, hey, there is a woman out there who will cater to my needs and my wants and at the same time I can cater to her needs and her wants, while both of us are on a learning curve, in a learning experience of trying something new.

This relationship of ours is very different from my last relationship. I pretty much leave all the financial matters to her – after discussion with her – because I figure she's got the noggin' for it. She's better at it than me!

B: What was your least favorite training process?

Stephen: Learning to dust before I vacuum. I used to go straight for the vacuum cleaner. I had years of experience with my kids, so housework to me was nothing new. I'd been doing it for a long time for my kids. I thought I knew how to be Mr. Mom.

B: But it sounds like Barbi did need to train you how she likes things done, what she thinks is the proper way to do it?

Stephen: Well, certainly. And I respected that. And it's a good thing. 'Cause the house stays cleaner!

But she learned how to accept a man's adaptability. I think that she thought, with her other marriages, that men were too rigid, that there's no flexibility in manhood. I showed her a different route. I call men like me sensitives...we're sensitive to women's needs and wants and I'm sure there are other men out there that are like me, that think men and women are equal.

In fact I think women are superior because they have the ability to focus on many different subjects, where we are just like a horse with blinders.

We see one thing at a time. You know, like, go to the store, get the item, and come home. That's the way we think – like a soldier – achieve your objective and get back as quick as possible.

There are guys like me out there who believe that women have a moral obligation, really, to teach us a few things. I am aware of the fact that my wife is more powerful than I am. Many women are more powerful than men when fully released to their ambitions. It's a changing world out there. It's a new century and a lot of thinking has to be changed all around, from political down to domestic and personal.

"Many women are more powerful than men when fully released to their ambitions."

B: When there is conflict, how is it handled?

Stephen: I don't think there is any conflict. I can't think of any real conflicts that we've had. Maybe me being aggravated and saying something and walking away.

B: What about emotional upsets?

Stephen: Depends on the outburst. If it's at the computer, which is about 90 percent of the time, then I just let it lie. I figure she's totally capable of taking care of her computer needs, and even though she's cussing a blue streak, it's not my involvement, so I just keep on doing what I'm doing.

B: So you feel conflict is pretty rare in your relationship?

Stephen: Yeah, pretty rare. You know, we see eye to eye on a lot of different things, I'd say 98 percent of everything. And if there is a conflict, it's usually something that's real asinine, mostly on my part. What we have to remember is that if one person is going crazy, the other one has to stay sane and centered. And that's a rule that she taught me.

"... If one person is going crazy, the other one has to stay sane and centered."

B: So only one person can go crazy at a time?

Stephen: Yeah, that was a valuable lesson that I learned from her.

B: So when you see your partner starting to go crazy then that's the time when you most need to stay centered and not participate in the craziness?

Stephen: It depends on who is driving the car when it happens *(laughs)*.

B: What could you say about the path that led you to being in a woman-led marriage and made you realize that's what you wanted to be in?

Stephen: I never thought that the man had to be the leader, even back when I got out of college in the early 70's. Like I said before, whoever is the more capable of the two should handle the finances. Just because you handle the finances, that doesn't mean you're the boss. Really to me, in a relationship, there should be no boss. If you're going to be boss, you should both be arm in arm boss over the kids.

B: So you don't feel like Barbi is your boss?

Stephen: No. Except when I do some office work for her, like sending out books. But boss doesn't really come into it. The word has no meaning for me. I was always pretty much my own boss, even when I worked for someone else; I had a lot of responsibility. That's why I was in business for myself for years and years.

B: What would you say to other men who might feel that this kind of relationship could detract from their manhood?

Stephen: I don't feel that way...there are a lot of Mr. Mom's in this country. And to me that's good training. We are all both male and female. Men have a male and female side, and women have a male and female side. That's what this book is about. So I don't think that there's any risk to my masculinity just because I take care of the house and do the things I need to do around here to keep the place clean, run errands and all. I also work on my own career and get a lot of support with that. Barbi does support me in my career and I really respect and appreciate that because I didn't have that in my last marriage, and that's something that's important to me.

Nobody can say he's more of a man or less of a man because he does a lot of the domestic work. I think that's just a natural part of being human. I did it when I had my apartment by myself. I had to wash the dishes, clean the tub, sweep, vacuum. Those things are a normal part of life, so for a man to feel that that hinders his masculinity doesn't make any sense to me. I think there are a lot of good marriages out there where the man helps the woman, they pitch in, and they clean together. I think that's more the norm than not. I am relaxed about my masculinity. I don't have a problem with any of it.

Nobody can say he's more of a man or less of a man because he does a lot of the domestic work.

B: What are the advantages and disadvantages of having a powerful woman as your wife?

Stephen: I don't think there are any disadvantages. I think they're all advantages. This is the 21st century and things are changing. I don't see any deficit at all in my relationship with my wife. One of the best advantages is peace of mind – knowing that someone is fully capable of taking care of whatever needs to be taken care of, and I don't have to worry about it at all.

I know that she's fully capable. And if she does have any problems and she needs my assistance, she comes to me and we hammer it out. I think that's a good thing. I think men and women should work together like that. To me that's normal. And because I did live another way for 20 plus years, it just gave me an insight into the other side. So I have both perspectives.

B: So you prefer having a woman who can stand on her own two feet and is not dependent on you?

Stephen: I know that every man wants a great helpmate and every woman wants a great helpmate, so it's a hand-in-hand type of thing. That's why the figure eight is a symbol of eternity. There's that communication between the two spirits and it's a closed link. When you have a man and a woman that are linked together that way it's a give and take relationship that's on a par.

The equilibrium in the marriage is like a gyroscope. It just stays centered and that's a good thing. I think men should want to be associated with powerful women. I think it's even glamorous to a lot of guys. I dated a lot of professional women and I was always delighted with their company.

B: In closing, is there anything that you'd like to tell the rest of the male population out there?

Stephen: Get with it, guys. Learn to recognize a powerful woman when you see her. A lot of us are stubborn and set in our ways, but if we open ourselves up a little bit we can see that there are women out there who are capable of doing our job or doing it even better than we do. Let's have more respect for women, and really see them as the wonderful and delightful creatures they are.

Appendix B

Five Steps to Peace

In his book called *The New Revelations*, Neale Donald Walsch offers powerful answers to the spiritual questions that have plagued the human race from our beginnings. He shows us that questioning the old beliefs and replacing them with the truth of your own experience is the way out. Every individual who chooses to awaken to their own divine nature is contributing toward changing their own future and the future of our planet. The following is an excerpt reprinted with permission from *The New Revelations*.

There are five things you can choose now if changing the world, and the self-destructive direction in which it is moving is what you wish to achieve.

1. You can choose to acknowledge that some of your old beliefs about God and about Life are no longer working.
2. You can choose to acknowledge that there is something you do not understand about God and about Life, the understanding of which will change everything.
3. You can choose to be willing for a new understanding of God and Life to now be brought forth, an understanding that could produce a new way of life on our planet.
4. You can choose to be courageous enough to explore and examine this new understanding, and, if it aligns with your inner truth and knowing, to enlarge your belief system to include it.
5. You can choose to live your life as demonstrations of your highest and grandest beliefs, rather than as denials of them.

These are the five steps to Peace, and if you take them, you can shift everything on our planet.

Appendix C

New Thought Resources

Affiliated New Thought Network (ANTN)
3505 Camino Del Rio South, Suite #160
San Diego, CA 92108
Phone: (619) 640-0826
www.newthought.org/

United Church of Religious Science
3251 West Sixth Street
Los Angeles, California 90020
Phone: (213) 388-2181
www.religiousscience.org/

Religious Science International
P.O. Box 2152
Spokane, WA 99210-2152
Phone: (509) 624-7000
(800) 662-1348
www.rsintl.org/

Association of Unity Churches
PO Box 610
Lee's Summit, MO 64063
Phone: (816) 524-7414 or (816) 524-7750
www.unity.org/

Association for Global New Thought (AGNT)
1815 Garden Street
Santa Barbara, CA 93101
Phone: (805) 563-7343
www.agnt.org/

Institute of Noetic Sciences
101 San Antonio Road
Petaluma, CA 94952 USA
Phone: (707) 775-3500
www.noetic.org/

Help the men in your life remember their duty.
Clip these signs and post them in your bathrooms.

Index

D

E

F

G

H

I

J-K

L

M

N-O

P

Q

R

S

T

U-V

W-X-Y

How to Order More Copies

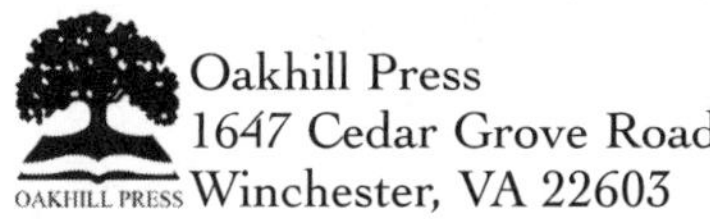

Oakhill Press
1647 Cedar Grove Road
Winchester, VA 22603

Please send me the following:

Quantity	Item	Price
________	Venus On Top/Softcover $14.95 (US)	________
	(Call for discount on 5 or more copies)	________
	Subtotal	________
	Shipping via Priority Mail - $5.00 each	________
	TOTAL	________

Ship to

____
Name

____
Company Name

____
Mailing Address

____
City State Zip

____
Telephone Fax E.mail

Note: We DO NOT SHARE your personal information with anyone.

Payment Method

____ Check enclosed made payable to Oakhill Press

____ VISA ____ Mastercard

Name on Card______________________________
Card # ____________ ____________ ____________ ____________
Expiration Date ____________(mo.)__________(year)

- **INTERNET** – Go to *www.VenusOnTop.com,* click on How to Order and follow instructions.
- **FAX** – Fill out this form and fax it to our secure fax number **503-289-7598** with your credit card information.
- **PHONE** – Call toll-free: **888-22-VENUS (888-228-3687)**
- **MAIL** – Send this form with your check payable to Oakhill Press (or include credit card information) to: **Oakhill Press, 1647 Cedar Grove Road, Winchester, VA 22603**